Joyce, Modernity, and its Mediation

EUROPEAN JOYCE STUDIES

1

General Editor: Fritz Senn
Associate Editor: Christine van Boheemen

Joyce, Modernity, and its Mediation

Edited by

Christine van Boheemen

AMSTERDAM - ATLANTA, GA 1989

This is the first volume of a projected series entitled

EUROPEAN JOYCE STUDIES

General Editor: Fritz Senn

Associate Editor: Christine van Boheemen

Contributions in the form of articles or monographs, etc., are invited and
should be submitted to the general editor c/o the Zürich James Joyce
Foundation, Augustinergasse 9, CH 8001 Zürich, Switzerland.

CIP-GEGEVENS KONINKLIJKE BIBLIOTHEEK, DEN HAAG

Joyce

Joyce, modernity, and its mediation / ed. by Christine
van Boheemen. — Amsterdam - Atlanta, GA : Rodopi. — (European
Joyce Studies ; vol. 1)
ISBN 90-5183-111-0
SISO enge 855.6 UDC 820"19"+929 Joyce, James NUGI 941
Trefw.: Joyce, James / Engelse letterkunde ; geschiedenis ;
20e eeuw
©Editions Rodopi B.V., Amsterdam - Atlanta, GA 1989
Printed in The Netherlands

Contents

Part III: Commentary

BIBLIOGRAPHICAL NOTE

In order to facilitate reading we have adopted the convention of the *James Joyce Quarterly*, and shall use the following abbreviations to refer to what we consider to be standard editions of Joyce's works:

CW James Joyce. *The Critical Writings of James Joyce,* ed. Ellsworth Mason and Richard Ellmann, New York: Viking Press, 1959.

D   James Joyce, *Dubliners*, ed. Robert Scholes in consultation with Richard Ellmann, New York: Viking Press, 1967. James Joyce, *"Dubliners": Text, Criticism, and Notes*, eds Robert Scholes and A. Walton Litz, New York: Viking Press, 1969.

FW James Joyce, *Finnegans Wake*, New York: Viking Press, 1939; London: Faber, 1939 and subsequent reprints. These two editions have identical pagination.

P   James Joyce, *A Portrait of the Artist as a Young Man.* The definitive text corrected from the Dublin holograph by Chester G. Anderson and edited by Richard Ellmann, New York: Viking Press, 1968.

SH James Joyce, *Stephen Hero*, eds John J. Slocum and Herbert Cahoon, New York: New Directions, 1944, 1963.

U   plus episode and line number(s). James Joyce, *Ulysses,* ed. Hans Walter Gabler, et al., New York and London: Garland Publishing, 1984, 1986. In paperback by Garland, Random House, Bodley Head, and Penguin.

INTRODUCTION:

JOYCE, MODERNITY, AND ITS MEDIATION

CHRISTINE VAN BOHEEMEN

The study of Modernism is one of the central concerns of contemporary literary scholarship; and in it Joyce stands central for several reasons. Whether we define Modernism as a style — an experimental reaction against nineteenth-century well-made fiction, whether we regard it as a movement led by a group of mostly expatriate writers who shared certain artistic ideals, or whether we try to avoid the pitfalls of definition and thus the need to account for troubling exceptions and take Modernism simply as a term referring to the literature written between 1910 and 1940, we always find that Joyce requires special attention.[1] This is so because he is at once exemplary as the pioneer of characteristic innovation, as well as the figure-head who eludes our attempts at pigeon-holing. Joyce is always already ahead of us, just as he was ahead of Pound, Eliot, Woolf, and Forster. An Irish writer, he seems to have made marginality into a strategic art of elusion, and preprogrammed elusiveness into the textuality of his writing.

Whereas the study of Modernism and Joyce's place within it has hitherto primarily concentrated on style, theme, and artistic intention, the waning of the ideology of the New Criticism which isolated the literary work from its context, in combination with the increased influence of cultural-historical, philosophical, and other non-formalist approaches to the text, also opens up new perspectives on Modernism — especially with regard to the *implica-*

---

1. We shall use "Modern(ism)" with reference to the literary-historical movement, and "modern(ism)" for Western thought roughly since Descartes.

4

tions of the stylistic features noted by close textual analysis. Thus the mythic method highlighted by T.S. Eliot, and the style of allusion noted by Weldon Thornton, to select two examples at random, are no longer simply regarded as the highly sophisticated and supremely innovative strategies of representation which confirm the transcendent iconicity of the Modernist work of art. We have lost some of our idealist innocence with regard to literature's power to embody the transcendent. Nowadays, it would seem, the importance of Joyce rests upon the fact that he has made his readers — and here I refer to the countless writers of fiction from China to Peru who have acknowledged his influence, as well as to the contemporary philosophers and theorists to whom Joyce is important as concrete example and living proof of their theories — aware of the philosophical implications of textuality. In general, we have begun to pay more attention to the use of the medium of language, as well as to the effects of specific stylistic features such as citationality. Indeed, Joyce threatens to make theorists, "philosophers", of us all. We find that the text, after our initial engagement with its portrayal of Dublin and its inhabitants which demands a complex moral, aesthetic, and emotional response, leads us beyond to ponder the nature of mimesis, the impossibility of representation, and especially the function and role of language (both written and oral) as the indispensable medium of human community, of selfhood, of artistic expression, and of thought itself.

It is not by gratuitous accident that Joyce should be the one English prosewriter to serve as example in several French discussions of the implications and meaning of twentieth-century writing. After Lacan's work on Joyce (referred to, e.g., by Jean-Michel Rabaté in the essay which follows), or Julia Kristeva's repeated reference to Joyce in *La révolution du language poétique,* Derrida's numerous references to Joyce deserve mention, and especially his 1984 Frankfurt Address, "Ulysse gramophone: L'oui-dire de Joyce". We note, most recently, Jean-François Lyotard's interest in Joyce and his use of him in the essay "Answering the Question: What is Postmodernism?"[2] There he states: "I shall call modern

2. "Answering the Question: "What is Postmodernism?" in *The Postmodern Condition,* trans. Regis Durand, Minneapolis: Minnesota UP, 1984, pp. 329-341.

the art which devotes its 'little technical expertise' (*son 'petit technique'*) as Diderot used to say, to present the fact that the unpresentable exists. To make visible that there is something which can be conceived and which can neither be seen nor made visible ...." (p. 337). This statement is given additional resonance in connection with the definition of the difference between Modernism and Postmodernism — according to Lyotard both aesthetics of the sublime, but in a different way. Whereas Modernism — and here his example is Proust — foregrounds the unpresentable as theme while preserving the sensuous gratification of aesthetic wholeness and form, the Postmodern "puts forward the unpresentable in presentation itself: that which denies itself the solace of good forms, the consensus of a taste which would make it possible to share collectively the nostalgia for the unattainable; that which searches for new presentations, not in order to enjoy them but in order to impart a stronger sense of the unpresentable" (p. 340).

We seem to have come a long way from the traditional, specifically literary perspective on Modernism, to a more general cultural appreciation in which the differences between Modernism and Postmodernism are not as clear-cut, or not marked by the containing demarcations of historical decades. In order to indicate that the subject of these essays is not "Modernism" as referring to the literary-historical period 1910-1940, nor to a set of stylistic features, but "Modernism" as a philosophical or theoretical concern with the problems and limits of representation, we have chosen the noun "Modernity", which is an English adaptation of the French "modernité". In contradistinction to the English term, this one is not delimited by temporal parameters, and can refer to texts as widely divergent as *Frankenstein* and *Finnegans Wake*.

Twentieth-century Modernity's fascination with the impossibility of representation historically coincides with the explosion of linguistics as a discipline, and may be related to the increased awareness of our indebtedness to language as *the* medium which makes us human. Joyce's special place in the group of Modernist writers as the only one whose work serves as paradigm for Postmodern textuality and thought, may very well have to do with the fact that he was the only one of the group whose work, in theme and technique, demonstrated a fascination with the nature and influence of the modern media — media of transportation. of communication, of entertainment, of expression. As Hugh Kenner points out in "Notes toward an Anatomy of 'Modernism'"[3], Joyce alone of his contemporaries seemed aware that "something *external to writing* has changed, and in changing obligated a change in artistic means" (p. 4). Not only is Joyce, in contrast to Eliot, for instance, the writer who *celebrates* modern city life with its crowds and the unwanted intimacy of "drying combinations", and who imitates the noises of machinery, the rhythm of new means of transportation; most distinctively, Joyce demonstrated a "continual involvement" with "the technology and economics of printing" (p. 13). Thus art turned towards reflection upon its own material substrate. It is not surprising that that self-consciousness should have extended itself to a concern with the mediating act of narration and of language in general. It ended in *Finnegans Wake* with an inventory of discourses, of narrative- and other effects mockingly mediated through several media, and with a mediated inventory of the collective narrative memory of Western culture, highlighting nothing so much as the discontinuity between the real and (its?) representation.

Finnegans Wake foregrounds the limitations imposed upon human aspirations to clarity and transcendence. The Fall keeps repeating itself; and this is not a pleasing message for those who wish to regard art as the embodiment of a higher vision, a truly meaningful expression which substitutes for the loss of religious values in a desacralized world. All art can do, *Finnegans Wake* would seem to argue, is to testify to human limitation. At best it can bear "witness... to the unpresentable" (Lyotard, p. 341). In contrast to what some critics seem to think, this is not the admission of moral defeat, or a narcissistic instance of "literature against iself", or the end of literature. This notion of Modernity, however humble its aspirations, implies an ethically demanding political program: to remain consciously aware of the insufficiencey of human means, however painful the realization, and "to wage war on totality" (Lyotard), to resist the political drive of bureaucratic government and the pacifying illusions of wholeness

3. E.L. Epstein ed., *A Starchamber Quiry: A James Joyce Centennial Volume 1882-1982*, New York: Methuen, 1982, pp. 3-42.

and satisfaction produced by our consumer culture (and the traditionally institutionalized form of reading literature). Instead of *placing* Joyce's modernity with all its seemingly negative effects of intellectual self-enclosure and awareness of paradox as the symptomatic effect of the erosive and devaluating influence of late capitalism as Frederick Jameson does,[4] the essays collected here focus with negative capability, thus without desire to proclaim or privilege a totalizing vision of either history or the text, on Joyce's universe "founded upon the void".

Most of the essays in this book were first presented in October 1987 at the University of Leiden. In order to avoid the associations with either theology or philosophy clinging to the noun "mediation", the noun "mediatization" was invented by means of the strategy which earlier gave us "Modernity" — "translation" from the French. Our purpose was to emphasize that the subject of these discussions is not "mediation" as preliminary step towards totalization. They concentrate on the limitations imposed upon representation by the necessity of mediation through the medium. This may be language in general, or, more specifically, the ideological structures of "secondary modeling" (Lotman's term) such as sexual difference and other conceptual configuations of opposition.

Ulrich Schneider's essay which opens this book provides an introductory discussion to the topic of media(tiza)tion which unifies the articles in this volume. He places Joyce's Modernity in the context of literary history and the criticism of the Yale School, to conclude with a suggestion which speaks for all the contributions in this volume: "[S]tudying the rich, multi-layered texture of Joyce's prose can be much more rewarding than digging underneath in search of naked truth or ultimate revelation".

The body of the book is made up of three sections, each approaching the general theme with a specific orientation. Section I, entitled "Representation and its Limits", collects a number of essays which define the nature of Joyce's Modernity as relating to his awareness of the limits of linguistic representation, and his self-conscious staging of the blind spot, the doubt, and the struggle

---

4. "Postmodernism, or The Cultural Logic of Late Capitalism", *New Left Review* 146 (1984), 53-92.

for certainty, which consciousness of the presence of language entails. Thus Jean-Michel Rabaté's analysis of *Exiles* argues that ontological doubt is the prime and central mover of Joyce's strategy of (re)presentation. Carefully analyzing the cunning with which the author — rebaptized the "arranger" following David Hayman's use of the term — weaves a textual web which gives the "name of Joyce to the process through which difference subverts representation", Rabaté's essay points to the central place of Joyce (or "Joyce") in understanding Modernity. The confrontation with Joyce's textuality forces the reader to the realization that the printed word, and especially that of Joyce, requires a complex act of memorizing anticipation. Indeed, careful reading of the works of Joyce entails a confrontation with what Derrida might call *"differance"*. This confrontation is highlighted by Fritz Senn's "Anagnostic Probes". As a progressive temporal act, our spelling of the meaning of the language of the text entails postponement of revelation and *anagnorisis.* When or if it comes, it may retrospectively subvert earlier conclusions, or even the very possibility of definitive epiphany. Senn's essay is followed by Van Boheemen's discussion of the function of the idea of Molly Bloom's feminity as a vehicle for the otherness of the style and composition of *Ulysses,* which continues the concern with Joyce's textual strategies, to argue the inevitably tautological nature of representation. Taking her clue from a newspaper car advertisement which displays a streamlined naked female torso as vehicle for its message, Van Boheemen explores the projective circularity governing the relationship between textual structure and the pre-conceived notion of the nature of "the other". Subsequently, Marilyn Brownstein points out that Joyce's self-consciously subversive strategy of representation echoes the insight produced by Plato's *Phaedrus.* Both *Finnegans Wake* and Plato's *Phaedrus* "turn away from the rationalizing proclivities of ordinary discourse, by presenting a particular view of memory as compensation and play". Basing her argument on recent neurological investigations into the nature of memory, she argues for the active presence of sensory memory in *Finnegans Wake* as a repressed double of representation.

Section II, entitled "Contexts", collects four essays which highlight the nature of Joyce's Modernism by placing it in a broader, historical context. Richard Brown adds to the discussion of doubt begun by Rabaté, by arguing that the idea of doubt, given thematic form as the topic of adultery, symbolizes the "deep and far-reaching uncertainty or *aporia*" of Modernism. He cautions us against interpreting the theme as the mere sign of the Modernist insight of the "undecidable abyss of all thought". Wishing to honour the concreteness of history, he invites us to consider the importance of the connection between textual process, the history of ideas, and the emergence of a certain theme at a specific point in (literary) history. Brown's concern with the historical reality also informs Mary Power's "Molly Bloom and Mary Anderson: The Inside Story". Power provides contexts for our understanding of the figure of Molly Bloom and her role in the action of *Ulysses*. Not the lazy housewife critics have sometimes called her, Molly might more profitably and correctly be seen as a *diva* "resting between engagements". Turning to the accounts of Mary Anderson in the media, Power drafts for us the discourse of feminine stardom around the turn of the century. Doing so she also shows that from a historical perspective the figure of Molly is better read as an early version of the career woman or working housewife. In the contrasting comparison of Joyce and Wyndham Lewis which follows, Peter de Voogd restages the fable of the Ondt and the Gracehoper of *Finnegans Wake* in terms of the debate between the sister arts, poetry and painting. His central concern is with the difference in style and form of representation between the visual and verbal media. Less one-sided than Joyce's spokesman the Gracehoper, De Voogd emphasizes that all media fall short of full representation, and concludes that both Joyce and Lewis "over-reached, both, in a sense, ultimately failed". The second section of the book concludes with Marius Buning's look at *Ulysses* as historiography. In the light of the current discussions in that field, Buning takes Joyce's fictional representation as a demonstration of the doubleness of historical narrative: in addition to rendering facts it also tropes the real in order to make it (re)cognizable.

The book closes with Section III, entitled "Commentary". The essays collected here focus on the mediation of Joyce's texts in criticism and annotation. All of them argue the insufficiency of the relationship between text and metatext. In fact, one might read these essays as a demonstration at metalevel of the point made so repeatedly in Section I: Just as representation, since it must inevitably resort to a medium, falls under the sway of the impossibility of its own endeavour, and manifests the presence of otherness even when it attempts to suppress or repress it, just so commentary manifests the structural *aporia* inherent in critical reference. The metatext will inevitably falsify the fullness and complexity of its object, rewriting Joyce in its own limited image. This discussion is begun by Marisa Gatti-Taylor, who demonstrates that Joyce's use of French and Italian profanities in *Ulysses* had not only not been adequately annotated; Joyce's use of foreign languages proves a way of driving a wedge into representation itself. The sections in a foreign language allow of an ironic double perspective on characters, actions, situations and narrative representation not available to the reader unfamiliar with French and Italian. Following this, Fritz Senn's "Protean Inglossabilities" surveys the effects and influence of annotation. Annotations alter our awareness of the primary work, they place the reader in a potentially endless web of textuality, they threaten to "litter our minds", and lead us away from an engagement with Joyce's text. In addition, any attempt at annotation, Senn wittily demonstrates, falls short of achieving its purpose. There are too many different readers with different needs. Accommodating the needs of all of them would entail rewriting the whole library of Western literature. In the next article, shifting focus from annotations to critical commentary, Geert Lernout points to the European-American divide in Joyce criticism and the International James Joyce Foundation. Offering the Belgian-Canadian history of his own introduction to Joyce as an experiential example, he postulates a critical difference in understanding and approach to the text which may have to do with differences in ideology as well as tradition. Alan Roughley's "The Mediatization of Joyce" also takes the critical responses to Joyce as its subject. Whereas Lernout places his discussion in the framework of professional politics, Roughley's reading offers an inquiry into the ideology of criticism. This begins with his doubling of Joyce with De Sade as a proto-modern precursor — both in his subversive mediation of Enlightenment rationalism, as well as his problematic textuality. The latter incites critical attempts to domesticate the protean meaning of the text by means of the *ratio* which we also note with regard to Joyce.

11

Roughley surveys British criticism of Joyce, confronting it with the nature of Joyce's textuality, to bring out its underlying assumptions. This Section is concluded by Jeri Johnson's staging of the debate between two feminist approaches to *Ulysses*. Like the preceding essays, she points to the polarization between an Anglo-American perspective (in her text exemplified by Sandra Gilbert and Sandra Gubar's recent criticism of Joyce in *No Man's Land: The Place of the Woman Writer in the Twentieth Century*)[5] and a European approach to Joyce's textuality (for which she chooses Kristeva's 1984 Frankfurt Address as representative example). Closely re-reading their arguments and *Ulysses* itself, Johnson points out that the two positions are themselves the effect produced by the pre-programming of Joycean textuality. Johnson's essay returns us to the doubt and otherness featured in the reading of *Exiles* which opens Section I; but the circularity of the focus and arrangement of these essays is not accidental. Not only is commodius recirculation a characteristic feature of Joyce's writings, the essays lying before us try, each in their own way and from their particular point of view, to suggest that Joyce's *praxis* of circularity is the effect of his recognition that linguistic mediation is at once impossible, unending, and specularly repetitive: "Echo, read ending!" (*FW* 468. 20).

The present volume is the first in a projected series. We hope it will stimulate readers of Joyce from all over the world to suggest themes, submit articles and monographs, or propose special numbers. Correspondence may be addressed to *European Joyce Studies*, c.o. Dr Fritz Senn, Zürich, James Joyce Foundation, Augustinergasse 9, Zürich CH 8001, Switzerland.

Leiden

5. Vol. 1, New Haven: Yale UP, 1988.

Part I: Representation and its limits

MEDIATIZATION IN "AEOLUS" AND "OXEN OF THE SUN"

ULRICH SCHNEIDER

The term "mediatization" of my title may not be immediately clear. For a German speaker the first associations the word might have are with medieval history rather than modernism: "to mediatize", according to the *Shorter Oxford English Dictionary*, means "to reduce a prince or a state from the position of an immediate vassal of the Holy Roman Empire to that of a mediate vassal". This is obviously not the subject of these papers on Joyce. Yet, the alternative, choosing the standard English term "mediation" as vehicle for my discussion of Joyce's modernity will not do either. This word is heavily charged with philosophical and theological connotations ("*Vermittlung*" in Hegel's dialectics, "*Vermittlungs-theologie*"). If, however, we take the root-word "medium" — in its contemporary popular sense — as our cue, we can institute a new meaning for "mediatization" which makes it applicable to modernity, and expresses our increased awareness of how the medium of language creates a problem for the twentieth-century writer.

If artists, as E.H. Gombrich citing Ernst Kris reminds us in *Art and Illusion*, never have immediate access to reality but can only translate experience into the terms of their chosen medium,[1] the modern artist seems to have become more conscious of both the restrictions and the possibilities of a chosen medium. Hermann Broch, for example, the Austrian novelist who wrote an important essay on Joyce and gave us the phrase "Welt-Alltag der Epoche" for Bloomsday, emphasized the significance of this repeatedly. At

1. London: Phaidon, 1960, p. 30.

the treshold of modernism, as he explains, the Impressionist painters discovered that the impression of reality was filtered through two intermediate layers: light and the colours of the palette. Impressionism arrived at a new perception of reality by discovering the reality and substantiality of the medium. When Broch asks, "Does not reality always and everywhere need a medium in order to manifest itself?", he clearly intends the answer to be yes.[2]

Broch's conclusions will not please those who believe that language, far from facilitating the manifestation of reality, functions as a distorting mirror, an epistemological evil, and not even a necessary one. The professors at the school of language in Swift's Lagado, advocates of the mathematical and scientific spirit of the time, were of the opinion that language should be as literal as possible. Thus they hoped to get rid of all the inconsistencies and redundancies of language "by cutting polysyllables into one, and leaving out verbs and participles, because in reality all things are but nouns".[3] Even better than such nominalism would be abolishing natural languages altogether: "An expedient was therefore offered, that since words are only names for *things*, it would be more convenient for all men to carry about them such *things* as were necessary to express the particular business they are to discourse on" (p. 150). This ingenious solution of the language problem has only one drawback: it does not work. Outside the academy the uneducated and women still prefer to use ordinary language, and it goes without saying that poets would also have refused to follow the principles of the academy.

Since the Romantic period, poets have been engaged in a battle against mediatization from a different perspective. In his book *The Unmediated Vision: An Interpretation of Wordsworth, Hopkins, Rilke and Valéry*, Geoffrey Hartman pursues the quest of the

2. *"Braucht Realität nicht immer und überall ein Medium, um zur Erscheinung zu gelangen?" Kommentierte Werkausgabe*, vol. 9,7., ed. Paul Michael Lützeler, Frankfurt: Suhrkamp, 1975, p. 121. Cf. Broch's essay *"Das Unmittelbare in Philosophie und Dichtung", Kommentierte Werkausgabe*, vol 10,1, Frankfurt: Suhrkamp, 1977, pp. 167-190.
3. *Gulliver's Travels and Other Writings*, ed. Louis A. Landa, London: Oxford UP, 1976, p. 150.

modern poet in the role of a new Perseus engaged in a relentless battle with reality. Perseus killed the Medusa with the help of Athene, who gave him "a resplendent mirror to escape the monster's direct glance, which would have turned him into stone". The modern poet "disdains or has lost Athene's mirror, and goes against the monster with naked eye".[4] Mistrusting the help of supernatural powers, he turns personal experience into his only shield. Paradoxically, "his real mediation is to accept and live the lack of mediation".[5]

Joyce's fight against conventions and authority, his self-reliance and self-confidence, which depended upon his decision to use, in Stephen Dedalus' words, "for my defence the only arms I will allow myself ... silence, exile, and cunning",[6] would certainly qualify him for the role of Hartman's new Perseus. His concept of epiphany has striking similarities with the unmediated vision of the poets chosen by Hartman. On the narratological level, the dismissal of an intrusive, mediating narrator and the preference for "showing" over "telling" in Joyce's early works make an important chapter in the history of the novel after Flaubert. Nevertheless, like other novelists of early modernism, Joyce became increasingly aware of the fact that, no matter how unmediated the writer's vision might be, he is bound to express it in mediated language. Even the young protagonist in *Stephen Hero* who believes in "sudden spiritual manifestation(s)" holds to the "doctrine" of the "literary tradition". Reading Skeat's *Etymological Dictionary* "by the hour", he develops a deeper understanding of this tradition and of what it means for the individual talent. When he tries to express his moods in poetry, he first reads "Blake and Rimbaud on the values of letters" and laughs at the "burgher notion of the poet Byron in undress pouring out verses just as a city fountain pours out water" (p. 37).

From the very beginning, but with increasing intensity, Joyce charges the language of his novels with mythological, literary, and historical associations. Tracing the allusions and quotations in his

4. New Haven: Yale UP, 1954, p. 156.
5. *Ibid.*, p. 173.
6. *A Portrait of the Artist as a Young Man*, ed. J.S. Atherton, London: Heinemann, 1967, p. 229.

18

works, we find ourselves suddenly immersed in Homer, the Bible, or Shakespeare. And usually it isn't enough to spot the origin of a quotation, since it has been mediatized through history. In his book on *Ulysses*, in a chapter paradoxically called "Immediate Experience", Hugh Kenner points out that the first words spoken or intoned in the novel, Mulligan's *Introibo ad altare Dei*, could be set inside six sets of quotation marks: Mulligan is "pretending to be a Black Mass celebrant, who is going through the motions of an Irish priest, who is reciting from the *Ordo*, which quotes from St. Jerome's Latin version of Hebrew words ascribed to a psalmist in exile".[7]

As we read onwards in a linear way, the process is interrupted again and again, and our understanding of what is on the page is slowed down and mediatized through other texts. In structuralist terms, Joyce's language becomes foregrounded so heavily that it no longer acts as a transparent medium, a window to the world out there. Instead, it becomes opaque. In the last two decades, the "transparency" of realism has almost become a dirty word for theoreticians who welcome opacity in literature as "a constitutive element of discourse, a quality that liberates it from the tyranny of the referent and from the traditional realistic demands of verisimilitude".[8] It has frequently been pointed out that *Ulysses* begins as a novel which still fits the realistic tradition and ends by flaunting its own fabrication, thereby moving from fiction to metafiction.

It should not be forgotten, however, that, from the very beginning, *Ulysses* highlights the linguistic medium through which we experience the world of the characters. In "Aeolus", for example, the narrator or arranger makes his presence felt through the insertion of headlines and the resulting segmentation of the chapter. But there are other hints for the reader pointing to the fact that *Ulysses* — and, indeed, not even a newspaper — does not contain an unmediated vision of the empirical world. We do not

7. London: Allen & Unwin, 1980, p. 35.
8. Sonja Bašić, "Transparent or Opaque? The Reader of *Ulysses* between Involvement and Distanciation" in *International Perspectives on James Joyce,* ed. Gottlieb Gaiser, Troy, New York: Whitston, 1968, p. 107.

find "life on the raw", as one of the headlines puts it, but life mediatized through the printing press. While Bloom is watching the typesetter at his work, he reflects: "Reads it backwards first. Quickly he does it. Must require some practice that. mangiD kcirtaP" (*U* 7.205-6). Even proper names, which Joyce could take from *Thom's Directory* without the slighest alteration, do not remain the same in the process of printing. Before they can be read, they must be written in reverse and thus placed at one remove from reality. The novel reminds us again how tricky the business of turning reality into print or fiction can be, when later on Bloom finds his name printed as L. Boom in the *Evening Telegraph*. Something has gone wrong at an even earlier stage of mediatization when Hynes wrongly lists M'Coy, Stephen Dedalus, and M'Intosh among the mourners at Glasnevin (*U* 16.1259-61).

Bloom is also very attentive to the noises of the printing machine, the "thump, thump, thump", and to the "sllt" of the flyboard. Language is nowhere more imitative than when it aims at onomatopoeia. But even in this case, the original noise has first to be spelled backwards and removed from reality before it can "speak in its own way" (*U* 7.174-177).[9]

Another instance of mediatization can be seen in the transformation of oratory into print. When J.J. O'Molloy recites a purple passage from a famous Irish speech, one listener comments: "that is oratory" (*U* 7.879). But Bloom's previous silent comment on another speech: "All very fine to jeer at it now in cold print but it goes down like hot cake that stuff" (*U* 7.338-9) — points to the difference between hot and cold media, as if Bloom had read some Marshall McLuhan: "The medium is the message".

Typesetting in reverse may be seen as part of the intricate

---

9. Cf. E.H. Gombrich's comments upon how onomatopoeia is mediated through language: "These so-called imitations are not imitations proper but approximations, within the given medium of language, to the sound heard. The sound of the drum, for instance, is imitated as '*rataplan*' in French; English lacking the nasal phoneme, uses instead the syllables '*rumtitum*' .... To me, at least, the cock says not '*cock-a-doodle-doo*', as he calls to the English in the morning, nor '*cocorico*', as he says in French, nor '*kiao kiao*', as in Chinese, but still '*kikeriki*', as he says in German" (*Art and Illusion*, pp. 306-307).

pattern of mirror images introduced into the novel with Stephen's aphorism on "the cracked lookingglass of a servant" as "a symbol of Irish art" (*U* 1. 146). These mirror images are not intended to support a traditional mimetic concept of art holding up a mirror to nature, but rather point in the opposite direction, towards the self-reflection of the modern novel. As Paul de Man claims, such mirroring techniques assert the separation of a work of art from empirical reality and free literature from the "fallacy of un-mediated expression".[10]

"Oxen of the Sun" confronts us with a different kind of reading backwards, a different retrospective arrangement. The chapter recapitulates the history of English prose and resembles a multi-layered palimpsest. The language becomes opaque to a degree which often makes it extremely difficult to find out what is actually going on, or what the characters are talking about. As Kenner observes, "thirty-five pages ... of loud and bawdy talk are so muted by indirect discourse that we would be hard put to reconstruct convincingly a sentence of it" (pp. 107-08). The personae of the narrator no longer serve to mediate as go-betweens between the respective worlds of characters and readers, but rather separate both spheres drastically.

Towards the end of the chapter Joyce includes a passage parodying Carlyle. Joyce puts him after the other Victorian writers and thus almost on the threshold of Modernism. In his works, but especially in *Sartor Resartus*, Carlyle cultivated a highly idio-syncratic prose which his contemporaries considered an affront against all stylistic standards.

Geoffrey Hartman, in *Criticism in the Wilderness,* calls it "a 'Babylonish dialect' made of Germanisms, Swiftian gusto, and a baroque simulacrum of the earthy, archaizing diction of Northern England".[11] From such a stylistic syncretism it is only a short step to Joyce's own "frightful jumble"[12] at the end of the chapter which

10. *Blindness and Insight*, New York: Oxford UP, 1971, p. 17. Cf. Brook Thomas' excellent discussion of mirror-images in *James Joyce's "Ulysses" A Book of Many Happy Returns,* Baton Rouge: Louisiana UP, 1982, pp. 44-55.

11. New Haven, Yale UP, 1980, p. 47.

12. *Letters of James Joyce*, ed. Stuart Gilbert, London: Faber, 1957, p. 139.

seems characteristic of modern English as an even more heterogeneous world language.

Another reason for Carlyle's modernity might well be found in his emphasis on mediation. The "Clothes Philosophy" in *Sartor Resartus*, as Hartman observes, distances humanity from its natural "Adamite" condition. Since Professor Teufelsdröckh's German manuscript is translated, excerpted, patched together or, in one word, "retailored" by the editor, the literary form of the work reflects the theme of mediation. According to Hartman, Carlyle reacts with disgust to "this potentially infinite regress of mediation" and finds his solution in "foreground[ing] the mediatory process, to make the writer's distance from any source so palpable that the retailored text is endowed with a factitious presence of its own …. It is as if something groundless were being foregrounded — which taken out of metaphysics or German *Naturphilosophie* and articulated as a theory of language, could evoke Heidegger and Derrida" (pp. 48-49).

Sartor Resartus is a patch-work and the combination of tailor and teller makes us realize that, in Hartman's words, "writers are in the second-hand word business" (p. 142). I think that the connection between such an insight and Joyce's patch-work or pastiche in "Oxen of the Sun" does not need belabouring. In fact, Hartman quotes from Joyce's Carlylese when he comes back to his theme of purity in language in another passage (p. 134-35). Let me conclude my own retailored reflexions on mediatization with a point which Carlyle's "Clothes Philosophy" might drive home to us, the point that studying the rich, multi-layered texture of Joyce's prose can be much more rewarding than digging underneath in search of naked truth or an ultimate revelation.

Erlangen

THE MODERNITY OF *EXILES*

JEAN-MICHEL RABATÉ

An experience common to theatrical audiences and directors, to actors, critics, and reviewers alike is that *Exiles*, Joyce's one play, remains for all its simplicity, its linguistic transparence, a very difficult text to stage, to perform, and even to appreciate fully. However, if the audience cannot help feeling slightly dissatisfied in spite of occasional insights provided by actors, the source of the uneasiness is hard to pinpoint. A recent exceptional performance of the play in Paris proved a discovery for those who did not know Joyce, and a bitter disappointment for those who identified Joyce with the avant-garde experiment of *Finnegans Wake*. Besides, it remains absolutely necessary to have witnessed at least one performance of *Exiles* in order to situate its global meaning and possible weak points. It will not do simply to denounce the play as a juvenile aberration (Joyce being 32 when he started writing it) or as one of those felicitous mistakes (or "volitional errors", which for Stephen Dedalus soon turn into "portals of discovery") which cannot but pave the way to a fuller mastery of the art of literature — an art which might be seen as bearing no relation to that of the stage. What should be stressed, is that Joyce wrote a play for the stage, refining the techniques of taking notes and preparatory associations already used for *A Portrait*, so as to take into account the new "public" nature of his meanings. And besides, has not Joyce created the most staggering play of this century, a play which is all the more fascinating as it is enacted in the reader's mind when reading the "Circe" episode of *Ulysses*?

Once one has seen the play performed, many prejudices and reservations appear in a different light, for the weaker sides of the text can also be explained otherwise, less in terms of Joyce's

24

evolution and linguistic fluency than in terms of a general dissatisfaction with representation as such. Thus the relation between the text and the notes accompanying it can be displaced or turned around: instead of reading the latter as notes which say little about the actual performance since they were written at an early stage in the composition when Joyce was still groping for the exact formula, the right balance between realism and symbolism, they may now be read as presenting the central problem Joyce faced when writing, which is the same as that of the staging of the text: how to represent something which eludes representation? In this case, the question of the precise dating of the notes would be less relevant to their meaning, although some of them are dated, and others appear plainly to have been jotted down between the writing of act I and of act II. The curious and fascinating mixture of dialogue drafts, personal comments on readings, dream-associations prompted by Nora's confidences, and dynamic programming of the play appears first as a set of projective patterns helping to control a work in progress, and also as a general interpretative frame for a completed work. The notes offer a second textual space, which does not privilege drama but rather philosophy (hence the references to Spinoza, Schopenhauer, Bergson, Sade and Sacher-Masoch) or literature: they derive their form from Flaubert's own notes for *Madame Bovary* in the then recent Conard edition.[1] This new space is a still potential space, opening vistas rather than closing the interpretation: "It would be interesting to make some sketches of Bertha if she had united her life for nine years to Robert — not necessarily in the way of drama but rather impressionist sketches" (p. 149). Joyce has to visualize a series of little vignettes in order to balance the choices still open to Bertha, torn between her indifferent husband and her devoted lover — this seen from her point of view, of course. Moreover, the notes disclose the main drift of the play, pointing to what could be called a "plot", if "plot" might be taken to suggest an effect on the audience rather than a narrative following a distinct pattern. The plot can be best approached through the dominant mood

1. See the notes by Jacques Aubert in the Pléiade edition of Joyce, *Oeuvres,* vol. 1, Paris: Gallimard, 1982, p. 1774. Page references throughout to Panther edn of *Exiles,* London, 1979.

underlined in the notes which disclose the key-note, the moral ambience of the play, its *Grundstimmung*, which is felt now and then in awkward passages or situations, and culminates in the uneasiness felt by the audience when the play reaches its climax in the famous profession of doubt which concludes it. Credible or not, the plot leaves us with this question mark.

A detour through Lacan's remarkable analysis of the play in his seminar of January 1976 will confirm the unity of all these questions. For Lacan, indeed, *Exiles* gives a privileged access to Joyce's "central symptom", since it discloses the "deficiency or lack proper to the sexual rapport".[2] The title thus alludes not only to the characters as exiles, but also to a situation of exile — or situations in the plural — which can have validity for everyone. Joyce could have anticipated Lacan's provocative slogan that "*il n'y a pas de rapport sexuel*", meaning that there is no sexual *relationship* and not just no sexual intercourse: sex cannot be expressed by a formula which would transform it into a "rapport", a relation between homologous or complementary subjects. The preparatory notes allow one to find the roots of this lack of rapport, since they primarily comment on the difficulty of portraying an absent relationship. This is why they directly lead to the most baffling and masterly pages of *Ulysses*, when the profession of doubt of "Ithaca" acquires cosmic overtones, while translating itself at the same time into a profession of faith in language as such. Doubt, which remains the key-note of *Exiles*, generates another type of textuality in *Ulysses*, where it underpins the whole gamut of the catechetic repertory of characters, situations, and relationships. Language becomes an almost autonomous medium and force, wrenching apart normal facts of everyday life and common assumptions of fiction, until the very elements, the most hidden wishes of characters, and the mathematical connections and the logical derivations between them set Stephen, Bloom, and Molly adrift like so many astral bodies whirling in infinity.

2. As Lacan's Seminar is still unpublished, I quote from notes taken during the lecture. See also the publication started in *Ornicar?*, "Le Sinthome", text established by J.A. Miller, numbers 6 to 12.

The constellation of the characters is no less rigorous in *Exiles*; and Joyce had probably learnt from Italo Svevo's *Senilità* the art of playing on the classical fourfold pattern which opposes two men (the extraverted lover and the introverted artist) and two women (the fragile spiritual "sister" and the sensual object of admiration and love). This pattern, combined with the agonies of erotic jealousy experienced by Joyce during his trip to Dublin in 1909, combined also with his intense work and meditation on Shakespeare's theatre in Trieste, explains how his first experiment with the theatre pushed him a long way from Ibsen. He is indeed entitled to believe, as the notes state, that "Europe is weary even of the Scandinavian women" and is waiting for the "Celt" heroine.[3] In fact, Richard and Robert oppose each other just as Shem and Shaun, while Bertha and Beatrice fight for the roles Joyce usually reserves for his women: inspiration on the one hand, physical attraction coupled with intuitive shrewdness on the other. The basic situation, in its simplicity, seems at first to fit a title such as "The Exiles' Return", and the notes stress the similitude between the plot and the story of the Prodigal Son.

Having returned from their Roman exile, Richard, Bertha, and their son Archie are still trying to find their bearings in their Dublin surroundings; for the past proves a heavy weight, and Robert and Beatrice's frustrated desires encroach on the tight family circle. Robert wishes to seduce Bertha, utilizing his otherwise sincere friendship with Richard to camouflage his devious intentions. Beatrice, once the confidante and addressee of Richard's thoughts, remains on the threshold of an adulterous passion, preferring the idealized role of an inspiring virgin to the worries of a real lover. The arrangement seems to suit Richard, who dominates Bertha's body, Beatrice's mind, and Robert's behaviour, even when the latter is engaged in making passes at his wife. For Richard may also need the vicarious thrill of feeling both the pleasure of possession by proxy and the indignity of being cuckolded. When his still faithful wife tells him of her relationship with his friend, Richard refuses to forbid her to do as they wish.

---

3. See B.J. Tysdahl, *Joyce and Ibsen: A Study in Literary Influence*, Oslo: Norwegian University Press, 1968, and Joyce's notes, p. 157.

Leaving them free to betray him, he goes so far as to refuse to be informed whether Bertha has yielded to Robert or not. Joyce's preparatory notes bring no key, no elucidation to the question of the reality of the sexual encounter between Robert and Bertha, left in tense tête-à-tête at the end of act two. All the formulations of the play are purposefully ambiguous. We see Bertha, who has accepted two kisses, rather liberally superimpose dreams, hallucinations, and possibly lies, so that no declaration can be taken at its face value:

> Robert. Were you mine in that sacred night of love? Or have I dreamed it?
> Bertha. (*Smiles faintly*) Remember your dream of me. You dreamed that I was yours last night.
> Robert. And is that the truth — a dream? That is what I am to tell?
> Bertha. Yes. (*Exiles*, p. 135)

The notes taken when Joyce was still composing show him as uncertain, meditating on the gaps left by his text. For instance, he goes as far as wondering whether Bertha, who would probably have refused normal coitus with Robert for fear of being pregnant, might not have accepted sodomy: "It is certain that her instinct can distinguish between concessions and for her the supreme concession is what the fathers of the church call *emissio seminis inter vas naturale*. As for the accomplishment of the act otherwise externally, by friction, or in the mouth, the question needs to be scrutinized still more. Would she allow her lust to carry her so far as to receive his emission of seed in any other opening of the body where it could not be acted upon, when once emitted, by the forces of her secret flesh?" (p. 156-7) The uncanny Jesuitical tone worthy of a prurient confessor provides a striking contrast with Joyce's unabashed frankness in sexual matters — evinced by his letters and other notes, such as the notes for *Ulysses*. Such casuistry may appear more experimental than prudish when compared with Bloom's musings in "Ithaca" on "the preordained frangibility of the hymen: the presupposed intangibility of the thing in itself ... the continual production of semen by distillation: the futility of triumph or protest or vindication: the inanity of extolled virtue:

the lethargy of nescient matter: the apathy of the stars" (*U* 17. 2212-26).

What really matters in distinguishing those two passages is that the note of uncertainty finally conveyed by the "apathy of the stars" in "Ithaca", is part of an answer to a scholastic mode of questioning, while in the unpublished notes for *Exiles* the sentence is left as a question which receives no answer. The answer is missing. Joyce does not know whether Bertha would allow her lust .... Joyce therefore remains in the same relationship towards his text as Richard is when facing his wife. In both cases doubt reigns, pervading all the exchanges between the characters. As Joyce explains in another note: "The doubt which clouds the end of the play must be conveyed to the audience not only through Richard's questions to both but also from the dialogue between Robert and Bertha" (p. 157).

This doubt programmes *Exiles* as a play, just as it rounds off "Ithaca" in its drifting relativistic universe founded upon the void. The constant modelling of the play by the notes implies that the play develops in the gap left by the absence of an answer; it multiplies dialogues, discourses, and interpretations so as to stage this lack of an answer adequately. Thus, although it is advisable to look for answers in the notes, one may consider them as a crystal, magnifying or amplifying the intimate doubts of each character, working to transmute a merely psychological hesitation — which, as we have seen, attacks even the cocksure Robert — into a quasi Cartesian, hyperbolical doubt. And the first of these notes sums up the whole process in a condensed and enigmatic way:

RICHARD — an automystic
ROBERT — an automobile. (*Exiles*, p. 147)

The notes explain what Joyce means by "mystic", for he mentions "Richard's mystical defence of his wife" which should convince Robert of the "existence and reality" of spiritual facts (p. 149). The paradoxical defence is identical to the logic of the gift which Richard explains to his son Archie, and then to his rival, in the long confrontation opposing them: You can only be robbed of what you own, therefore, if you give something to someone else, at the level of symbolic transaction, you both keep something and you are safe, since no one will steal what has been handed over to someone else. Consequently, anything that is offered without resistance cannot be snatched away by force and violence; and passivity is the best weapon against the hard dialectics of power and possession. This is why Richard cannot come out with the words Bertha begs him to utter. Nor can he pronounce the absolute ban on her seeing Robert because, by so doing, he would be contradicting himself and undermining his whole philosophy of existence. Bertha tells Richard: "Tell me not to go and I will not" (p. 69) and Richard refuses, throwing her back on her own freedom of choice. The refusal to forbid constitutes this "defence of her soul and body" functioning as "an invisible and imponderable sword" (p. 147).

And when the notes develop the idea of "the weapons which social conventions and morals put in the hands of the husband" (*ibid*), the play itself rules out any such social temptation, since it is clear that Richard and Bertha are not married. On the contrary, it is this transgression of the religious code which has incited Richard's mother to reject him, thereby leading him to choose exile instead of a literary career in Dublin. This is stressed at various points in the play, and even recurs in the mouth of Robert, who has a revealing hesitation. Richard makes it plain that he knows everything about the affair and Robert's love-letters; and he cruelly quotes from the last letter, asking his friend to define the nature of his feelings for Bertha. Robert answers: "I admire very much the personality of your ... of ... your wife. That is the word. I can say it. It is no secret" (p. 74). He hesitates to allude to Bertha as Richard's wife, which she is only in the meaning of concubine, or a permanent partner who lives with a man; but this comes from his guilt which shifts the object of expression, for he could have said "I love your wife" instead of "I admire her". If, however, he also wishes to designate and place her as Richard's wife, it is because he prefers to situate her and himself in the bourgeois situation of adultery. In this game, the stock responses to typical situations allow people to go on playing a role, while he feels totally unsure of himself in Richard's mystical and perverse play.

Richard then refuses to prescribe his wife's actions or to pro-scribe anything. Therein lies his "defence" of her. But why is he called an "automystic"? Does this imply "self-mysticism", or a mystique of the egoist self, engaged in artistic self-begetting? The traits pertaining to masochism in Richard are clearly adduced by his evident narcissim. But the important point is the coupling of the two men of the play: "*automystic*" and "*automobile*" function as a parodic couple of concepts which provides the engine of the mechanism, so to speak, and creates the *perpetuum mobile* of personal interactions. Ironic duality is reduplicated theatrically at least, for Robert really and truly believes in the possible exchange of desire. In this, he is indispensable to Richard, as a counterpart, in order to prevent the latter from succumbing to the temptations of a morose delectation or an illusory sense of mastery. Richard is an anxious Prospero trapped by his own tricks, while Robert is an Irish Caliban, still eager to emulate his master. This is why Richard comes back from a walk along the beach with the Shakespearian hint that the "isle is full of voices" (p. 125); but unlike Prospero he seems unable to break his wand in the end. The final gesture asserting complete mastery can only come from a woman embodying both the isle and the voices.

Robert appears as Richard's former disciple, a disciple who has kept and fossilized adolescent dreams of power and creation. He has neither matured nor aged; and when he quotes to Richard his own tags and echoes from former conversations, the prodigal exile back in his home city can measure the full difference. Their opposition is basically one which poses the law of nature on the one hand against the law of spiritual freedom and creation on the other, according to one of the major polarities hereafter to be found in *Ulysses*. In one of those rare author's *bons mots* which were so dominant in Ibsen's plays, Joyce puts the matter in a nutshell when he has Robert exclaim wildly that desire and passion are "nature's law", to which Richard superbly answers: "What is it to me? Did I vote it?" (p. 78)

The debate between Platonic idealism and Aristotelian realism will find a more appropriate locus in Bloom and Stephen's speculations on perception and on the symbolic function of naming in paternity. A telling detail here is that Bertha is the only character in the cast to be deprived of a family name, as if she was still waiting for a name to be given her by marriage with any one of her possible partners. The pattern of names and places, which has so often been commented upon, nevertheless supposes that there is one name too many. The automystic and the automobile must finally cooperate in bringing about the exclusion of one of them. This is why the plot of the play requires that the past exile of Richard be continued by the exile of Robert, who leaves Ireland at the end: "Exiles — also because at the end either Robert or Richard must go into exile. Perhaps the new Ireland cannot contain them both. Robert will go. But [Bertha's] thoughts will they follow him into exile as those of her sister-in-love Isolde follow Tristan?" (p. 156) The end is thus perhaps not a real conclusion, since the roles are merely exchanged, Bertha pining for an absent Robert .... But this is only one of the many potentialities contained in the plot, and with which the notes so generously play.

If desire then only blossoms and takes on its lyrical, rhetorical, and written form in the triangle of adultery, love is fulfilled by the immolation of sexual desire on the altar of doubt. This is what allows a symbolic order to take over from sexual, "natural" desire, an order which will put the artist's Christlike daydreams of redemption back in place. When Richard tries to free himself from all his social and sentimental ties, he seeks to advocate a law which will write absence and treachery into a code based on the Name. Therein his self-mystification will meet its ultimate defeat, because, once mobilized and brought back into play, it will finally afford him access to a way of writing which is free from all narcissistic smugness, and cleansed of all perverse traps.

This remains on the level of programmatic considerations, however, and we shall have to learn later, with Stephen, to steer our way between Charybdis and Scylla, between dogmatism and empiricism, between Plato and Aristotle, in order to think and to live the full function of naming in the perpetual symbolic debt names entail. The production notes reveal the direction in which Joyce would have liked to have gone, but which the framework of the play did not always enable him to indicate. Thus he underlines the difficulty of portraying characters that are off-stage: "During the second act as Beatrice is not on the stage, her figure must appear before the audience through the thoughts or speech of the others. This is by no means easy" (p. 158). This is, in fact, one of the stumbling blocks of the play, one of the points where we can assess the immaturity of the author as a dramatist. Joyce also remarks that the effect the play produces hinges on the willingness of the audience to believe in the suffering of the characters: "Critics may say what they like, all these persons — even Bertha — are suffering during the action" (p. 148).

Absence and suffering: two "conditions" which cannot easily be signified by the mediation of the bodies of actors on a stage and yet they reveal the themes treated by the text as a whole. Thus Richard's masochism must not seem to give him too intense a pleasure, because the suffering portrayed would then disappear. Yet if either pleasure or pain appear too gratuitous, then the interest is lost.

Indeed, the plot of the play seems peculiarly narrow if it is reduced to the torments of an introspective writer who wonders if his partner slept with his best friend. On the other hand though, if the plot is taken as the first level of a bottomless spiral of questioning about the positivity of doubt and uncertainty, which, as we have seen, does not exclude Joyce in his role as author, then the play takes on its full shape. Therefore, the question shifts. Why doesn't Richard want to know? How does this not-knowing become another form of knowing? Does Richard know he does not want to know, and knowing this, does he suffer all the more? And after such knowledge, what forgiveness?

Any such knowledge of non-knowledge, the existence of which must remain hypothetical for the time being, might be located between Stephen's confused perception of bodily shame and sexual embarrassment in A *Portrait*, and the paradox of paternity defined in *Ulysses* as the area of shadow represented by the mother's sexual organs traversed at least once by father and son, the one in begetting, the other at birth — a shadow which must be forgotten in order to clear the father-son relationship of all these carnal dealings. Between these two extremes reigns the despotic aura of jealousy, which is as valid for father-son relationships as for the extra-marital temptations of Bloom and Molly, making no exception of the vague incestuous desires of father for daughter. Now the point is that jealousy seems to be absent from all that Richard actually says: jealousy with its train of perverse fantasies, of which Bloom gives a few wild examples in "Circe", presupposes the basic stability and reality of the sexual rapport. In the notes, Richard is said to be jealous because, as Spinoza sees it, he derives pleasure from imagining the woman he loves deflowered by contact with the private parts of someone else; but above all, and beyond any "sensationalist" approach, he wants to overcome his jealousy in order to inhabit that new territory it has provided for him: "He is jealous, wills and knows his own dishonour and the dishonour of her, to be united with every phase of whose being is love's end, as to achieve that union in the region of the difficult, the void and the impossible is its necessary tendency" (p. 148).

The paradox of *Exiles* lies in the fact that the jealous partner uses doubt to outflank jealousy — contradicting all classical approaches to jealousy, Proust's included — and finds enough seeming reality in "the difficult, the void and the impossible" to base his suffering on an excess which no discourse can redeem, since he reaches the limit of his male sexuality in this movement. That is why Bertha, Richard's true "bride in exile" (p. 143) is given the final speech of the play, and in a manner which it is fitting to analyse more closely. Richard says to Bertha: "I have a deep, deep wound of doubt in my soul" (p. 144) and she asks: "Doubt of me?", to which Richard asserts. But then he elaborates: "I have wounded my soul for you …. It is not in the darkness of belief that I desire you. But in restless living wounding doubt" (*ibid*). And he finishes with his "wound" which tires him out, slumping exhausted and silent on the lounge.

There is a four stage semantic progression: the first step is that of the "wound *of* doubt", a wound caused by doubt of the loved woman. She is the cause and the object of the doubt, which is reduplicated by the second moment, when the doubt of is transformed into a doubt *for* her. Doubt becomes a gift, and this hollowing of uncertainty affirms desire as a withdrawal from knowledge. The wound of doubt is proffered to the woman who has caused it to show her that it is not because she has caused it that she is a cause of desire: the offering *presents* doubt, not as a presence, but as a gift. The third stage insists on the impossibility of representing the "living wounding doubt" harped upon by an obstinate repetitive complaint: hyperbolical doubt is seen as a living, active, incessant wound, indefinitely reopened and regenerating. This allows a return to the first level, but in a fourth step, which replaces the grammatical determinate of "wound of doubt" by the non-determinate of a wound incorporated in the subject: "my wound"; the wound is synonymous with the subject, just as with the "agenbite of inwit" which qualifies a conscience-stricken Stephen in *Ulysses*.

The outcome of this delicate dialectic is that Richard can only utter his discourses of doubt and desire in the separation of saying from seeing, for he has to address a partner who is absent and present at the same time; the text states plainly that Richard, even though he is gazing at Bertha when speaking, speaks "as if to an absent person" (p. 144). He then brings about the fusion of a wife who is present and abandoned, and the absent lover to whom he used to write from Rome. In the same way, the final "monologue" of Bertha soliloquizing lulls Richard and drives out Robert at the same time; indeed, this final song of love and desire wavers between the second and the third persons. "I want my lover. To meet him, to go to him, to give myself to him. You, Dick. O my strange wild lover, come back to me again!" (p. 145) The rapid shift from "him — you — Dick" bypasses the logic of the excluded third element in the eternal triangle. The couple opens up to this triangular logic, without being committed to lover-swapping, of course (although I have stressed the ambivalence of the scene, which can be read as a renewal of fidelity as well as, perhaps, a hint of possible foursome relationship), and changes the mode of discourse: the personal pronouns thus bear the onus of a new, internalized exile through language. As Richard was telling Beatrice in the first act, referring to her adolescent tryst with Robert: "I was a third person, I felt". This feeling of exclusion from the world of women (represented both by Beatrice and his mother) led to his exile. Now that he is back, he steps forth as an "ex-he" coming back from the continent to his "ex-isle", Ireland. Place and subject, "ex-him" or "ex-he" and "ex-island" fuse now in the assertion of a desire spoken by two voices simultaneously.

To Prospero, returning from the magic isle built out of dreams and mystifications, in a phoney game of total mastery over the others' fantasies, a lover who cries that desire is reborn from its ashes, purified by a temptation whose reality need not be stated, replies: "Forget me and love me again as you did the first time" (p. 145). Just as Molly blends into one real and ideal lover the lovers she knew in Gibraltar with the recent impressions left by Boylan and Bloom — who flows with his floral name among the flowery words of sweet nothings — thus Bertha begins a new cycle and ends the old one in a speech which unlocks desire.

Therefore Richard does not want to know, because there is nothing to know, there is nothing to see. Bertha closes her eyes and the play ends. There is nothing to see, move along please "automobiles" and "automystics", move along, because what is being given is the act of giving itself, that which does not exist but ex-is in the exile of language. We have thus shifted from a first disjuncture (has there been, or hasn't there, sexual rapport?) to a new mobilization of the differences: "there *is* no" ... rapport, relation, there are only inequalities, excesses, we are always dealing with too-much or too-little, which hastens knowledge to its doom. A doom, a loss, or an end which founds literature on the void, the difficult and the impossible, putting in parenthesis, by a king of literary phenomenological reduction, the primary confidence we tend to place in "there is ....". Such a suspension opens the space of textuality to the Other in exile.

The play then commits its "staging", the scene of all scenes, the scene of three-way desire and all the combinations and permutations which it involves, to what soon becomes a quest for the impossible: how to mimic, to capture, to represent the central void around which all the speeches hinge? The scene *par excellence*, the staging of the "*romanesque*", as Girard means it, is confronted by that in it which resists representation. It is in the notes that these difficulties are thought out. Much more than notes for production, they are markers, traces of a detour or a route of routes, pieces of a travel journal which can only be completed in *Ulysses*. It is as if the narrative mode alone had been able to open up its mirror to the crossed beams of parabolic and hyperbolical doubtfulness. This doubt oddly appears as the only firm ground on which the edifice of the work steadies and secures itself. In that, perhaps, Joyce's symptom is disclosed. For doubt, even if it gives rise to a whole realm of emotions or even passions, a wringing of hands in the agony of never-being-sure of the truth, the climax of pain shared and communicated to the audience, in this very process, it does not lead to obsession or psychosis, far from it. On the contrary: the psychotic would be the one for whom the basic questions dealing with the truth of a situation (Am I alive or dead? Am I a man or a woman? Can I believe any one else?) are no longer asked, because the subject has the answer: in fact, he *is* the answer, immediately, without any speech to distance himself or herself. On the other hand, doubt, which impels the parabola or the parable of *Exiles*, turns morbid jealousy and its attendent psychotic symptomatology (such as the *Beziehungswahn*, or interpretative delirium) into creative uncertainty, an uncertainty which prevents any one signifier — even the word "betrayal" — from becoming the major one. This place can only be played by the signature of the divided subject who feels the pain of the division, but enjoys the exile through language.

For to want uncertainty is also to want to be uncertain and to nurture in one's body and in one's language the "mystic" primacy of the creation of the Name. When the "automystic" takes pleasure in his fortunate fall or dispossession, and when the "automobile" delights in his speed on the spot, they are playing cat and mouse with the desire of the Other, the Other who sets the exile in motion. "The play is three cat and mouse acts" (p. 155) writes Joyce towards the end of his notes. But in this almost too mathematical "plan" of three stages and four performers, we can read underneath more than a scene which stages the impossibility of representing the scene, because we find the very blue print of doubt. This working out and drawing out of impurities means that the "doubt" which becomes "doubt-for" finally becomes pure, unadulterated doubt, a moving doubt for sure... *Eppur si muove...*? Am I now both "the doubter and the doubt"? As a reader, as a spectator who has perhaps been moved by the play to the writing of those rapid and sketchy notes, I still hesitate on the threshold; but I cannot help acknowledging the masterly waddling of Lautréamont's *"canard du doute aux lèvres de vermouth"* at work in the play, and at a remove, a cunning arranger capable of giving the name of Joyce to the process through which difference subverts representation.

Dijon

ANAGNOSTIC PROBES

FRITZ SENN

This essay is one of several attempts to present and characterize
instances of postponed clarification: later passages throwing light
on earlier ones. This is nothing new in fiction (in life too we often
understand long afterwards, or too late). Joyce seems to have
given the disruption of smooth sequences more functional
prominence; it becomes an essential, restless animation of the
reading process as a halting temporal progression with inevitable
glances backward that reinterpret what was apprehended before,
in perpetual retroactive resemantification. Enlightenment trails
behind. We *also* read from right to left. *Finnegans Wake* changed
Dubliners and — in a loose, sweeping way — all preceding
literature into the bargain. At least the eyes of the beholders have
changed. In the following observations the focus will be on the
impact that, microscopically, subsequent words, phrases, passages
may have on those that precede them.

Girdling

An attentive reader might well be slightly puzzled over the second
sentence in *Ulysses*: "A yellow dressinggown, ungirdled, was
sustained gently behind him on the mild morning air"[1] (*U*. 1.2),
where the movement comes to a halt with the highlighted attribute
"ungirdled", framed between pauses in a movement of static
observation. What is it that Mulligan's dressinggown is not? Does
the word suggest that, against unstated expectation, there is no

---

1. Former editions of *Ulysses* used to read: "*by* the mild morning air".

"girdle" in sight, or else that the one Mulligan has he wears loose, untied? Dictionaries will not decide this.

But what is a "girdle" in the first place? A term that obviously belongs to the elevated, ceremonious, churchly diction of the opening paragraph. No further real girdles will turn up in *Ulysses*, unless in imagination or in parodistic passages.[2] The seemingly unwarranted negation has lured annotators to the word, but with a tendency to instant symbolism: "ungirdled — an inversion of priestly chastity".[3] This gives an ecclestiastical meaning to what still has not even been determined on the simplest of all possible levels: whether "ungirdled" implies an absence of a girdle/belt or its not being fastened. Is the prefix **"un"** privative, as in "unattired", or does it connote a reversal, as in "unfolded" or "undone"? Questions of this kind, easily disregarded by critics in search of higher and more general truths, have to be faced squarely by translators. We can check whether they take "ungirdled" to be something not present or something not done. Their views differ. Some think there is no girdle around: in French we find **"sans ceinture"**, in Swedish **"utan knuden"**, in modern Greek **"chôris zônê"**. The Dutch version is **"zonder ceintuur"**. Others claim the girdle is there, but not fastened, as in German **"mit offenem Gürtel"**, Norwegian **"Uomgjordet"**, or in Hungarian **"oldott övvel"** ("with loosened belt"). Translators are, collectively, of two minds; the Danish one even changed sides in the course of revisions from an earlier **"snorløs"** (beltless) to a mere loosening: **"Uomgjordet"**.[4] The point is not that we inherently cannot know the meaning of "ungirdled" (some native speakers may never entertain any doubt

---

2. Stephen Dedalus: "marybeads jabber on their girdles" (*U* 3.388); in a Cyclopean interpolation we find "a girdle of plaited straw and rushes" (*U* 12.169). "From. his girdle hung" (*U* 12.173); in one of the transformations of the 14th chapter; "a point shift and petticoat with a tippet and girdle" (*U* 14.600).

3. Don Gifford and Robert J. Seidman, *Notes for Joyce: An Annotation of James Joyce's* Ulysses, New York: Dutton, 1974, p. 6.

4. **"En gul, snorløs slaabrok"** in *ULYSSES*, trans. Mogens Boisen, Copenhagen: Martins Forlag, 1949, p.7, was changed, lexically and syntactically, to **"Uomgjordet bases en gul slåbrok"** in a revised edition of 1970 (p.19).

to begin with), or that there is some designed ambiguity, but that uncertainty is on record.

The sacerdotal symbolism of "ungirdled", if not immediately evident, will be borne out only a little later when Buck Mulligan intones his chant from the Mass, and even more so when Stephen Dedalus internally remarks on Mulligan's "shaking gurgling face" and his "light untonsured hair" (*U* 1.15). It is Stephen with his preoccupations who notices that Mulligan's priestly parody does not extend, after all, to his hair: there is no tonsure. "Untonsured" is doubly negative, it makes a point of the absence of a shaven crown, of hair that is not there. It also reinforces a liturgical portent in "ungirdled". The parallel, negative, uncommon participles form a pair. So the annotators had a point, but were perhaps just a little hasty in forcing a priestly resonance on unsuspecting readers *before* Buck Mulligan had a chance to display his persistent mimicry. The annotators are right after all; they are right **AFTER** all. A later "untonsured" affects a previous "ungirdled". We might now conclude, by analogy, that just as untonsured means "no tonsure", "ungirdled" might reinforce "no girdle" and dispel lingering lexical doubt?[5]

As it happens, semantic resolution will come in the same chapter when Mulligan, reverting to his ceremonial play-acting, "stood up, gravely ungirdled and disrobed himself of his gown, saying resignedly: — Mulligan is stripped of his garments" (*U.* 1.508). Here the identical shape operates as an active verb that clearly presupposes a girdle in order to become unfastened. We now know for sure that Mulligan was wearing a belt or girdle all along, but that he first wore it untied (and must have fastened it in the

---

5. Perhaps another absent word is conjured up, the Latin, also priestly, prototype of "ungirdled" — "*discinctus*", "ungirt", with the same meaning of "having no belt", or having one that is slackened. Fittingly, it could also mean easy-going or loose, the type of figure Mulligan is. Horace refers to a "**nepos discinctus**" (*Epod.* 1,34) — a loose, feckless, spendthrift (literally: "nephew"; Mulligan is a nephew). Ovid confessed *in propria* or as a literary *persona*, "*discinctaque in otia natus*" — that he was "born in careless leisure" (*Amores* 1,9,41). A modern version has: "born to leisure *en deshabillé*" (Ovid, *The Erotic Poems*, trans. Peter Green, Harmondsworth: Penguin, 1982, p. 102).

meantime). We can NOW claim that the several beltless translations in existence are, on the basis of intratextual consistency, in need of correction. The participle, epithet, "ungirdled" can be tied — fastened — buckled to the subsequent past tense "ungirdled" and clarified by it.

What at first may not have been evident now has become so by circumstantial completion. Earlier understanding can be revised and modified, always supposing that the former occurrence is remembered and recognised (some translators evidently did not make the connection between the two related passages). Under-standing proceeds in time. Meaning accrues, changes, with the progress of the reading. So a question becomes not only what something means, but HOW and WHEN it may mean what, and HOW meaning comes about.

At times, as in jokes, we may deliberately be led astray. There may be an unforeseen twist. One of Lenehan's facile quips, referring to the prospective father of a new-born child, is that a Jewish parent is "Expecting every moment will be"... If we have not heard it before, we will be surprised though not necessarily amused by the sequel: "will be his next" (U 12. 1649). Expectation, truistically, is connected with the next moment that may or may not fulfil it. Joyce supplies us with many next (or future) moments of semantic momentum, or, etymologically, Latin *momentum* — motion, alteration, impulse. Some hindsight impulses are worth passing attention.

Circumdation

We normally understand in the light of what went before. Memory enables us to make sense of odd collocations. As English teachers, stylists, purists, we might not accept an expression that tells us that a woman "smiled *tinily*"[6]. The immediate context, however, justifies the unusual adverb: "A tiny yawn opened the mouth of the wife of the gentleman with the glasses. She raised her small

---

6. Translations tend to iron out the irregularity, or paraphrase: "elle...eut un petit rire de rien de tout".

gloved fist, yawned ever so gently, tiptapping her small gloved fist on her opening mouth and smiled tinily, sweetly." (*U* 10.125-27) This shows a simple progression from a "tiny yawn" to "smiled tinily". The manner of smiling appears to be a stifled yawn transformed and brought about by the same mechanics, such as those impassively reported in the "Wandering Rocks" chapter. We see that what "tinily" does, above all, is to link the resultant smile with its analogous origin. [In a similar transition Davy Byrne had "smiledyawnednodded all in one" (*U* 8. 969)]. We read from left to right, most of the time. But it was C.G. Jung who once observed that *Ulysses* could be read from anywhere in either direction.

We know what he had in mind and how he exaggerated, but at times the reversal is literally true. "Metempsychosis" follows "Met him what?" (*U* 4. 336), but also explains it from behind, inverting the accustomed order. All reading is in part backwards, and in some cases more pointedly so. Poetry and prose in the classical languages do not make immediate sense at each turn; much has to be held in mental storage until semantic circuits are closed. In the sequential release of information, English has to be more orderly and explicit than highly inflected Latin. Joyce switches to Latin right after the first paragraph of *Ulysses*, but it is the relatively straightforward syntax of the Old Testament rendered into the Vulgate and used in the Mass: "*Introibo ad altare Dei*". This reads almost like its vernacular equivalent: "I will go in to...". Except that our Latin reader or audience would have to wait, minimally, for the last syllable of the first word, the terminal **-o** of "*introibo*," to know who will be going.

When Stephen Dedalus obsessively remembers the death of his mother, he conjures up, visually: "Her eye on me to strike me down", and then, audibly, Latin words from a Prayer for the Dying, words that have become a haunting, excruciating memory. Imagine you want to know what those words actually say as you hear them one by one. For purposes of demonstration the verbal sequence is here broken up into slow motion semantification — which cannot pretend to simulate in any way the serial processes of listening or reading. How much could we "understand" at each singular step forward?

"**Liliata** (*U* 1.276): a participle, in its nature the result of some process. Something undetermined as yet has been "lilied": made into a lily? made to resemble a lily?, been provided, perhaps decorated, with lilies? The verbal derivative of a noun for a flower is dangling without any semantic anchorage. The sentence ironically begins with a word that suggests the end of a process. We have to wait for the sequel; it does not yet clarify:

"**rutilantium**" "glowing red". Another participle, this time present tense and active voice, unrelated to the preceding one. There is no immediate connection between something "lilied" ("**liliata**" is feminine singular — *or else* neuter plural) and an unidentified genitive plural participle, perhaps a contrast in colour: something white juxtaposed to something reddish.

"**te**": Neither participle meaningfully coheres with the pronoun **te** (you, accusative). The three disparate words add up to a cluster of contingencies. No plot, or pattern, or syntactical shape is discernible. Indeterminate (as yet) activities precede identities.

Comprehension is brought about by the next three steps, one by one, backwards.

"**confessorum**": this supplies "confessors" in a plural genitive that we now can join to "**rutilantium**" — confessors are shining with some ruddy light. The light effects have run ahead of their source. The next moment offers

"**turma**" (*U* 1. 277): a crowd, which reveals the delayed subject and a theme, to which "**liliata**" can be attached. This crowd is, perhaps, of lily-white appearance, or else each with a lily in hand, or perhaps emblematically purified. Grammatically it may be the subject or else have some ablative function. Up to that point it remains obscure what a whitish group of reddish confessors does, until

"**circumdet**" finally relieves a suspended **te** from indeterminacy: the crowd may, or should, "*surround you*". It also says what kind of sentence the whole is. In exaggeration, it is the very last vowel that gives the tone of the whole away. The final syllable, the conjunctive "e" in "-det", indicates a wish, a petition, a prayer, and not a statement of fact.

Sense leaps out at the last possible moment. It is oddly fitting that, with the delayed verb "circumdet" meaning is in fact rounded off, "circumdated": previous data link up. A semantic circuit is closed.[7] With the syntactical matrix in mind, we can now navigate the continuation with far less perplexity, right from the start: "iubilantium te virginum chorus excipiat". Transient obscurity has given way to light.

The translations of the Latin prayer available to Joyceans are not quite in agreement about the first word, "Liliata": it is considered to mean "lilied" in the sense of decorated with lilies, or perhaps provided with lilies, and also more metaphorically: "bright as lilies".[8] More intriguing is the inherent untranslatability of the dynamics. Modern European languages like English must rearrange the process and forgo the suspenseful choreography of delayed matchings in favour of instant, step by step, pre-orientation. We inevitably begin with an optative signal like "May" and are directed, right away, towards an appeal, with an identifying subject following soon after. This is a wholly different cognitive development, without the puzzles or mysteries that seem indicative of the many that are yet to follow in this book. Orderly, streamlined translations of "Liliata rutilantium" are as adequate to the motion of the sentence as a plot summary would be to the actual explorative experience of reading *Ulysses*.

Novices learning how to read *Ulysses* make laborious headway

7. This mimetic "circumdation" sounds a bit like *Finnegans Wake* in action: "long the" and "riverrun" could be illustrated by a term like circumscription. A meaningful sentence is patched together by surrounding, encompassing, beginning and end.

8. "May the lilied throng of radiant Confessors encompass thee: may the choir of rejoicing Virgins welcome thee", Weldon Thornton, *Allusions in* Ulysses: *An Annotated Word List*, Chapel Hill: U. of North Carolina Press, 1968, pp. 17-18; "May the glittering throng of confessors, bright as lilies, gather about you. May the glorious choir of virgins receive you" (Gifford, p. 10).

not unlike students spelling out a Latin period — a complex tissue of anticipations and delays, with pauses and retrogressive reassurances or revisions. Some of the most disturbing modernist features of *Ulysses* were routine in classical languages. In its first chapter we will figure out, not in the conventional, expositional order, but by circumstantial links, the setting on top of a historical tower, somewhere near Dublin, at a certain time. The last two chapters, "Ithaca" and "Penelope", above all put much of what we had taken for granted into a different light. Adjustment takes patience and circumspection, many retracings in an Odyssean progression of trial and error — unless such indigenous processes are short-circuited by outside information or tutorial interference. So the spelling out of **"Liliata rutilantium"** seems typical and representative, except that the resolutions do not tend to be as neatly satisfactory as in Latin grammar. As often as not we may still be waiting for the final, redeeming **"circumdet"** that makes everything fall into line.

She Could See From Where She Was

What we learn later may change what we thought we knew before, even when we did not feel in need of explanations. *"If youth but knew"*, Mr Deasy quotes sententiously to Stephen Dedalus in an entirely unrelated context (*U* 2.238), but as a matter of fact we never know NOW what we may come to see differently only a few insights later. Joyce's works tend to make such truisms poignantly appreciable.

Nothing appears puzzling in the first part of a chapter we call "Nausicaa". What we read is, moreover, and this is unusual in the chapters that came before, presented in a conventional manner, with a handy exposition and plenty of descriptive asides. It is easy to visualize the scene, the strand, and to know the time, evening. Girl friends, we read, "were seated" on the rocks (*U* 13.9). Not sitting, but "seated" — a suitably elevated, dignified style for the sort of dignified poses that are on view. Of the three girls, one, Edy Boardman, is soon witnessed with little Tommy behind the pushcar, so she must have left her position; another, Cissy Caffrey, seems to move about a great deal with the twins; at one time she walks over to a gentleman opposite. One moment "she jumped up ... and ran down the slope"; and she ran, we learn from the internal, unflattering comment of Gerty MacDowell, "with long gandery strides it was a wonder she didn't rip up her skirt at the side ... to show off and just because she was a good runner she ran like that so that he could see all the end of her petticoat running and her skinny shanks.... It would have served her just right if she had tripped up over something...." (*U* 13.474-85). The observations are a bit less than friendly. When all the others leave, Gerty still remains behind: "If they could run like rossies she could sit so she said she could see from where she was" (*U* 13.688). Much of this we take in as a tinge of jealousy and perhaps natural rivalry for attention. Gerty adamantly stays behind to watch, at which stage she is also conscious of being watched. It is only later, when Leopold Bloom eyes Gerty as she walks away, precariously, in a carefully delayed exit, with a limp that is no longer to be concealed in a becoming posture — it is only then that we learn of an additional reason for Gerty's resolution to remain on her rock, "seated" indeed, leaning back, at her immobile best. She was right in a way we could not then guess: the others, they *can* run like rossies, but not she. She attempts to elevate her stasis into a superior attitude. The pose she lets herself be caught in for half a chapter is an optimal one. We can now see, *from where we are*, what it was not possible to notice when we were limited to a point of view that refracted her own selective mind, and what it chose not to admit.

Once we are conscious of her handicap, what she does and does not do makes more pertinent, pathetic sense, and invites more understanding and empathy. With the hindsight of later readings, we can even review the sentence that introduced her in a previous chapter: "Passing by Roger Greene's office and Dollard's big red printinghouse Gerty MacDowell, carrying the Catesby's cork lino letters for her father who was laid up, knew by the style it was the lord and lady lieutenant but she couldn't see what Her Excellency had on because the tram and Spring's big yellow furniture van had to stop in front of her on account of its being the lord lieutenant" (*U* 10.1205-11). We now know that this early vignette does not show Gerty at her attractive best; impeded motion is matched by impeded vision. We may reinterpret the passage as a halting one, and can now give it a corresponding rhythm and turn the prose into one that drags its feet, in a possible imitation of the walk, "with a certain quiet dignity characteristic of her but with care and very slowly" (*U* 13.769). Whether such an intensification is justified or not, it could not even be attempted without the postponed knowledge that this woman's locomotion is seriously impaired. Once having witnessed Gerty MacDowell's lameness, we will never recapture that pristine, innocent perspective of before. That "one shortcoming", the limp, is going to stay as a part of all further readings. We cannot read the same chapter twice.

Invalidation

In one of the sections of "Wandering Rocks" we find Hugh Boylan supervising a blond shopgirl filling a wicker basket with fat pears and shamefaced peaches on top of a "bottle swathed in pink tissue paper and a small jar". He wants it all sent immediately to an address he scribbles down while he adds a discretionary explication: "— Send it at once, will you? he said. It's for an invalid" (*U* 10.322). At that stage, most readers may guess at the identity of the supposed invalid and only wonder, perhaps, about the particular kind of subterfuge.

The shopgirl's wholly unexciting response to this is worth a short digression: "— Yes sir. I will, sir" (*U* 10.323). Nothing remarkable: pure, though maybe flustered, politeness; but potentially no longer so for readers who have the end of *Ulysses* with Molly Bloom's closing "I said I will Yes" in mind. They may impose belated significance on the coincidental echo. For what it is worth, a shopgirl now says to Boylan, or nearly so, what Molly Tweedy 16 years ago said to Bloom in a different context. The end of the book enables us to pause, midway, at a commonplace phrase.

Boylan erects a little smokescreen of an invalid or, as some translators slightly magnify it, to a sick person.[9] We hardly worry

---

9. **C'est pour une personne malade — Het is voor een zieke — 'E per un infermo — Es ist für einen Kranken.** These last two translations overdo the pretence by making the recipient of the basket a male, which, given the name and address, is somewhat improbable.

over such a trifle. Parallactic confirmation of Boylan's gifts will come later. On the Blooms' kitchen dresser we again find the wicker basket with one remaining pear (and learn it is a "jersey" pear) and, again very specifically: "a halfempty bottle of William Gilbey and Co's white invalid port, half disrobed of its swathe of coralpink tissue paper" (*U* 17.306). The "Ithaca" chapter keeps minute track of concrete details. We discover what it is that Boylan sent ahead to pave the conqueror's way — a bottle of port (Lenehan, referring to his own, very minor and external conquest of Molly, thought of her as "well primed with a good load of Delahunt's port under her bellyband" (*U* 10. 557). More specifically, the bottle contained "invalid port", and it seems clear now that this word triggered off the evasive misrepresentation "for an invalid". This gain of postponed comprehension is minimal; a tiny source has been disrobed, an earlier scene becomes more ordinarily real. The brand name, perhaps even remembered off the actual label, gave Boylan the idea: what would be more natural and less original than invalid port being sent to an invalid? One might even imagine a voice inflection like "It *is* for an invalid". All of this looks quite in keeping with the nature of the "Wandering Rocks" chapter — transferences on the surface. At the time, no matter how closely we scrutinized the scene in the fruit shop, we would never have guessed such a trifle.

Such hindsight elucidation only works if we match a later occurrence with a prior one. An act of recognition is required which may or may not take place. It often doesn't, given the wealth of details to pay attention to.[10] Uninformed by external nudges, we may never connect Bloom's "I was (just) going to throw it away" (*U* 5. 534 and 537) with the outcome of the Gold Cup race — but officious commentators usually take care that we do before we were prepared.

For easy reference, what is common to all the above processes shall be denoted by means of a Greek verb which simply means to recognise: **"ana-gignô-sk-ein"**, "to know again." The noun suggested for retroactive modification is **"anagnôsis"**, "recogni-

---

10. Not all translators remember, when they come across "invalid port", that this ties up with a casual remark hundreds of pages before.

tion". The term is similar to the two Aristotle used in his *Poetics*: "**anagnôrismos**" or "**anagnôrisis**", for very specific revelations or discoveries. The Greeks, with fine insight, extended the meaning of the verb "**anagignoskein**" to the analogous cognitive activity of reading. By common sense, reading depends on knowing again what we come across, on *recognition*. We are less likely to lose sight of this platitude in a book like *Ulysses*, where non-recognition often frustrates us. Making our way through a later chapter like "Circe" is largely a matter of recalling earlier events, phrases, motives. The episode is, vitally, an elaborate orgy of anagnostic distortions and permutations. "Circe" depends on its own past.

Anagnosis, by definition, is always secondary — *re*-cognition. Reading the Gerty MacDowell parts again allows us to see them readjusted. When Mulligan ungirdles himself we can project back and verify that he did have a girdle, by anagnosis. We do not always understand at once. Joyce instructs us to wait. Bloom remembers a night in the box of the Gaiety theatre with Molly, when he "Told her what Spinoza says in that book of poor papa's. Hypnotised, listening.... She bent". (*U* 11.1058) Even though we cannot make out whether she was hypnotized by his talk or perhaps listening to the music before or after, she appeared attentive. Her own point of view will set this right: "and him the other side of me talking about Spinoza and his soul thats dead... I smiled the best I could all in a swamp leaning forward as if I was interested having to sit it out then" (*U* 18.1114-16). Not Spinoza, but menstruation was on her mind, and ever after, with this now in *our* minds, we may find Bloom's "What do they think when they hear music?" or "Nature woman half a look" (*U* 11.1049 and 1061) obliquely expanded.

The most elaborate passage sorely in need of elucidation is the verbal jumble at the beginning of the "Sirens" chapter. "Understanding" these pages (called "Ouverture", "Prelude", or "tuning up") pragmatically consists in discovering the parts later on in the chapter from which the opening fragments look extracted. Conventional order is inverted. "Bronze by gold heard the hoofirons" (*U* 11.1) makes sense since we have already come across bronze and gold and can identify them as Miss Kennedy and Miss Douce (*U* 10.962). Otherwise we would be at a loss:

"bronze" does not normally "hear". The second item, however, "Imperthnthn thnthnthn" (*U* 11.2) remains cryptic until we find an insolent bootsboy who turns a haughty voice saying "your impertinent insolence" into a mocking variation "Imperthnthn thnthnthn" (*U* 11. 99-100). Ever after, we are likely to think that "Imperthnthn thnthnthn" actually *means* "impertinent insolence", but it only does so in proleptic and unwarranted foresight. In this way the "Overture" is being read backwards. The technique could be termed, by misappropriation, one of functional "afterclang" (*U* 11.767).

Protean Postcreation

Where Joyce differs anagnostically from most other writers is in the vitality of these retroprocesses, in the postponed modification. Seasoned Joyceans may, in fact, forget how much of what they know is tacitly and rightfully projected onto the pages. We all know that Stephen on Sandymount beach is writing a poem. Or do we? What we are given is a muddle of associations: "He comes, pale vampire, through storm his eyes, his bat sails bloodying the sea, mouth to her mouth's kiss" (*U* 3.397-98). Then a new paragraph says: "Here. Put a pin in that chap, will you? My tablets. Mouth to her kiss. No. Must be two of em. Glue em well. Mouth to her mouth's kiss. His lips lipped and mouthed fleshless lips of air: mouth to her moomb.[11] Oomb, allwombing tomb. His mouth moulded issuing breath, unspeeched.... Paper... Old Deasy's letter... Turning his back to the sun he bent over far to a table of rock and scribbled words. That's twice I forgot to take slips from the library counter" (*U* 3.399-407). We realise that Stephen, after experimenting with sounds and enunciation, *scribbles words* — words, presumably, that grow out of what he turns over in his mind. The passage is sketchy; we see nothing of the writing nor do we, at this moment, read the composer's thoughts (as we usually do in a stream of consciousness chapter). No reader could tell what exactly the words are that Stephen

---

11. Pre-Gabler editions of *Ulysses* said: "womb".

records, except that "mouth" and "kiss" are probably featured. Revelation has to await a scene in the newspaper office of the "Aeolus"chapter when a bit of paper torn off elicits comment. It is then that we read, this time in Stephen's mind, but arranged as though they were laid out on paper, four neat lines of verse: "*On swift sail flaming / From storm and south / He comes, pale vampire, / Mouth to my mouth.*" (*U* 7.522) So this seems to be what was taken down on the beach in moments of narrative inattendance. Now the processes that went into the making of a short stanza can be reconstructed, in part. We can NOW tell — or at least tell with some assurance — what it is that was thought THEN.

We could never have inferred from the "Proteus" passage that "He comes, pale vampire" was taken over unchanged. Surprisingly, what was *twice* "mouth to her mouth's kiss", and the variant "Mouth to *her* kiss", has become "Mouth to *my* mouth".[12] The female element has evaporated completely, three *hers* have been replaced by *my*. There is, in other words, more Stephen and less woman. Similarly, "kiss" has disappeared in the final version, and all that experimenting with oomb-womb sounds went for nothing.

We can also potentially recognise an addition unsuspected before, most likely the unconscious recall of Douglas Hyde's English translation of an Irish poem from the *Lovesongs of Connaught*, which ends in "His mouth to my mouth" to rhyme with "south". Both the borrowings and the differences from Douglas Hyde's metric pattern and wording are now more evident. We also see what has fallen by the wayside: sails are not bloodying, but "flaming" (this was lifted from "the sun's flaming sword" (*U* 3. 392). Other elements like "swift" and "south" have been added.[13]

The finished product throws retrospective light on the process of

12. Ironically, Deasy's letter, the part not usurped by Stephen, also contains "mouth". Ireland's agricultural threat and Stephen's fictional conceit seem to chime when, just after we read "*Mouth to my mouth*", professor MacHugh puts his foot in: "Foot and mouth?" (*U* 7.527).

13. Retrospective comparison can point to a minor thematic permutation: What in "Proteus", was "the sun's *flaming* sword — *sails* bloodying the sea — the *southing* sun" (*U* 3.391; 397 and 442, italics added) has been realigned into: "*sail flaming ... south*" (*U* 7.522-23).

51

its finishing, but not too much. We cannot tell, of course, whether
the version given in typographical arrangement (suitable for a
chapter dealing with printing and newspapers) is what Stephen
wrote down on the beach. For all we know, he could have
transformed the four lines several times over in Protean perpetua-
tion. We only know that selective and compositional changes were
being made.in between.

Without the later passage, the earlier one would remain highly
opaque. This is especially so if we compare it to its analogue in *A
Portrait*, Stephen's elaborate, and elaborately recorded, composition of the villanelle. What is of interest here is not only that a later
occurrence anagnostically elucidates its counterpart, but that it
may prompt us to modify our views of Joyce's technical
procedure. A chapter like "Proteus", almost entirely given over to
the interior monologue, might suggest *an almost unbroken stream*
of perception and associations. We might easily think that — in a
kind of psycho-transcript, or a translation of thought into words
— we are consistently told what goes on. We later find out what
mental processes (composing even four simple lines is a highly
complex web of interactions) were silently elided, outside of our
range. The processes of selection and matching and structuring
were much more intricate than a sentence that directed us to the
writer's shadow — "His shadow lay over the rocks as he bent,
ending" (*U* 3.408) — would have indicated. Hindsight discloses a
major narrative omission.

In retrospect we become more knowledgeable and at the same
time perhaps more skeptical. More accreted knowledge implies an
increased sense of what further may elude us. Elusiveness itself
becomes part of the meaning.

On the Boil

We cannot be aware of what we do not know. Many passages do
not seem to require clarification at all. In the first bedroom scene
of the Blooms, few of the trivia we witness raise questions. Molly's
imperative "Poldy!" hastens Bloom up to her bedside. "Who are
the letters for?" she asks. "— A letter for me from Milly, he said
carefully, and a card to you. And a letter for you" (*U* 4.250). On a

first exposure we can hardly notice how carefully, indeed, Bloom contrives his answer. On a return reading the studied casualness of his enumeration is striking. He first mentions his own letter, then Milly's card. "And a letter for you" sounds like an afterthought; it is, however, we now realize, what he knows Molly wants to know above all. The letter, picked up on the hallfloor, with its address "Mrs Marion Bloom" in a "Bold hand", has already made "his quickened heart [slow] at once" (U 4.244). It made him lose his composure. His plain answer is a careful act of dramatic retardation.

Having deposited Molly's mail on the twill bedspread, he might well leave, his duties done; but he lingers behind and asks "Do you want the blind up?" and, unbidden, proceeds to let more light into the room. A deviously appropriate word, "blind": all during the day Bloom will shut any thought of the man who sent that letter to his wife out from his mind. Moreover, in the course of the novel, "blind" will acquire a sense of Odyssean subterfuge. With "The courthouse is a blind" (U 12.1550), Lenehan suggests that Bloom's words are a pretext.[14] It is easy to overemphasize such subsidiary connotations. What makes them possible is a memory of their future.

When we know what the consequences of Molly's letter are, we appreciate her impatience better than we did on our first encounter, and understand why she hurries Bloom out of the room so she can read its contents: "Hurry up with that tea, she said. I'm parched." He answers: "The kettle is boiling" (U 4.263-64). As he reaches the kitchen soon after, with Molly's "Scald the teapot" still in his ear, he finds the pot "On the boil, sure enough" (U 4. 270-71). Domestic routine, all of this, sure enough. For readers alerted to the nature of the rival who will bring the programme and generally manages Mrs Marion Bloom's impending concert tour, and familiar with Bloom censuring perturbing thoughts, the doubling of "boiling" and "on the boil" is less of a harmless repetition. Mind you, at this point the name Boylan has not yet surfaced; but Bloom knows, as his reactions indicate, who sent the letter. Anagnostic substitution enables us to interpret a haunting

14. Molly Bloom will also think of "some blind excuse" (U 18.695).

non-presence. For this we do not depend on later alignments like
Lenehan's "I'm Boylan with impatience," or its near-resumption
"I'm off, said Boylan with impatience" (*U* 10.486; 11.426), but the
two resounding occurrences infuse the morning's "boil(ing)" even
more. In other words, we understand much of *Ulysses* by what is
not yet there on the page.

As he fiddled with the blind, Bloom's "backward eye saw her
glance at the letter and tuck it under her pillow" (*U* 4.256). His
"backward eye" can be taken out of context and interpreted as a
tacit reading instruction. Backward glances allow us to interpret
what we do not understand, and to reinterpret what we think we
did. Backward eyes are the subject of this essay.

Pointing to the Title

Titles, in their annunciatory nature, are proleptic. They direct,
anticipate, raise expectations. They are *pro*gnostic. True to
promise, *Dubliners* is in fact about Dubliners; there *is* a mother in
"A Mother". In the first story we may wonder, afterwards, why
Father Flynn's sisters should be singled out for mention in the
title, if in fact they are; but the sisters, though perhaps off centre, at
least are there. On the other hand, "Counterparts" is more tricky
— what does it project? The title "A Painful Case" turns out to be
a phrase lifted from a newspaper, though it then radiates beyond
its immediate context to include Mr James Duffy himself. We can
hardly foretell, at the outset, what "Araby" is going to be about.

The announcement "Grace" might promise various things, none
of them too clearly (possibly a name like Eveline). The subsequent
tale will define it; in the course of our reading we will narrow it
down, theologically, to a gift of God, against which we can measure the various more secular occurrences of the word. We
understand the title *after* the reading. "Grace" becomes a handle
to talk about the story, the story explains the title, the title in turn
gives incongruous weight to a merely prepositional "By grace of
these two articles of clothing" (*D* 154). By anagnosis — *and*
prognosis — title and story interact. "A Little Cloud" is a different
case, with, apparently, no anagnostic epiphany to emerge from
textual insights. So far no interpreter has revealed by a plausible

elucidation what exactly the Old Testament echo achieves. What it does is to help create unrest.

The headlines Joyce added to the seventh chapter of *Ulysses* at a late stage also serve, in journalistic fashion, to anticipate, summarize and whet the appetite. Headlines prepare for something. Interestingly enough, the "Aeolus" episode also includes the opposite direction: Stephen puts a "vision" into words, spontaneously, it appears. He makes up a story that ends abruptly and is then asked to supply a title for it. Three revisionary names are then suggested — afterwards — as alternatives (*U* 7.1057). So in a temporal sense it is not true that Stephen *tells* "The Parable of the Plums" — what he has told *becomes* a "Parable" or a "Pisgah Sight" by annexion. The appended labels in turn open dimensions the tale itself might otherwise not have had. Similarly (though not by authorial hindsight) a fictive Dublin day changes some of its constrictions by being named "Ulysses".

Aeolian headlines prepare for what is to follow, often in conventional proclamation ("RETURN OF BLOOM"), but more and more also in phrases ("HELLO THERE, CENTRAL!") held in suspense of which the import has to be determined retrospectively. A certain type of newspaper thrives on distortive anticipation. Occasionally, an event is featured only in the headlines, not in the subsequent text. There is nothing in the last section of the chapter that would bear out the titular promise of "ANNE WIMBLES, FLO WANGLES" (*U* 7.1070). It will turn out that this information, if anything, already *is* the story, displaced and perverted from the body of the text, where all we read is "Tickled the old ones too", an item that was already taken care of by "DIGITS PROVE TOO TITILLATING". The wimbling[14] and wangling is self-sufficient and paves the way for an anagnostic blank.

Aeolian headlines become progressively more titillating and self-

15. If indeed, as Stuart Gilbert claims (with an alleged nudge from the author), that "WIMBLES" is a *hapax legomenon* (*James Joyce's Ulysses*, New York: Vintage, 1955, p. 198), the situation becomes even more tantalizing. A *hapax legomenon* is a lexical unit that occurs only once and has to be defined from that one context alone. Only wimbling Anne could know then what it is that she is doing.

perpetuating. A sentence like "ITHACANS VOW PEN IS CHAMP" (*U* 7. 1034) takes part in two contexts. The immediate one is the environment of the excessive headline itself which includes such pointers as "SOPHIST — SPARTANS — HELEN" as well as "PROBOSCIS". A Hellenic flavour may help to pinpoint "PEN". The Greeks, discordantly, never abbreviated their names in such a crass manner; "PEN" remains indeterminate. In the major context of the chapter, such a word has already figured rhetorically in an earlier headline: "THE CROZIER AND THE PEN" (*U* 7. 62), as well as in metaphorical dialogue ("that was a pen" (*U* 7. 630); a member of the staff was seen with a real "pen behind his ear" (*U* 7. 34). None of these potential meanings are valid of course, nor does "CHAMP" refer, as it did earlier in *Ulysses*, to horses. The excessive headline owes its origin to a wholly tangential remark: Stephen is compared to Antisthenes, the sophist, who is credited with "a book in which he took away the palm of beauty from Argive Helen and handed it to poor Penelope" (*U* 7. 1038). It is this aspect which has suffered inflation into the heading — inflated as well as dislocuted, changed. The beauty contest has been transferred to a splurge of parochial pride. "PEN IS CHAMP", an anachronistic jumble, can be understood, once more, in hindsight. "Penelope" postdefines "PEN", without, however, entirely deleting a hovering surface sense of a dominating writing pen, which still functions thematically in a chapter that pits oral skills against written or printed ones.

From another angle or by Homeric conditioning, "ITHACANS VOW PEN IS CHAMP" could be read as a paraphrase from the *Odyssey*, where one of the suitors, speaking for all the others (all Ithacans) vows to poor Penelope: "You excel all women in comeliness and stature" (*Od.* 18:248-9).

By their privileged positions, titles and headlines demonstrate the interaction of before and after even better than other parts. Everything we find in *Ulysses* may still, potentially, contribute to the significance of its powerful title.

Coming Events Cast Their Shadows Before

Often a shadow precedes the event, an echo its origin, a distortion its prototype, a rumour the reality. We hear the mass in parody before we attend one in All Hallows Church absorbing fragments of the real thing. Stephen's opinions on *Hamlet* are first offered in Mulligan's mock exaggeration ("He proves by algebra that Hamlet's grandson is Shakespeare's grandfather...." (*U* 1.555). They have to wait several chapters to be unfolded in a less facetious and more extensive form. An important key term in *Ulysses* is introduced by, literally, nothing, by sound not recorded, a blank in the text that we would not even perceive if it were not followed by a request for completion: "Met him what? he asked" (*U* 4.336). Right afterwards the word becomes visible and is spelled out, defined and implemented — "Metempsychosis?" (*U* 4.339). We hear of Bloom's potato long before we can guess why he should take it on a tour in his pocket.

In the third chapter Stephen calls up his "consubstantial father's voice" (*U* 3.62) as it comments on the in-laws, the Goulding faction: "The drunken little costdrawer" (*U* 3.66), and then again, Crissie, "Papa's little bedpal. Lump of love" (*U* 3.88). Uncle Richie Goulding himself is partial to superlatives: "The grandest number, Stephen, in the whole opera" (*U* 3.100). This happens in an environment of thematic change, the voices heard may be unreliably transformed by memory or by imagination. When later on we hear a live Simon Dedalus say "the drunken little costdrawer and Crissie, papa's little lump of dung" (*U* 6.52), or when Richie Goulding rhapsodies to Bloom: "Grandest number in the whole opera" (*U* 11.828), we realize that the pre-echoes were substantially true. The first part of *Ulysses*, at any rate, offers parallactic confirmation and a texture of realistic coherence.

A minor character, Tom Kernan (known to readers of "Grace"), first turns up as a subject for thought or conversation. His favourite expressions, on Ben Dollard's singing of "The Croppy Boy", are imitated by Martin Cunningham "draw[ing] him out....pompously": "— Immense....*His singing of that simple ballad, Martin, is the most trenchant rendering I ever heard in the whole course of my experience. – Trenchant*, Mr Power said laughing. He's dead nuts on that. And the *retrospective arrangement*" (*U* 6.146-50). This prospective characterization will be validated, the parody justified. When Tom Kernan appears in person he lives up to this mimicry: "When you look back on it all now in a kind of retrospective arrangement" (*U* 10.783) he thinks; and "Ben Dollard does sing that ballad touchingly. Masterly rendition" (*U* 10.791); and again: "Most trenchant rendition of that ballad" (*U* 11.1148). Report this time has been proven right. Kernan's cherished phrase, "the retrospective arrangement", is a key term for the techniques that are examined in this sketchy survey; it illustrates acts of "anagnosis". Most examples presented are retrospective arrangements.

True to type, Tom Kernan will in fact propose "The Croppy Boy" to be sung in the Ormond bar (*U* 11.991), its masterly rendition will be set forth in refracted quotation. As readers we can retrospectively appreciate that, with its teary emphasis on the death of Irish rebels, the ballad fitted very well into the "Hades" chapter where it was first brought to casual notice as not much more than an attempt to keep a conversation going.

Terminal (Un)certainties

A later occurrence, as has been abundantly reiterated, may throw light on, or modify, an earlier passage, or reveal a surprising turn. When the documents in Bloom's second drawer prove his financial basis (including £900 government stock *U* 17.1864) to be reasonably secure, all his little economies during the day take on another aspect, and he becomes a bit of an Odysseus laden with treasures. When, on the other hand, we hear that "it was Bloom who gave the ideas for Sinn Fein to Griffith" (*U* 12.1574), this entirely new angle need not turn him into a political schemer or grey eminence or clandestine agent, for the rumour is unlikely to be based on fact; and yet one wonders to what accidental fire this particular smoke may be due. The role projected on Bloom in this instance is potentially adequate and, for all its practical unlikelihood, helps to characterize him and displays how the others view him with suspicion as someone not to be categorized, a dark horse.

Postponed information, if reliable, often clarifies very little; it does not of course automatically, in an ultimate epiphanic flash, put everything into place or remove all doubt. Not all of us would agree with the following conclusion on "How Joyce Ends": " 'Two Gallants' was written so that the story's central idea — that Corley

and Lenehan have conspired to defraud a servant girl out of a gold
sovereign to finance an evening in the pubs — eludes the reader
until the final line, when Corley displays the coin."[16] One
assumption is that "Two Gallants" has a "central idea", another
that it is manifested through the coin in Corley's palm, the last
thing we read. Consequentially we recognize, so the argument
seems to go, that Corley and Lenehan have been hatching a plot,
with malice aforethought, and with success. So we can reinterpret
the whole story and see how Lenehan, with whom we are detained
most of the time, was in the know all along (but we were not). We
are finally assured that "a gold coin eliminates any ambiguity
about their motives," and "that the story is another indictment of
the Irishman's preference for clambering over a woman to get a
bottle of stout" (Herring, p. 96 and 51). All of this may well be part
of the story's meaning and the characters's motivation, but it does
invest a final disclosure with inordinate anagnostic trust in
wholesale disambiguation. Perhaps Joycean motives — and that is
something the stories might also reveal — are a trifle more
intricate. Anagnosis is not a finite process.

Not everything will resolve itself in hindsight. Hermeneutic
gains induce new turbulences. Postponed clarification may never
take place, often simply for lack of further evidence. Most of us,
for instance, assumed from Bloom's memory of his father-in-law,
"At Plevna that was" (*U* 4.63), that Major Tweedy took part in the
battle of that name and fondly used to reminisce about it. Molly
remembers "Groves and father talking about Rorkes drift and
Plevna and sir Garnet Wolseley and Gordon at Khartoum" (*U*
18.690). Several scholars have documented that no British troops
took part in that battle of Plevna in Bulgaria (December 1877). It
seems assured that a major of the Royal Fusiliers, or a drum major
or sergeant major for that matter, could not possibly have first
hand knowledge of it. What does this mean for us? Was Joyce
careless or sloppy; was Brian Tweedy dishonest or bragging to his
own family; or is he "the product of such fantastically loose
historical manipulation that at no point can he be taken seriously"

16. Phillip F. Herring, *Joyce's Uncertainty Principle*, Princeton:
Princeton UP, 1987, p. 196.

(Herring, p. 135)? Or should we perhaps give up the *prima facie* notion that he did claim, on several recorded occasions, to have participated at Plevna? After all he might have been retailing something picked up from army talk, or out of Hozier's *History of the Russo-Turkish War*[17] that he appropriated from the Garrison Library of Gibraltar. There do not seem to be anagnostic pointers for plausible reconstruction of this sort, and so we might have to reserve judgment.

Ten Pages of Notes

Anagnostic insights are a matter of temporal disposition. Postponed revelation or modification entails a very practical, didactic dilemma for those who provide outside information in the form of annotation, commentary, glosses, or in the class room. Assuming that not every reader nowadays knows of the Ascot Gold Cup in 1904 (in fact it takes some time for us to find out that the date of Bloomsday *is* 1904 — when do we really first know?), of the battle of Plevna, "The Croppy Boy", the Latin of the Church, Irish history, Dublin topography, etc., what sort of data should be given out WHEN? Annotators tend to anticipate, to pre-identify, to shortcut the explorative processes of reading that have here been likened to the parsing of a Latin sentence. For the benefit of instant enlightenment, commentators officiously put **"circumdet"** before **"Liliata"**, an orderly horse before the nebulous cart, since this is also what is expected of them.

On the first page of *A Portrait* we come across two names, "The brush with the maroon velvet back was for Michael Davitt and the

---

17. This book, we learn, contained: "The name of a decisive battle (forgotten), frequently remembered by a decisive officer, major Brian Cooper Tweedy (remembered)" (*U* 17. 1419). The contrastive array of remembering, forgetting, and decisiveness is far from clear. It might mean that Bloom does not remember (though he did earlier on) the name of the battle, but that major Tweedy often did since he played a decisive part *in it*. Or else the adjective indicates no more than that Tweedy was a decisive officer with regard to professional aptitude. Ironically, it is factual meaning that is not decisive.

brush with the green velvet back was for Parnell" (*P* 7); and as readers of the late 20th century we may have to rely on commentary. But of course Stephen himself does not yet know who these people are; he will learn later. That is, among much else, what the *Portrait* is about, learning. The reader is still to hear a lot about Parnell in scenes to come, but practically nothing new will be added regarding Michael Davitt, a historical figure far less known than Parnell. So a note has to be supplied, and supplied right on the spot, at the first mention of the name. Premature information can hardly be avoided, yet it goes against the developmental grain of the transformative novel which, after all, begins with **"ignotas"** in its epigraph. External Annotation replaces inherent Ignotation and must do so, unfortunately, often far too soon.

As the funeral carriage gets under way in the sixth chapter of *Ulysses*, "The wheels rattled rolling over the cobbled causeway and the crazy glasses shook rattling in the doorframes" (*U* 6.30-31). Our guiding commentaries hastily inform us that this refers to a song, "The Pauper's Drive", whose refrain is "Rattle his bones over the stones". Is this sufficient, pertinent, or convincing? It is likely to become more so as we rattle along and, pages later, come upon "Rattle his bones. Over the stones. Only a pauper. Nobody owns." (*U* 6.333) These are the actual words of the song, echoing in Bloom's mind to the rhythm of the carriage. From there on the song accompanies Bloom for a short while, and of course it is now possible to say that, perhaps, the previous rattling (without either bones or stones) already alluded to a song few of us would ever know or recognize without its subsequent direct quotation. At best, the early rattle is a vague adumbration, an echo before the sound is turned on. The untimely note makes sense on the premise that Annotation must translate a sequential progression into spatially available simultaneous knowledge.

When, in the first chapter, Mulligan talks to an acquaintance who tells him that he "got a card from Bannon. Says he found a sweet young thing down there. Photo girl he calls her" (*U* 1.684), our *Annotations* inform us, helpfully, that "Alec Bannon is an associate of Mulligan's circle and has met Milly Bloom down in Westmeath" (Gifford p. 15-6). That this Bannon is called Alec will surface in the 14th chapter, and readers who make the connection themselves will be mildly thrilled by subsidiary recognition. Who "Milly Bloom" is, even the most ideal reader simply cannot know at this stage. There is, in the first chapter, no Milly Bloom. Certainly, in some way, the Blooms in *Ulysses* may be said to grow out of this sweet young photo girl, but her precipitate exposure also counteracts something as insignificant as the dynamic spirit of the whole work. It is as useful as telling the reader of a detective novel in the first scene what the gardener has got hidden in his pocket.

Quite apart from depriving novice readers of the oldest literary pleasures of suspense and surprise, such anticipation implies that a first chapter is not really first, but coequal with all the others. This state of panoramic synopsis and readerly omniscience may be a distant goal. It is an aim of annotation to spare its readers trouble and save them time, but this time is then also removed from the reader's engagement with Joyce's works, the time of incubation, exploration, discovery, qualification, and renewed questioning and probing. All that this peroration wants to do is to balance the tutorial intervention and the prognostic remedies (that are often pragmatically necessary) against the ingrained anagnostic enjoyment of progressive reading as well as the frustrations of failed anagnosis.

James Joyce Foundation, Zürich

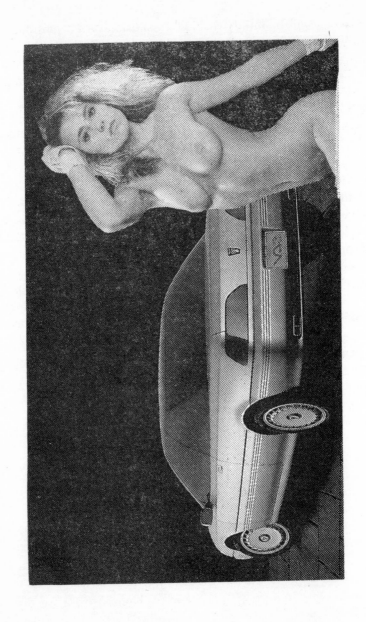

"THE LANGUAGE OF FLOW":
JOYCE'S DISPOSSESSION OF THE FEMININE IN *ULYSSES*

CHRISTINE VAN BOHEEMEN

In front of me lies an advertisement clipped from a recent newspaper. It displays a smoothly streamlined car — rounded hood and tail-lights, curving bumpers. The image of the car partly disappears behind the photographed torso of a naked, prominently busted young woman who twists her body to give the impression of extreme streamlining: buttocks rounded out to the back, the taut belly and breasts curving to the front. The text of the advertisement announces "exciting news" of a national automobile show, and does not mention the woman. The function of her image in the composition is to lend the image of the car, and beyond that the automobile show, the excitement suggested and proclaimed. To the student of literature the rhetorical strategy of the advertisement should be very familiar. We are dealing with a visual metaphor. If in "my love is like a red, red rose", the rose stands for the woman, in the ad the woman stands for the car, and expresses the excitement to be attributed to it. The image of the woman is the *vehicle* of communication for an associative idea — excitement. The aspect of the woman's figure that makes her image appropriate for that function is its sexy streamlining.

What is the connection between advertising and Joyce's *Ulysses*? Is there not a wide difference between the world of high art and the vulgar expressions of contemporary advertising? There certainly is. Still, the structure of the advertisement helps me communicate my notion of the function of the image of woman in *Ulysses* in two ways. First of all, my reading of the ad in the previous paragraph foreshadows my approach to Joyce's novel. Instead of the traditional scholarly question "What is the meaning of the text?" or "What does the text say?" my perspective is more critical. The central query of this essay will be "What is the function of the image of woman for the coherence and prestige (the "stream-lining") of *Ulysses*?" It is a way of reading which I first saw advocated in Pierre Macherey's *A Theory of Literary Production* which taught me that the question "What necessity does this literary work embody?" often reveals aspects of structure and internal coherence which we might not have noticed otherwise.[1] A reading which thus focuses on rhetorical or persuasive intention no longer regards the work of art as a mimetic icon or the representation of a transcendent truth. Once we raise the question of purpose and function, the literary text is already seen as a speech act. It seems to me that feminist literary criticism of Joyce, in its attempt to advance beyond the thematic annotation of Joyce's images of women and their sources or biographical research into his relationships with women, must dare to break the enchanting mirror of seeming reality which keeps us locked in illusion, and scrutinize the literary text with analytic objectivity and an awareness of its constructed nature.

Secondly, then, the advertisement helps me to clarify my insight into the function Joyce's use of the image of woman has for the architecture of *Ulysses* both as imaged reflection of our world, and as the intentional act of authorship, the signature, of James Joyce. Though the connotation of womanhood in the literary text (I shall focus exclusively on Molly Bloom) differs from that in the advertisement, its function seems similar. As a convincing image of feminine flow, and the *mise en abyme* of Joyce's own flowing style, Molly Bloom functions as warrant and proof of the authority of her author and his prestigious place in the tradition of the English novel as the writer who ended the realist tradition by carrying it to its limits.[2]

One of the most striking qualities of *Ulysses*, in addition to its difficulty, is its subversion of the conventions of realism. At first sight this may seem an odd statement since Joyce did everything possible to ensure that his fiction confirmed the actuality of life in

1. Trans. Geoffrey Wall, 1966; London: Routledge, 1978.
2. The argument of this essay relies upon chapter VII of *The Novel as Family Romance: Language, Gender, and Authority from Fielding to Joyce*, Ithaca: Cornell UP, 1987.

Dublin, June 16, 1904. Moreover, to extend the grasp of his realism, he devised a technique of interior monologue which allowed the novelist to bring the most intimate and hidden details of private life and personal experience into public view. Yet the aspect which begins to demand attention — more and more the better we get to know the novel — is its irregularity, its violation of conventions, its unsettling of identities, its subtle frustration of readerly expectations, and its apparent desire to create uncertainty and doubt rather than distinct clarity and meaning.[3]

To take a well-known interpretative crux central to our sense of the meaning of Joyce's story: How does the plot of son seeks father end? What does the meeting of Stephen and Bloom signify? Opinions are divided and diverse.[4] Secondly, where does the story end? With "Ithaca", the chapter of definitions as Joyce himself indicated? Or is "Penelope", the chapter of feminine flux and dreamy reminiscence which closes the text, its true end? I raise these questions not to answer them, but to show that even if we do not focus on individual words or fragments of sentences, much of the weaving of *Ulysses* remains polyinterpretable. Indeed, *Ulysses* may well be a deliberately unsettling, ambivalent text, sublimating the principle of doubt upon which it is founded into a textual strategy which leads the reader to an experience of that doubt. If Homer is noted for his exemplary clarity, Joyce's version of the story about Odysseus, (ambivalently named *Ulysses* rather than *Odysseus*), seems remarkable for its perversion of single meaning. Rather than Homer, it is Penelope, weaving and unweaving her web, who may have been Joyce's model of authority. Her example is a style of weaving which suggests and promises closure, but simultaneously postpones and subverts it, in defiance of full definition and definite choice. Unwilling to continue the paralyzing tradition of English realism — in his eyes that is —

3. See Karen Lawrence, *The Odyssey of Style in Ulysses*, Princeton: Princeton UP, 1981, for an analysis of the stylistic idiosyncracies of *Ulysses*.

4. See Richard M. Kain, "The Significance of Stephen's Meeting Bloom: A Survey of Interpretations," in *Fifty Years Ulysses*, ed. Thomas F. Staley, Bloomington: Indiana Univ. Press, 1974, pp. 147-160 for a survey of different readings and interpretations.

Joyce may have devised a way of writing fiction which would at once be more truthful than and different from the tradition — and the model for this "otherness", and for this notion of truth, was in Nietzschean fashion, it seems to me, the idea of otherness provided by the feminine. Just as woman is the complementary "other" to the "Man of Reason" of Western thought,[5] hence alogical, erratic, undecidable and flowing, just so Joyce presented himself as the other (and better half) of the tradition of novelistic authority, writing an epic which at once continues and subverts the generic convention as its complement and other in its doubtful undecidability.

Our question may well be, "Why did Joyce choose this unprecedented style of authority? Would it not have been more sensible to stick to the realism of the first chapters of *Ulysses* which sufficiently demonstrate Joyce's mastery, as Pound advised with irritation? In order to clarify Joyce's choice I should like to turn to the words of Leopold Bloom, who, in "Circe", desires to hear woman speak: "Speak, you! Are you struck dumb? You are the link between nations and generations. Speak, woman, sacred lifegiver!" (*U* 15.4647-50). Suddenly brave, meek Bloom conquers his fear of women, and starts giving orders. One could interpret these words in the psychological frame of Bloom's characterization. But in addition to being an illustration of a certain type of personality (who may resemble the author), these words also refer to a more general, cultural-historical issue: Woman, defined as "sacred lifegiver" is reproached for not speaking, and receives the command to do so. As the "link between nations and generations" after all, she possesses the knowledge of the mysterious secret of life and death. In Bloom's mind the time-honoured Christian image of woman as the passive (and silent) fleshly house of passage of the masculine and transcendent spirit, has made way for a new myth, the modern biological myth of woman as "lifegiver", which seems no less one-sided than the earlier one. Whereas traditionally

5. In *The Man of Reason: "Male" and "Female" in Western Philosophy*, Genevieve Lloyd provides an analysis of the consistency with which masculinity has defined itself as "rational" in Western thought, and the necessary semantic complementary of the feminine (London: Methuen, 1984).

in Western thought the role of "lifegiver" had been reserved for God the Father, now woman is suddenly promoted from *medium* to *origin* and source of life; and it is Bloom's desire to hear this voice of origin speak, as if *vox feminae* were *vox dei*. If we also remember that Stephen Dedalus desires his mother to supply him with the one word known to all men, we begin to sense a pattern which may not merely inhere in the attitude to women taken by the actors in the story, but may also apply to the point of view of their text.[6]

Regarded from this point of view, Joyce provides in "Penelope" the actual realization of Bloom's desire. Molly's scabrous fantasies and recollections are almost literally the voice of blood, the voice of life — life as sexual instinct and biological continuity. It is as if the locus of authority not only shifted from Father to Mother, but moved from spirit to matter, from transcendent origin to physical reproduction; and did so with the vengeful intention to finally expose the repressed dirty secret.

Thus "Penelope", a chapter of words instead of events, fantasy rather than fact, libido instead of ratio, seemingly Joyce's afterthought, may be central to our understanding of the nature of the text as a whole. It is perhaps not accidental that this chapter should have been selected for repeated stage dramatizations. It may be worthwhile, therefore, to pause and study the distinctive features of Molly's language and style, and their relation to the inscription of otherness and the principles of doubt in *Ulysses* as a whole.

The most striking *stylistic* quality of Molly's monologue is its scarcity of punctuation marks. The flow of the eight sentences (8 as the symbol of Mary, Mother of God, as well as the lemniscate denoting infinity) is often read, as Joyce said he intended it to be read, as the representation of feminine language — alogical, flowing, inconsequential. In every way this language is the counterpart to the masculine logos/logic of predicative meaning which ever since God's example of masculine behaviour in

6. If Joyce indeed identifies his desired style of linguistic authority with the feminine, he is part of a larger movement which is characteristic of modern writing, as Alice A. Jardine argues in *Gynesis: Configurations of Woman and Modernity,* Ithaca: Cornell UP, 1985.

Genesis, makes sense and meaning through the strategies of exclusion, division, separation, and opposition.

Undermining the possibility of discrimination, distinction, and denial, "Penelope" suspends the either/or of logic into a both/and (or neither/nor). But this unsettling preclusion of final meaning and identity is, as I already implied, also a characteristic quality of *Ulysses* as a whole — even if embodied or articulated differently than in this chapter. Thus the final episode of the fiction is not merely different from the body of the text in that it stands apart and outside as an "ek-static" *ricorso* (to use Vico's term for the movement of return to beginning). It is, simultaneously, its continuation, almost the concentrated apotheosis of the stylistic tendencies — and the desire — of a text which wishes to inscribe itself as "other". In repeating, intensifying, and thus clarifying the style of writing of the body of the text, "Penelope" gives us the distilled essence of Joyce's style — and here its extreme realism of physical detail as well as "profound" psychological penetration are as relevant as its apparent flux. Its successful achievement retrospectively affirms and confirms the deviant identity of the work as a whole — in theme, structure, style, and intertextuality. In a very sly and cunning way "Penelope" functions as both the cap-stone and corner-stone of *Ulysses*, its *alpha* and *omega*, *arche* and *telos*.

Here the car advertisement returns to my memory. What is the function of the idea or image of woman (Molly Bloom and her speech), for the rhetorical intention of the novel as a whole? In the ad, the image of woman helped to suggest, to give presence to the attractiveness and excitement of the car. The peculiarity there was that in order to do so, the figure of the woman had to be doubly appropriated. Not only is she used as medium of communication, she is also deprived of an autonomous physical identity and appearance. Her body is displayed as streamlined — but that notion of armoured streamlining is already suggested by the smoothness and coldness of stainless steel. It is not an intrinsic quality of the soft irregularity of human, especially female, flesh. The idea of perfect instrumentality which clings to the car is *projected upon* the woman's body; it is not intrinsic to her human identity. She is already the connotation produced by the desire for technological mastery. What about Joyce's image of Molly

Bloom? If Molly's style is to serve as emblem of the text's new and perverse identity, the question rises whether the otherness attributed to her is the intrinsic identity of (a) woman. Is it, perhaps, as we noted in connection with the ad, already the projection of a (modern and "masculine"?) desire for alternative authority?

Let us scrutinize the *Darstellung* of Molly Bloom more closely. In addition to the connotion of flow mentioned above, Molly is characterized by her mocking deflation of cultural and spiritual ideals and icons. In an earlier chapter in *Ulysses* we learn that she parses "metempsychosis" as "met him pike hoses." Thus the transmigration of souls, a principle of eternal spiritual life, is rephrased as a loose but obliquely meaningful reference to "pike hoses" evoking sexuality rather than spirituality. Molly turns Greek into the speech of an uneducated middle-class Irish housewife. (Just as Joyce transforms the *Odyssey* into an obscene Anglo-Irish novel.) Her voice utters the written word — the text of culture — with an echo of deflating difference, as if what it repressed suddenly returned. *Ulysses* gives more examples of Molly's debunking and revisionary speech, but the reader of "Penelope" will hardly need a demonstration of its radical novelty which violates all contemporary bourgeois taboos regarding propriety and the parameters of fictional representation. Molly's speech proves body language — not gesture, which is always mute — but talk about physical processes: digestion, urination, copulation, menstruation and orgasm, represented and structured as flow — the flow of urine, menstrual blood and a repetitious, continuing form of orgasmic response.

The question is whether we think that alogical flow and physical secretion are (the) truly essential feminine qualities. It is a question which, let us face it, we cannot answer because we do not know what *the* or *a* real, essential, feminine identity is. If it is true that "femininity" has always been defined as the "other" or "opposite" of man (connoted as the rational and spiritual creature), then the connotation of "fluidity" may not be more than the counterpart necessary to give the masculine connotation of rationality self-identity and meaning — just as without the concept of death, the idea of life is meaningless. Should we desist, then, from exploring this question? I think not. Even if we cannot solve the conceptual problem, and provide a definition of an essentially true feminine nature, we can analyze the semantic function connotations of gender difference have had through the ages, and articulate *why* and *how* certain connotations predominate in a certain epoch. This involves the demonstration that what we now recognize as arbitrary connotations of femininity which are culturally determined were once taken for essential truth, and had to be taken as naturally self-evident, in order for the illusion of rational, masculine self-identity to survive unscathed. Thus they served to support the illusion of transcendent subjectivity — not only of men, but by vicarious identification also of women.

Especially since we have grown familiar with the work of Lacan, Foucault, Derrida, Deleuze, and Lyotard who have demonstrated the collusion between rhetorical configuration and man's illusion of transcendent subjectivity, the exploration of these signifying structures has become possible and grown urgent. Thus my endeavour is no longer just a feminist one, it is part of a poststructuralist enquiry into signification and subjectivity.

What now, more than fifty years later, seems arbitry to us, may not have been so to Joyce. It seems fairly obvious that to him the image of woman as flow and responsive and infinite feminine receptiveness represented a natural truth, which had been concealed perhaps until he first revealed and staged it. I conclude this not only from his more or less casual remarks about women as they have been recorded in Ellmann's biography. There is ample evidence in *Ulysses* itself to warrant the conclusion that Molly is indeed to be regarded as the realization of hypostatic feminity, a strikingly novel but essentially true notion of feminine presence, not metaphysical but physical, not spiritual but fleshly, not phallic but uterine, not logical but flowing. The suggestion is implicit in the teleological movement of the discourse. While *Ulysses* voids the traditional and expected happy ending of the epic quest, and while it perverts the notion of a climactic *coniunctio oppositorum*, it preserves a linear progression from episode to episode which implicitly lends pride of place to "Penelope". Vulgar prejudice holds that women must always have the last word, and "Penelope" is the overwhelming embodiment of that idea: "The last word (human, all too human) is left to Penelope" Joyce wrote to Frank Budgen in February 1921, confirming the suggestion implied in the syntax of the text.[7] In addition, there is Budgen's confirmation that Molly is a version of the *Gea Tellus*, Good Mother Earth. He assures us that "there is none of the coldness of an abstraction in Molly Bloom, but she is more symbolical than any other person in *Ulysses*. What she symbolizes is evident: it is the teeming earth with her countless brood of created things."[8] Thus, even if *Ulysses* subverts the classic effect of discovery and knowledge implicit in the structuring effect of plot, and in the process avoids the mimetic representation of ultimate origin, Joyce nevertheless gives us the substitute revelation of Molly Bloom as an emblem of original otherness.

Moreover, it is precisely because the text takes Molly as the embodiment of essential origin and truth, that the fiction can portray her as debunking received ideals and ideas of origin. Wondering about the word "arsenic" she concludes that her husband would say "its from the Greek leave us as wise as we were before" (*U* 18. 241-42). She is also beyond the need of postulating a point of absolute origin or beginning: "Who was the first person in the universe before there was anybody that made it all who ah they dont know neither do I so there you are" (*U* 18. 1569-72). Thus her critique of the futility of the need to know and have origins and hierarchies, rests upon the understanding of Molly as already fully self-present, not in need of affirmation of identity. She can voice her charmingly ignorant feminine views, because in the world of the fiction she is seen as *embodying* essential origin and truth: no longer the logos as spirit, but the word become flesh.

How do I know that Joyce was not correct in this definition of the essential nature of femininity? After all, the psychoanalyst C.G. Jung wrote Joyce to say that he "learned a great deal from it". Though his comments are in general not very laudatory (elsewhere he speaks of Ulysses as a "transcendental tapeworm"), he especially mentions "Penelope": "The 40 pages of non stop run in the end is a string of veritable psychological peaches. I suppose the devil's grandmother knows so much about the real psychology

7. Richard Ellmann ed., *Selected Letters of James Joyce,* New York: Viking Press, 1975, p. 278.
8. Frank Budgen, *James Joyce and the Making of Ulysses,* 1934; rpt. Bloomington: Indiana Univ. Press, 1972, p. 262.

of a woman, I didn't."[9] More recently, Colin MacCabe's *James Joyce and the Revolution of the Word* defined *Ulysses* as a text which liberates the speech of female desire. Joyce, a man writing as a woman, is placed antagonistically over against George Eliot (MacCabe's emblem of the realist literary tradition), a woman writing as and like a man; and Joyce is praised as the friend of woman in that he opens the possibility of expression of her (always the "mother's"!) otherness.[10] There also is the suggestive fact that Hélène Cixous (who wrote her dissertation on Joyce) may have tailored her notion of *écriture féminine* after Joyce's example; while Luce Irigaray takes woman's fluidity as model for her textuality.

It would indeed be very gratifying to accept these interpretations and versions of a true femininity as correct and intrinsic. Joyce's seeming celebration of womanhood as myth would place *Ulysses* in the unique position of the feminist's vindication of the exclusion of women from literary history. It redresses the traditional fear, and lends the idea of woman a power and centrality which is unprecedented. Molly Bloom, as emblem of the eternal feminine, is the inert centre of the action of *Ulysses*, its still point in a turning world. Stephen Dedalus' question, "Was that then real? The only true thing in life?" "*Amor matris*: subjective and objective genitive?" (*U* 2.143 and 165), scintillates with meaning as the possible suggestion of the text as a whole: that the feminine, the biological is to be regarded as true and ultimate "genetrix". The "hand that rocks the cradle" is upgraded to being the prime mover of the world no less than the stylistic principle of the fiction.

However appealing this attribution of authority and transcendence to the feminine principle may be to the old-fashioned feminist type, I at least can no longer regard it the truth Joyce, Jung, or MacCabe hold it. And perhaps the fact that they did ought to make us suspicious. French poststructuralism teaches that man's sense of full subjectivity is an illusion which he owes to his use of the medium language. It would be illogical to assume

9. Richard Ellmann, *James Joyce,* New and Revised Edition, New York: Oxford Univ. Press, 1982, p. 629.

10. Colin MacCabe, *James Joyce and the Revolution of the Word,* London: Macmillan, 1978.

that the image of transcendent female subjectivity would not be more than a mirage produced by language if the notion of masculine subjectivity is so. Language may suggest the viability of a full and original identity and self-presence, but it cannot embody it. It is not surprising, therefore, that the image of Molly, scrutinized more closely, proves a fallacious, ambivalent, in fact mythic construction, like the fetish made up from the conflation of contradictory qualities within the compass of one entity.

To my knowledge this was first pointed out by Mark Shechner in *Joyce in Nighttown*, where he argues that Molly is a female with phallic qualities, who fits the gallery of Joycean "phallic mothers" such as ALP, Gretta Conroy, Bertha in *Exiles*.[11] She is what Stephen Dedalus calls "an androgynous angel", and has the power of the word which turns her into Joyce's as well as Bloom's agent of vengeance against masculine rivals and castrating females alike. Thus Molly can get the better of Aunt Dante, for example. Moreover, as Shechner points out, Joyce's "androgynous angels" are sketched with a profusion of fetishes. Shoes, stockings, drawers, gloves etc. clamour for attention, and prolifically compensate the absence of what, by implication, must have been a vitally essential organ for Joyce. At issue is not a psychoanalytic reading of the implied author of *Ulysses*; I am interested in Joyce's creation of that contradictory type, the "phallic mother", only to the extent that it helps us understand the constructed nature and mythic function and form of Molly Bloom. What Shechner helps me see, then, is that it is Molly's sexual ambivalence which entitles her to function as the central agent of resolution of opposites in *Ulysses*. In her, as image and idea, the ontological contradiction between the masculine and feminine (or fidelity and infidelity, freedom and dependence, art and Ireland) is resolved. Like "the grave, the womb, or the Freudian id," Molly sublates logical contradiction (Shechner, p. 199). Instead of the image of a "real" woman (whatever that may be), she is, indeed, the very symbol of reconciliation which stands, indifferently, and neutral, above the limitations of masculinity and femininity as "sane full amoral

11. Mark Shechner, *Joyce in Nighttown: A Psychoanalytic Inquiry into Ulysses,* Berkeley: Univ. of California Press, 1974.

fertilisable untrustworthy engaging limited prudent indifferent *Weib*. 'Ich bin das Fleisch das stets bejaht!'"[12] Though grammatical gender is arbitrary, of course, it is interesting to note that both the nouns *Weib* and *Fleisch* are neuter.

The mythic, or imaginary quality (in Lacanian terms) of Joyce's idea of woman is perhaps best illustrated with reference to her association with water imagery in *Ulysses*. In the first chapter we find the invocation to the sea, *"Thalatta Thalatta!"* (*U* 1.80), in relation to Stephen's mother; the novel ends with "the sea the sea" (*U* 18.1598) as Molly's consciousness dissolves into dream. Her thinking of the sea at the moment of surrender to sleep foreshadows the ending of *Finnegans Wake* where the river ALP flows into the ocean, the "cold mad feary father" (*FW* 628.2) at the moment of death. The peculiarity of *Ulysses* is that it combines two contradictory aspects which remain separated in *Finnegans Wake*. In *Ulysses* there is no distinction between water as fertile sea ("our great sweet mother" (*la mer/la mère*) the source of life; and water as the cold and impersonal paternal ocean, the agency of death. For Stephen, the mother, and the sea with which she is associated by symbolic identification stand for both the idea of nature as complex inexhaustible life, as well as the threat of individual extinction through engulfment. The sea is at one and the same time Swinburne's "great sweet mother" as well as the "scrotum-tightening" agent of castration. And if we try to reason this paradox away, placing it as a peculiarity of Stephen's late adolescence, for instance, we find the constellation repeated in the consciousness of Leopold Bloom. For him too, woman is at once the elusive Heraclitean *panta rhei* ("Woman. As easy stop the sea. Yes: all is lost" (*U* 11.641), as *Lacus Mortis,* the Dead Sea in the Promised Land: "A dead sea in a dead land, grey and old. Old now. It bore the oldest, the first race. A bent hag crossed from Cassidy's, clutching a naggin bottle by the neck. The oldest people. Wandered far away over all the earth, captivity to captivity, multiplying, dying, being born everywhere. It lay there now. Now it could bear no more. Dead: an old woman's: the grey sunken cunt of the world" (*U* 4.222-227). Always: woman as source of life

12. Budgen, p. 266.

and image of death. And the antidote to the horror of that final vision is the scurried return to the vital, affirmative living warmth of female flesh. Thus the tautological circularity of the text, which takes Molly's style as matrix and as final objective of representation — is mirrored in the ambivalent image of woman projected by the text.

Most significant perhaps, is the oddity with regard to Molly's connotation as flow. Rivers, seas, oceans, and women of childbearing age flow. In *Finnegans Wake*, ALP flows down from the mountain to the ocean. But Molly too is shown as a "flower": When her monthly period begins, she seems in the grip of a supernatural force flowing from her body "O patience above its pouring out of me like the sea" (*U* 18.1122-23); or, "O how the waters come down at Lahore" (*U* 18.1148). She remembers that her husband called her "flower of the mountain yes so we are flowers all a womans body yes (*U* 18.1576). My conflation of the two possible pronunciations of "flower" may shock linguists as unorthodox, and of course it is. It is, however, suggested by the playful undecidability of the text itself: A fragment such as "Got your lett and flow" (*U* 11.861), forces the reader to readjust his pronunciation. This oddity helps us understand the *reason* for the semantic conflation of masculine and feminine qualities in Molly as "flower". For Joyce, the notion of flow relates on the one hand to the flow of urine and the non-erect penis — Bloom's "languid floating flower" (*U* 5.571-72). On the other hand, it is associated with menstruation, the colour crimson, and feminine fertility (the language of flowers is for Bloom the language of women). Thirdly, it is related to writing and language. We read: "the flow of the language it is" (*U* 8.65), or, "means something, language of flow" (*U* 11.297-98). What we have then, in Molly Bloom, is not just the image of a woman with masculine traits. The complex cluster of meanings related to "flower" suggests that what Joyce gives us is the imaginary fusion of notions of masculinity and femininity, in the central, embracing image of the crimson flow of Molly's blood, the flow of the fertility of life which is obliquely seen as a symbol

13. See Patrick Parrinder, "These heavy sands are language....", *James Joyce Broadsheet,* 7 (February, 1982), p. 1.

for a language, a textuality and a perverse form of writing against the grain. Indeed, my earlier surmise is wrong. *Ulysses* is not a text which tries to shift the *locus* of the idea of origin from the paternal to a maternal principle. It wishes to sublate sexual difference and banish alterity to turn everything into a mythic notion of flow which the fiction itself imitates and practises in its weaving/ unweaving of the image of Dublin — the flow of woman is both the paternal and maternal instance of Joyce's fiction, both the self-styled source of inspiration as well as the goddess for whom the tribute is intended, origin and end. Just as in the car advertisement the notion of streamlined efficiency determined both the shape of the image of the woman and the car, just so Joyce's revisionary notion of a new flowing style of authority informs both the style of the novel and its representation of womanhood.

But then the depiction of Molly's flow is necessary as proof of the viability and actuality of a manner of writing behind, beyond, or outside the realistic tradition, just as the image of the woman in the ad mediates the message sent there. Joyce can generate a deconstructive text like *Ulysses* owing to his identification with the self-generated notion of woman as original presence, an idea seemingly confirmed by the successful creation of the figure of Molly Bloom (while forgetting that she is the contradictory product of language and imagination).

As its date of publication recedes in the past, the tautological, ideological nature of Joyce's idea grows more obtrusive. Simultaneously, the perverse oddity of Joyce's textuality gains outline and clarity. Is the peculiar unsettling echo of *Ulysses* which always gives and takes in one movement the resonance of the peculiar place from which (and through which) the author speaks? Is *Ulysses* ventriloquated through the womb of Molly Bloom? Is the mystery of the womb — the "incertitude of the void" of which both Bloom and Stephen, the masculine protagonists, are acutely conscious (*U* 17.1015 & 1020), and which Molly never need acknowledge because she is thought of as experiencing the womb as fulness and flow — the mythic source of Joyce's fiction? Is for Joyce, "a conscious reactor against the void of incertitude" (*U* 17.2210-11), the womb a "portal ... of discovery" (*U* 9.229)?

However this may be, there seems little doubt that the function of the image of woman in *Ulysses*, and her "last word (human, all too human)," is not only the "indispensable countersign to Bloom's passport to eternity" as Joyce argued,[14] it is at once the countersign of Joyce's passport to immortality as the author of *the* novel to deconstruct the self-presence of realistic fiction; but it tells us little about the true nature of women, and the question remains whether any text can give us an image of true femininity or true masculinity for that matter. Our project must remain, not *cherchez la femme*, but to study the mutual determination of notions of authority and connotations of gender.

Leiden

---

14. Letter to Budgen, in Ellmann, *Selected Letters,* p. 278.

AGAINST MEDIATION: THE RULE OF THE POSTMODERN IN THE *PHAEDRUS* AND *FINNEGANS WAKE*

MARILYN L. BROWNSTEIN

A simultaneous playful and serious meddling with the ordinary mediating function of language characterizes the linguistic subversions of both Plato's *Phaedrus* and Joyce's *Finnegans Wake.* These texts, moreover, are not so peculiarly paired once we recognize the nature and motives of a discourse constituted by linguistic occurrences which regularly and systematically block language's natural effect. In the jargon of the twentieth century we call such texts "Postmodern".

The distinction, modern — postmodern, particularly as it occurs in Jean-François Lyotard's *The Postmodern Condition,* best serves this view. Lyotard does not restrict his terms to the literary history of the twentieth century but suggests that modern art is the predictable concomitant of any historical moment that recognizes the unrepresentable nature — "the lack of reality" — of reality[1]: "I shall call modern the art which devotes its 'little technical expertise' ... to present the fact that the unpresentable exists" (p.78). Modern art nostalgically seeks recompense for the unrepresentability of content, in the "solace of good forms" (p.81). The postmodern, itself a response to modernity's foregrounded and overdetermined forms, copes with reality's unrepresentability by attempting its representation.

Postmodern discourse, thus, abandons the linear, the hier-archical, the binary orderliness of an ideal form — the logic of

---

1. *The Postmodern Condition: A Report on Knowledge,* trans. Geoff Bennington and Brian Massumi, Minneapolis: U of Minnesota P, 1984, p. 77.

language's forms — in pursuit of the real, of "what will have been done". It represents, after the fact, what has been occurring all along; "*Post modern*", in Lyotard's estimation, "would have to be understood according to the paradox of the future (*post*) anterior (*modo*)" (p.81).

Discourse which takes for itself the character of an event is language in defiance of a principle linguistic effect, the ordering of reality as a hedge against the world's uncanny strangeness. In Plato's late work and in that of Joyce, doubled forms of memory offer respite from language's strictest mediations. These distinctively doubled forms push at the margins of language in order to radically re-establish the possibility for "Being" — in Heidegger's terms — situated "always and everywhere throughout language".

The radical nature of this postmodern project, the remembering of what in fact the protective mediations of language conceal, is disclosed not only in the subversive functions of *Finnegans Wake* and the *Phaedrus* but in a criticism — at least in the case of the *Phaedrus* — which attempts to normalize, i.e., de-radicalize, the text. As readers and teachers and critics of Joyce, we need to study this example and to be wary of our own too good intentions, of the natural propensity to correct the purposeful disruptions of the postmodern text (to undo the essence of "what will have been done").

Finnegans Wake and the *Phaedrus* turn away from the rationalizing proclivities of ordinary discourse, by presenting a particular view of memory as compensation and play. In linguistic forms that incorporate all that is unsafe, all that language ordinarily attempts to control, both texts challenge convention. What is truly dangerous in language rather than what is apparently so, is addressed in Socrates' speech near the end of the *Phaedrus*. In a myth of Plato's invention (except for the character of Theuth, who, according to Egyptian legend, invented the alphabet), Socrates reveals the response of Thaumas, king of Thebes, to Theuth's treasure: "... the invention will produce forgetfulness in the minds of those who learn to use it, because they will not practise their memory. Their trust in writing, produced by external characters which are no part of themselves, will discourage the use of their own memory within them. You have invented an elixir not of memory, but of reminding; and you offer your pupils the appearance of wisdom, not true wisdom, for they will read many things without instruction and will therefore seem to know many things, when they are for the most part ignorant and hard to get along with, since they are not wise, but only appear wise" (275B).[2]

Although Plato's criticism of the Sophist is the topical heart of this passage, the linking of memory and wisdom, in the larger, metaphysical context, requires our attention.

In *Finnegans Wake* Joyce similarly seems to comment on speech and writing and, like Plato, at the same time raises the larger issue; he too makes the case for sensory memory. "To put it more plumsily. The speechform is mere sorrogate" (*FW* 149. 28-29).[3] The speechform is not only surrogate parent (substituting paternal symbols for the maternal body) but also a sorrow-gate, and even, perhaps, a sœur-gate, a walk-through or passage, from mother to sister. "Plumsily" is a matter to take up at length elsewhere, but I will suggest here that besides the plumb-line or seeming straight-forwardness of the declaration, "plum" in Joyce refers to human plumbing, anal and vaginal — and in the latter case linked with "silly".[4]

2. Plato, *Phaedrus,* trans. H.N. Fowler, London: William Heinemann, 1914.

3. It is worth noting what would appear to be a fortuitous coincidence here; on line 20 of this same passage, a complaint about "sophology" is part of the "Answer".

4. Much of the fruitiness of *Ulysses* is captured in Stephen's parable of the plums, the tale of two crones climbing the column of the "onehandled adulterer". In its location in the windy (Aeolus) episode, this narrative with its interruptions conflates the gypsy whores of Proteus, vestal virgins, sexual acts, sex role confusions, defecation and breaking wind as well as "raising" it. To put anything "more plumsily" then would certainly be to hearken to such coincidences. "Plumsily" moreover recalls "dumbillsilly" of an earlier passage of *Finnegans Wake*: "...and the duncledames have countered with the hellish fellows: Who ails tongue coddeau, aspace of dumbillsilly?" (15. 18). Besides the French version of Tindall's analysis ("Où est ton cadeau, espèce d'imbécile?") — a "confusion of history" worked out in a "confusion of tongues", there is also the (un)mixed blessing or gift of the purely applied English tongue — *a tongue-cod, Oh!* ("Pluck me whilst I blush!") — operating in *a space of dumbillsilly,* (If ordinary language mediates the real, Joyce's resonates

The distinction between memory and reminding, or remembering and reminding in the *Phaedrus* and in Joyce's mixed view of "the speechform", opens onto a particular view of memory. In the *Phaedrus* Socrates rejects artificial memory, the memory forms of the art of rhetoric; Plato refers neither to artificial nor, in fact, to linguistic memory of any sort here. Similarly, when Joyce told Frank Budgen, "The imagination is memory", he did not allude to an exclusively linguistic memory but to the linking of linguistic and sensational memory which the lines cited above make corporeal. Anticipating a Lacanian rather than a Freudian context, these lines yield a view of linguistic mediation — the replacement of desire for our mother with the symbols of our father — as a mixed blessing at best[5]; for sorrow's gate opens to us all in language's utilitarian rejection of the real — as well in the (limited and limiting) solace of linguistic play with which these lines are marked. Memory, in the postmodern text, survives as the urgency of a primary nostalgia reified, an etymological restoration, a reversal, in which *algos*, the grieving or longing for *nostos*, for homecoming, is renewed as a kind of corporeal eloquence — a speaking of the body through disruptions in the body of language. Thus the authority of the unconscious, the submerged life text which sanity — or culture —demands we repress, is, in part, restored.

In other words, postmodern texts strive for language which corpo-realizes the real. These texts possess the character of an event as they superimpose the activity of the unconscious, of submerged memory, on language. It is as if the layers commonly called conscious and unconscious have shifted; or, in the "notlanguage" (not, knot, nightlanguage) of *Finnegans Wake,* "Who in his heart doubts ... that the feminine fiction stranger than

---

with its restoration; "the longest way round is", indeed, "the shortest way home".)

5. From a Freudian perspective it would seem that desire's triangulation, the symbolic solution, is the sign of recompense for and acceptance of the incest taboo while the Lacanian formulation contains the subject's division, the ubiquity of lack or the impossibilty of satisfying desire, and concomitant ruptures in language are thus necessarily a part of all experience.

the facts, is there also at the same time, only a little to the rere? Or that both may be contemplated simultaneously? Or that each may be taken up and considered in turn apart from the other?" (*FW* 109.31-34)

To manage such a transposition involves the reversal of the mediating role of language. In Joyce, the alternative begins in feminine or maternal memory, the recovery of the playful and dangerous (infantile) remembering of the origins of *eros* in direct relation to the maternal body. In that sense *Finnegans Wake* recovers all that is forbidden: the maternal body, the sisters' bodies, and in fact, (here comes) practically every bodily act imaginable as *Finnegans Wake* reinscribes the activity of an infantile dynamic upon adult experience. In Plato, the memory of ideal beauty offers another version of this alternative. The *Phaedrus,* in the strangeness of the text, offers, just as *Finnegans Wake* does, a view of a feminine memory, not merely discursively, but as the natural event of the text itself; that is, the language of the text enacts the dynamic of feminine desire, the dynamic of the ideal union of infantile and maternal bodies — partaking of a characteristic and peculiarly mirrored doubling of forms and a favouring of spatial and non-hierarchical arrangements over the ordered dynamic of languaged forms.

The powerful figuration of feminine or sensational memory in the *Phaedrus* is Plato's discursive version. The centerpiece of the dialogue is the myth of the soul's constitution in a celestial chariot ride: the soul (consisting of the reason of a driver, the appetite of a dark horse, and the emotion of a white horse) struggles to ride along with the gods, close to the rim of the universe. If the dark horse of passion can be managed sufficiently, the charioteer is rewarded with a glimpse of perfect forms beyond the dome of heaven. In successive incarnations, souls who have glimpsed the forms are privileged to return in human bodies. On earth some special humans may be significantly stirred by beauty in the form of a beloved, an experience which contains its own ethos: "Now in the earthly copies of justice and temperance and the other ideas which are precious to souls there is no light, but only a few, approaching the images through the darkling organs of sense, behold in them the nature of that which they imitate" (250 B 484).

Sensual memory triggered by vision, by seeing beauty on earth cannot remind the soul of the perfection of the forms, for memory before incarnation (like most preverbal memory) is lost to consciousness. Instead the soul remembers, that is, recollects in physical affect, sensations inherent to the experience of perfection. Sensational memory, remembering in the body, is also ethical memory, however. In his appreciation of the beauty of the beloved, the lover discovers responses in himself that are productive of wisdom. He admires the beloved and treats him well in order to be loved in return. The beauty of the beloved, thus, initiates goodness through its resemblance to perfection, and the goodness of the lover mirrors that beauty, ensuring the wisdom which is to follow. Love, moreover, is divinely inspired; it only seems inexplicable, irrational, but in fact represents wisdom close to that of the gods, for the lover approaches the ideal (which only the gods completely know) in the beauty of his beloved.

In describing ethical memory, Plato, in a reversal of his position from earlier dialogues, defends the irrational as the only legitimate source of inspiration and wisdom, and prescribes a sustained erotic tension as the basis of both the getting and giving of such wisdom. The nature of this erotic tension, a love in which ego boundaries between lover and beloved disintegrate, a "folie à deux",[6] resembles most closely the union of mother and infant during life's earliest months. Such a conception, introduced in the *Phaedrus* in Socrates' second speech and in his treatment of Phaedrus throughout the dialogue, most unceremoniously lifts the *Republic's* ban on poets.

The poet is banned in the *Republic* not because he is not wise, but because his wisdom is not rational, because it may be divinely inspired. Martha Nussbaum observes that in dialogues prior to the *Phaedrus* the fact that the poet has no *logos* for his *episteme* indicates that he is not a philosopher, although he may indeed, at times, know the truth.[7] Clearly, then, all of the dialogue

6. I am grateful to Dr. James Grotstein for sharing in a written communication this insight on the mother-infant relationship.

7. "'This story isn't true': Poetry, Goodness, and Understanding in Plato's *Phaedrus*", in Julius Moravesik ed., *Plato: On Beauty, Wisdom, and the Arts*, Totowa, New Jersey: Rowman and Allanheld, 1982, pp. 83-84.

distinguishing speech from writing in the *Phaedrus* serves two, seemingly competing, truths. At the narrative level, Plato preserves Socrates' teaching —for Socrates, it is conventionally believed, did prefer speech to writing. This view counts, however, for only part of what we may learn here. Equally important — if not more so — the examination of speech versus writing serves to display the dynamic of the Socratic dialectic in all its erotic-ironic fluctuations while silently scoring Plato's point: a celebration of the irrational, the mute or extralinguistic, as a means of knowing. This reevaluation of the irrational is key to Plato's postmodern position.

Besides the narrative linking of the irrational and wisdom in the myth of Platonic invention (the story of Thavmas' response to the invention of the alphabet), Platonic irony resonates throughout with the ambivalence of the irrational. So long as we understand that irrational simply means without benefit of the logic of linguistic mediations, then we can identify — and eventually, conflate —ethical memory in Plato and what Joyce calls the feminine in *Finnegans Wake*. In both cases, the special nature of sensory memory provides for a reenactment of an ambivalent (maternal) dynamic. In the *Phaedrus*, Socrates' seduction of Phaedrus works in the same manner as the description of the relationship between lover of wisdom and his beloved in Socrates' second speech.[8] Attention which awakens lust but denies consummation becomes the source of the irrational, or, in Lacanian terms, the occasion of the loss of subject position. This disruption of the rational, this disordering of the speaking subject, is key to Socratic method, for Socrates, antiquity's great tease, practiced maternal love as pedagogical principle. Paul Friedlander assesses the effect of such treatment: "it is Alkibiades who expresses this in almost extreme terms in the *Symposium*: 'How badly he deceived me. And he has done this to me but also to

---

8. It is interesting to note that many key Platonists, including Robin, Hackforth, DeVries, and Rowe reject the possibility of seduction between Socrates and Phaedrus. Paul Friedlander, *Plato*, Vol 1, trans. Hans Meyerhoff, New York: Pantheon, 1958, is a notable exception in this century.

Charmides and Euthydemos and to many others. He pretends to be their lover and then turns out to be the beloved rather than the lover' (222B). In the beginning Socrates appears as the pursuer and Alkibiades as reluctant; in the end Alkibiades says: 'Our roles seem to be reversed. ... From this day, it shall be I who shall wait upon you, and you who will be waited upon by me' (135D). Thus eroticism, not as a mask, but permeated with irony, and the probing dialogue manifest themselves as the highest expression of Socratic nature: he transforms, he educates in the sense of leading upward. ... The more susceptible Alkibiades is to Socrates' education, the more does attraction tend to include its opposite as a sting" (p. 142).

Thus, the occasion of Alkibiades' ambivalence, his admiration for Socrates and his disappointment in Socrates' bed, yield the subject-object confusion at the heart of infantile desire. Socrates begins as lover and becomes beloved. Platonic love or the ideal teacher/student relationship of the *Phaedrus*, the interaction of the lover of wisdom and his acolyte, replicates the maternal and moves beyond. Sensational-ethical memory in Plato is maternal in its dynamic — a sustained desire without consummation — as well as in its *ethos*, a mirroring of the nurturing behaviour of the other as the means to wisdom and goodness. Socrates' seduction, however, is only initially maternal — outside of language — while its consummation, an intellectual rather than physical acting out, moves the beloved from a maternal/sensory axis to a paternal/rational one. Similarly, in *Finnegans Wake*, if we consider the lines cited earlier as paradigmatic, we find that Joyce's inter- and intra-linguistic puns consistently function as a language game, tapping the resources of the subject's stability, while at the same time exploiting a corporeal insouciance in a polymorphously perverse remembering of the activities of sensory experience.

There is a neurological definition that is useful here in confirming the postmodern dynamic. Current neuroscience revises the notion of an unconscious in distinguishing languaged from sensational or spatial memory. All of experience is stored both as linguistic and sensory memory. All of life experience, in fact, is stored in separate modules in the brain which are not randomly but idiosyncratically activated. This means that at any given moment perception occurs as a series of linkages among a large number of locations in the brain. We have access to linguistic memory as thought, but thought receives input not only from linguistic but also and *necessarily* from mute or sensational memory, memory whose origins are in preverbal life but are ongoing as any and all non-linguistic storage.[9]

In this context a ubiquitous rationalizing habit is revealed as one extreme of linguistic mediation. For example, there are, quite ordinarily, occasions when we experience ourselves as divided. Since sensational memory is mute, we often know it only as affect. When we find ourselves ambivalent — in a culture which insists we make up our minds — the so-called rational mind goes into action. Intolerant of ambivalence or cognitive dissonance, the rational mind makes up what it cannot know. Observing affect, it generates context-responsive explanations: "it may be that I like you, but today you are wearing the same perfume as my mother's over-bearing elder sister". Not aware that it is your smell I don't like and feeling suffocatingly unhappy with you, I break our lunch date, wondering if in fact we are meant to be friends at all.

Along with the neuroscientific recognition of the continuity of sensational memory goes an account of the mechanics of the brain's extraordinary plasticity.[10] In addition to the predictable development through puberty, the quality and number of connections between the languaged and unlanguaged portions of the brain, it would seem, show a quite amazing adaptability to environment. The result is a full range of cognitive strategies among individuals. Neuronal networks in idiosyncratic combinations and of various emphases connect sensational memory, the limbic system (seat of emotions), and linguistic memory. Different individuals remember differently. Some people recognize Aunt Ethel's perfume.

9. An account of sensory memory most accessible to the lay reader may be found in Michael Gazzaniga and Joseph Le Doux, *The Integrated Mind,* New York: Plenum P, 1981.

10. The former is documented in W. Penfield and P. Perot, "The brain's record of visual and auditory experience: a final summary and discussion", *Brain* (1963), 595-696. See Oliver Sacks, *The Man Who Mistook his Wife for a Hat,* New York: Summit Books, 1985, for an anecdotal account.

The uses of mediation then (implementations of the rationalizing effect of language) are both individually and, very likely, culturally determined. Some research suggests, for example, that the Japanese, whose alphabets are both ideogrammatic and phonetic, seem to make more balanced use of both memories than westerners do.

Freudian theory, in locating sexual differentiation in feminine difficulties in resolving the Oedipal dilemma, prepares the way for Lacan's version. In Lacan's (linguistic) analysis of sex difference in Oedipal resolution, he concludes that women remain in the "real", that is, in relation to the maternal body while entering the symbolic order. Lacan distinguishes between "threat" and "nostalgia" as components of castration anxieties which activate the Oedipal struggle. "Threat" alludes to the male response, the agent of compulsory symbolic solutions, while "nostalgia", the feminine choice, represents a longing to return to the body from which she was born.[11] In the masculine recoil from difference, in the opting for similarity even in the spectre of the large and threatening form of the father, lie the roots of the symbolic, a system which replaces the real with linguistic substitutions based in categories constituted out of similarity. The feminine version is one that both accepts the linguistic solution but also remains attached to the maternal body. This would include access to sensational recall based in systems of perception prior to language, systems which are ambivalent (in the fluctuating subject I-object I of infantile desire) as well as spatial and non-hierarchical — in the

11. I suppose that in a more orthodox reading of Lacan, "nostalgia" could also be construed as a longing for her lost penis, since both Freud and Lacan insist upon castration anxiety as the key component of sexual differentiation. My model assumes an object relations orientation to preverbal life, an ongoing connection of the girl to the maternal body rather than the Freudian/Lacanian formulation in which her Oedipal task involves relinquishing her earlier (universal-infantile) "masculinity". Theoretically, both views lead to the same conclusion, that the girl, in her acceptance of the symbolic, maintains her hold on the real. The male, who cannot accept castration, must substitute the symbolic for the real. See the Mitchell and Rose introductions to *Feminine Sexuality* for a good introduction to this problem.

nature of the perceptual field and its objects. The feminine system thus seems to be constituted from a more balanced combination of sensational and linguistic memory.[12]

In the *Phaedrus* Plato initiates an ideology as well as a politics of such balance. As a postmodern writer, Plato worked against a prevailing modernity, the linguistically over-determined speeches of the Sophists. His fear is articulated by Socrates in the Theuth myth — the concern that languaged memory obscures the real. In Plato, ethical memory, the activation of the ideal without conscious memory of perfect forms, is the privilege of few — the few whom he designates as the lovers of wisdom, the teachers and rulers of the ideal state. Plato creates an ideal social hierarchy which he presents as a political ethic. Reminiscent of the one in the *Republic*, this one differs in that poets of divine inspiration as well as lovers, identically inspired, are accorded the same esteem as philosophers; in fact, it would seem, according to this scheme in the *Phaedrus*, that they are all one and the same. True lovers and lovers of the truth are among the highest order of humankind.

Although most of us might reject Plato's postmodern social or political hierarchy, we seem not to be rejecting his values. Current revisions in methodology in the arts and sciences are in fact turning to non-hierarchic, multidimensional, pluralistic, i.e., postmodern forms. "Chaos" or the investigation of algorisms for random phenomena in the physical sciences, computational theory in artificial intelligence and in brain science, the concept of the rhizome in semiotics and in psychoanalysis, the new historiography, and the wild and often seemingly random eclecticism of postmodern architecture, music, and performance art represent what is amounting to a revolution in the history of ideas.

What seems hopeful is that between the overdetermined formalism of the modern and the sometimes disconcerting wildness of the postmodern, we glimpse attempts at epistemologies that reflect what Feminist and Marxist and other revisionary criticisms suggest may be the memory or cognitive strategies of

---

12. It is well to note here that the term "feminine" is one of gender distinction. Biological sex is not at issue. Clearly, the full range of individuals includes very masuline women and very feminine men.

large parts of the world's population. Subordinates in any culture depend heavily on coping with events perceived in a non-hierarchical and less categorical fashion, on, if you will, a less mediated real. Survival means coping with difference. The rage for order and the concomitant solace of good forms are tropes of minds whose principle function is management. Brain research moreover confirms the mechanistic possibility of such models.

As postmodern innovators, Joyce and Plato represent the most radical solutions. In revolt against the Sophists, Plato creates a dangerous text; in extolling sensational memory, he advocates the irrational as productive of wisdom and, its essential agent, protracted and highly sexualized desire, as the means of transferring such wisdom. In the elaborate description of the relationship between lover and beloved in Socrates' second speech, we discover the love that is both the occasion of and the agent for transmission of such wisdom. The lover is the lover of wisdom and his beloved a beautiful boy. In the juiciest literary description of *eros* — at least until *Finnegans Wake* — wisdom is awakened in the boy by the attentions of his lover. Here love's contracts are sealed in soulful glances which pump floods of water, mostly from under the arms, to spill over sprouting wings. The experience of growing wings, moreover, is compared to the emergence of teeth, with all the mystery, misery, moisture (and potential mastery) that such development holds.

This extravagantly infantile dynamic is coupled with Socrates' insistence on sexual continence: love between the lover and beloved should not be consummated; self-control and its difficulties, expressed in the figure of the dark horse and the detailed narrative of its suffering, produce a vulnerability and a mastery as requisites to wisdom. Prolonged and (even) anguished desire is the guarantee of wisdom. ("Writing", Roland Barthes tells us, "is the science of the various blisses of language, its Kama Sutra").

"Gricks may rise and Troysirs fall": Joyce confirms, invoking a history of not necessarily forbidden acts in not necessarily forbidden language. Thus he engages us, as Plato does, in a text of bliss; the postmodern text, in its maternal love, desires us, and like young philosophers, we participate. *Finnegans Wake* in its circularity surrounds us, and, like any ordinary life event, we can only assess meaning, shape, pattern, from a distance, in a rereading. In the presence of the text, the linear is interrupted by a multidimensional space in which infantile memory — sensational memory which is infantile sexuality — is recovered, or I should say, uncovered. Desire in *Finnegans Wake*, like desire in the *Phaedrus*, is unconsummated — not so much as commentary on HCE's inability to "wet the tay", but as a celebration of desire's protraction, the inevitable longing which linguistic triangulation, the mediation of language, prevents. In this sense both *Finnegans Wake* and the *Phaedrus* may be called postverbal texts. Both employ ordinary language as background to contiguous sub-versions which constitute the infantile or postmodern arrangement as the foreground of the text.

The experiential formula for such bliss — infantile experience, preverbal experience — is the product of an unsynchronized brain; that is, right and left hemispheres are not in concert, and most notably, right and left eyes are functioning separately and simultaneously. To be of two minds then, a vulnerable body, and the sensations of early life (alternately wet, warm, hungry, comforted, not comforted, in a state of perpetual desire, satisfied mostly through the mouth and eyes and in liquid forms) returns us to the relations between the lover of wisdom and his beloved in the *Phaedrus* and the complications, finally, of *Finnegans Wake*. In languaged forms both writers force the doubled, juicy, prolonged desire that organizes the spatial mind.

And just as a text whose overdetermined or mediating forms would be paranoid — breaking the links between word and world —the text which functions exclusively in terms of sensational memory would be schizoid, blurring the distinctions between inner and outer. Texts made from languaged attempts to subvert the ordinary role of language shift intermittently between the two functions or entertain both possibilities simultaneously. In the case of the *Phaedrus*, Plato manages the simultaneous solution in representing Socrates' view — his preference for speech over writing. Plato, in the meantime, confirms the other advantage, that of a written discourse — thus mirroring the ambivalence of the infantile mind. Doubling of this nature is, of course, the basis of the Socratic dialectic as well as that of Platonic irony. So in having it both ways, advantages proliferate — along with the particular dangers of such confusions.

Consider the "biografiend" of *Finnegans Wake*. Named by his desire, by "choice of need", that is, by Joyce of need or inevitably, he writes at the "selfabyss". At sanity's edge and abusing himself, he finds "funferal" in the "funnanimal world". A matter of life and death, *Finnegans Wake*'s author writes of the personal/ universal, "unlivable, transaccidentated through the slow fires of consciousness into a dividual chaos, perilous, potent, common to allflesh". Schizoid and paranoid, s/he finds everything doubling, parting, and doubling again. One name is all names and of all nations —"Europasianised Afferyank" — masculine and feminine — "Jesuphine and fraur". "I am she she sherious", the finnature puns, stuttering through many names and occupations — a butcher, a baxter, a penman, and sons — both Shem and Jaun — while the body is persistently superimposed on history — the bisexcyles and the vicocyclometer, not surprisingly, are one — and history is similarly imposed on the flesh which becomes the matter of writing and its material — the world's fool'scap.

This dunce cap, however, fools no one; it doesn't make us dumb. Possibility includes silence and language, sensory and linguistic memory. And their coincidence, in Joyce — "coincidance" is the word's dance and also the world's dance. Joyce's cultivation of coincidence, the irrational reciprocity of colliding forms, re- members the arrangements of a postmodern epistemology. Rather than linear and branching linguistic models (taxonomies), in each circular motion of Joyce's collideorscape, new categories, or more appropriately, constellations — gather. There the world turns as a sexual body and the body of language, creating evershifting arrangements in which "contrarieties reamalgamerge", in which the "chiarascuro coalesces". In Joyce and in Plato, difference, thus, is not reconciled in the creation of categories forced from a pernicious (i.e., strained) similarity, but instead doubling forms on all levels of language provide combinations which bespeak an altogether appropriate variety and ambivalence. Coincidence in *Finnegans Wake* creates links just as contiguities in the *Phaedrus* do to disclose the simple truth of human experience — a crowded world of doubled or ambivalent forms. In a sense (or five of them) this world is made whole from the faith or innocence of an infantile ideal: a trust that something out there mirrors perfectly our own desire. This faith preserves not a world without difference but one in which difference operates freely (without linguistic mediation), a world in which our apprehension of difference is not grounded in distance or, necessarily, in distrust.

Herein, of course, lies possibility for an ideology — and its subversion. The history of *Phaedrus* criticism until quite recently has been a history of mediation; it is my hypothesis that the threat of the unmediating text brings a prompt reply.[13] The language of the *Phaedrus* is ambivalent much in the manner of the language of *Finnegans Wake*. It takes on the forbidden not as topic but as event in Socrates' seduction of Phaedrus — and in the enactment of their love for each other that is their love of wisdom in which we, as readers, participate. The nature of the Socratic dialectic — a dialectic which requires no synthesis — is as threatening as the Socratic seduction itself. Both, of course, thrive on the ambivalence rejected by the rationalizing intellect. And, finally, in his recovery of such a method, Plato deserts the contingencies of consistent style and rhetorically appropriate (i.e., familiar) forms for a language that subverts convention in both its form and content.

The style of the *Phaedrus* is poetic — associative, metaphorical rather than linear, binary. As a result, the work caused dismay before this century in a criticism which could not place it chronologically within Plato's œuvre; some believed it to be an early work and the result of a yet undeveloped writing style; others argued that Plato bowed to the conventions he hated as illustration of what not to do. Only within a revisionist commentary do we have complete acknowledgment that the poetry of Plato's style is crucial to our understanding.[14]

As to the poetry of the text: we know that poets had been excluded from the *Republic*. Clearly then it would be contradictory

13. By this term I mean a text that operates simultaneously within and outside of language, affirming in some balanced way the relationship between sensory and linguistic memory — or from another perspective, a text whose language is informed by internal and external reference.

12 — the "anti-Platonist" Derrida and the feminist Platonist, Martha Nussbaum, to name two.

to believe they might have a place near that of the lover of wisdom in this dialogue. Plato's lyrical language, moreover, is viewed as suspect and even clumsily parodic. The setting also represents an inexplicable — and therefore entirely discountable — break with convention; Socrates — and dialectic — ordinarily operate within the city. The sensuality of the location and its history as a place where girls romp and play thus create disturbing discontinuities — problems not to be resolved in their obvious dialectical relationship to past dialogues, history, common sense, and memory but in their extinction. To pursue a consensus among Platonists then is to eliminate disquieting elements of the *Phaedrus* and to be left with a short discussion on the virtues of speech rather than writing near the end of what can only be judged as a formless and digressive work.

Finally, I would like to note that *Finnegans Wake* criticism has not, of course, ignored unconventional textual elements. *Finnegans Wake* is billed in fact as the world's best compendium of unconventional textual elements. And readers of *Finnegans Wake* do write about the history, the setting, the mythology, and the poetry of the text. But I wish also to note that one need not establish a criticism of mediation in order to mediate a crazy text. Another method is silence. *Finnegans Wake* is a sacred text; shortly after its publication — or actually even before its complete publication, it had been elevated. But if we were to review university curricula and student interest — not to mention the reading list of any ordinary, well-educated individual — from then to now, we might wonder when, if at all, anyone might read this radical text.

Finnegans Wake thus comes, in Lyotard's sense, both before and after, "before" the literary postmodernism of this half of the century, temporally, and in the range of its inventiveness, and "after" both as it attempts the representation of the unrepresentable (that which has already occurred); and most crucially, it represents the future, in its potential, in that it is hardly read or taught, at least in proportion to its notoriety as a sacred book. I wish to suggest that *Finnegans Wake* needs to be taught more and, specifically, more casually. *Finnegans Wake* needs to be read a lot. *Finnegans Wake* should be demythologized.

Joyce's last work is important because of its postmodernity, because it is a radical text, and because it is subversive. What has been unspeakable needs to be spoken — for the *ethos* and *logos* of fun, of politics, of culture demand the remembering of Joyce's exile as well as our own. The return of this particular unmediated real remembers, at the margin of pleasure, the body in pain: the body of the mother and the father, sister and brother, the body of poverty and alcoholism, of illness, depravity, idleness, victimization, incest — despair, crime, revelry and love. *Finnegans Wake* remembers the body of the family and the family of man, the body sexual and the body politic. Perhaps for Joyceans, the time has come to ignore the setting, the mythology, the history — the literary aspects of the text — in order to confront the madness of the text, its schizophrenia, its destruction of boundaries between what can be said and what is ordinarily unspoken. Perhaps it is time to face radical difference in a world not innocent but fully cognizant of and vulnerable to the threat of such difference.

The language of *Finnegans Wake* urges a return to the "self-abyss", to the margins of thinking and being. Reading it demands that we "glypse at and feel for ourselves across all these rushyears the warm soft short pants of the quickscribbler: the vocative lapse from which it begins and the accusative hole in which it ends itself; the aphasia of the heroic agony of recalling a once loved number slip by slipper to a general amnesia of misnomering one's own" (FW 122.1-6). Thus the Platonic *ethos* is realized; we are not *reminded*; we *remember* as glyphs and glimpses meet in a linguistic ideal where intelligence is knowing and feeling. Sensational memory, the memory of the *Phaedrus*, informed by the vision of ideal beauty, recurs in Joyce as a greedy and infantile recovery of *jouissance*. To live in the mind as if it were the body produces autoerotic and infantile "short pants" — the gear of childhood and sexual noises; the childwriter (is scribbling drawing or writing?) is postverbal. The inability to speak — a preference for writing, perhaps, or silence —leads to forgetting what to count on (a deracinating cultural order and the incest taboo) as well as who, in "misnomering one's own" — a sure route back to the maternal body for the innocent, the aphasic, one free of a stubbornly linguistic memory.

Such remembering recalls such vulnerability. When boundaries dissolve, all pains, all pleasures of the other, become mirrors of our own. We are afflicted with life — all and only self-inflicted. As hierarchies fail, ambivalence remains the one sure thing. Such *jouissance* is distinctly not our privilege.

Georgia

Part II: Contexts

"PERHAPS SHE HAD NOT TOLD HIM ALL THE STORY...": OBSERVATIONS ON THE TOPIC OF ADULTERY IN SOME MODERN LITERATURE

RICHARD BROWN

"...this most strange and unexplained 'hiatus'
In Don Alfonso's facts",

Elsewhere I have argued that Joyce's modernity needs to be defined in relation to his treatment of sexual subjects as well as in relation to his experiments in literary form.[1] That is not, of course, to ignore the formal innovations of his work so much as to provide a *context* for them. In what follows I intend to explore a little further one of the topics in relation to which his modernity may be defined and to extend the discussion to a number of other modern authors. The topic is that of adultery, one that received challenging and innovative attention in the work of Tony Tanner who discerned in the nineteenth-century modern European novel of adultery a dynamic pattern of contract and transgression, relevant both to the social situation of adultery and to the constraints and innovations of the novel as a literary form.[2] I take the topic of adultery to be of central importance for Joyce's work and for that of a range of other modern authors, though not only in the sense that Tanner has pointed out.

In his handbook for rhetorical and logical expression *The Topics*, Aristotle defines the object of a philosophical discourse as

---

1. See: *James Joyce and Sexuality*, Cambridge: Cambridge UP, 1985.
2. Tony Tanner, *Adultery in the Novel*, London: Johns Hopkins University Press, 1974.

a puzzle or problem: a discourse is founded on an uncertainty, a question, an *aporia*[3] or else should contest some established thesis or belief. I wish to argue that at the very centre of his topos of adultery in modern literature can be found a deep and far-reaching uncertainty or *aporia* — to use Aristotle's term which has become something of a commonplace of recent deconstructionist literary criticism. Yet I do not wish to suggest that the issue of adultery is in itself unimportant, or a mere expendable sign or cover for the Postmodernist or deconstructionist recognition of the undecidable abyss of all thought. It seems to me, on the contrary, to be a matter of considerable critical and historical importance that this *aporia* should be experienced in relation to these particular topics in these particular literary works.

It was, of course, precisely Joyce's treatment of certain "sexual subjects" that defined and oriented his first relationships with publisher and audience, through Grant Richard's censorship of *Dubliners*, the seizure of the *Little Review* instalments of *Ulysses*, and the 14-year delay before the legitimate publication of that book in an English-speaking country. The issue has always been present. Indeed, if we wished to adopt the terms of Aristotle's account of the mechanics of argumentative discourse in the *Topics*, we might say that the established or understood thesis against which much early criticism of Joyce was posed was the idea that *Ulysses* was unfit for reading because it was about sex. The defence posed by Eliot, Stuart Gilbert, and other critics was to deny that this was the case, to talk not about content but about form, structure, and Odyssean analogy. This, besides perpetuating a rather tired-seeming distinction between form and content, had the effect of dividing Joyce's audience into high-brow and low-brow camps: the latter searching for smutty passages in the texts (just as certain of Joyce's characters do in the books that they read) and the former denying the importance of these things. By this division

3. Aristotle, *Organon: Topica*, trans. E.S. Forster, London: Heinemann, 1960; but see, for instance, the essay by Terence Irwin in Dominic J. O'Meara ed., *Studies in Aristotle*, Catholic University of America Press, 1983, p. 195, where conflicting uses of the term in the text are discussed, and it is suggested that "Aristotle does not seem to be clear about the exact role of aporia".

of audience, sophisticated and intelligent literary critical analysis of Joyce's achievement in terms of its sexual subject matter was made impossible.

So what if we ignore, for the moment, sophisticated and intelligent literary critical analysis. Stephen Joyce, Joyce's grandson, has gained some recent visibility among the burgeoning academic discussions of his grandfather's work and has, of course, some claim to our attention, — not just as heir but perhaps also as a rare living embodiment of that problematical entity, Joyce's audience, on what was, perhaps, the only occasion when Joyce can be said to have had an audience clearly in mind; for it was for Stephen Joyce that Joyce wrote the children's story *The Cat and the Devil*. Stephen Joyce's contribution to Joycean debates has been notable, among other things, for its intellectual caution: demurring first of all, at the publication of Joyce's explicitly masochistic and coprophiliac letters to Nora of 1909 and, more recently, appearing at the Joyce Foundation's International Conferences to speak disapprovingly of excessive or misguided attention to the works. As an antidote to criticism, Stephen Joyce offered a reading of the famous closing passage from "The Dead", beginning "She was fast asleep", and ending "His soul swooned slowly as he heard the snow falling faintly through the universe and faintly falling, like the descent of their last end, upon all the living and the dead" (*D* 224).

Stephen Joyce finished reading and made no further comment; the lines, it was his purpose to imply, have a special power that transcends any critical comment. Many commentators might agree with him here and certainly have agreed that the passage represents an especially powerful affective core of the works, since it has become one of the most common of commonplaces in Joyce criticism. Various interpretations have been offered attributing its power to a moment of "epiphany", to new special perceptions on the part of character or author concerning love, life, death, resurrection, symbolic snow, journeys westward and so on. A few critics have even found it an example of a kind of deliberately bad "purple passage" that prefigures the fondness for parody in the later works.

It is indeed remarkable that after so many re-readings the passage still stimulates and disturbs. A traditional analysis might note the way that Gabriel's repeated affirmations build to a restrained climax, the trick of personification which makes the snow tap on the window like ghostly fingers; or the partial chiasmus which adds that warm note of closure to the final sentence. The animate and inanimate merge throughout as Gabriel's identity fades into the 'grey impalpable' and deaths of the past and future pass before his eyes. No doubt one reason that the passage has become so central is because it seems to offer a vindication of the human power of imagining and, indeed, of the morality of imagining, since Gabriel's ability to perceive Gretta as the centre of her own world for the first time, to visualise the funeral of Aunt Julia, the dripping figure of Michael Furey and 'the vast hosts of the dead' is offered as, or at least has been taken as, an indication of some kind of moral growth on his part. Moral positives underline the affective point here: Gabriel looks "unresentfully" at Gretta's sleeping body and "generous" tears fill his eyes. But perhaps we should notice, more than we have often done, that they are positives with a strongly Larkinian negative or passive flavour. And indeed Gabriel's affirmations may not be so emotionally convincing as the manner in which his feelings are passed through a Freudian filter of denial: 'It hardly pained him now to think how poor a part...'.

Neither should this attention to observable features of language and the necessary generalizations that follow, lead us to neglect the central dramatic situation to which Gabriel's feelings are a response. This situation consists in a moment of lover's doubt, the sudden recognition of his wife's past love of (and continuing affectionate memories for) another man, a situation which is one of a series recurring at climactic moments throughout Joyce's work. Denis Donoghue has interestingly pointed out the oddity of calling these situations 'adulterous' ones, since in many cases no actual adultery takes place.[4] It is suspected, imagined, remembered or avoided adultery that echoes throughout Joyce's work from this scene to his play *Exiles* and, of course, in *Ulysses*. In these latter two works the possibility of adultery forms the central focus of the

4. Denis Donoghue in a review of *James Joyce and Sexuality* in *The London Review of Books*, 18 April 1985, p. 7.

action and yet in neither is it described. The private meeting between Bertha and Robert in *Exiles* takes place off-stage. It is a gap in the play's action that neither Richard nor the audience fills. In *Ulysses* we need not have quite the same doubt about Molly's utter rejection of the "faithful Penelope" role and yet the narrative sequence is artfully figured to avoid it: describing it in anticipation, in Bloom's hallucination and in Molly's prostrate retrospection. In the most relevant part of *Finnegans Wake*, Book 2, Chapter 4 where the story of Tristan and Isolde is narrated, Joyce typically begins not with the young lovers but with the aggrieved husband, King Mark of Cornwall, and his interest is displaced from their loving encounter to the doddering, historical digressions of the four old men who tell the tale.

The manipulation of form in *Exiles* and *Ulysses* ensures that adultery is perceived as a kind of gap in the consciousness of a central character and as an absent or displaced centre in the awareness of the audience. This is strikingly prefigured in the passage we have been discussing. The tissue of narratorial refraction in the passage is complex. Gabriel is the medium through which the narrative purports to communicate its informations to us. According to the decorum of this kind of narrative, nothing he is unable to see or imagine or know may be related to us, and yet his testimony is far from reliable in this moment of extreme feeling as he "swoons" and his very identity "fades". He only knows about the incident at second hand from Gretta Conroy's brief, uncertain, and reluctantly offered memory of her girlhood romance. She has perhaps romanticized, one may suppose, or else she edits for Gabriel's protection and, by her own account, she did not know Michael Furey well. He feels she knows something he does not but she is "fast asleep" and cannot be called on to supply corroboration or denial.

Gabriel and the reader of the passage will never know the truth. There is a gap, a bottomless residue of doubt in the record, a doubt which Gabriel communicates in the rhetorical figure of assumed dubiety that the Renaissance rhetoricians named with Aristotle's term for the question on which a rational discourse is based: the figure of *aporia*: "Perhaps she had not told him all the story...".

Interestingly, the gap in Gabriel's consciousness is promptly filled with objects: "A petticoat string dangled to the floor. One boot stood upright, its limp upper fallen down: the fellow of it lay upon its side." The meaning or relevance of these objects, starkly described, animated, unglossed, may seem a puzzle to some readers. How can their presence be explained? At one level, the reference to Gabriel's "riot of emotions" and the phallic suggestion of the flaccid upper of the boot give us a clue, and a clue to another absence: the sexual act between Gretta and Gabriel that has not taken place. On the other hand it is precisely as objects, self-sufficient and unexplainable, that they appear, suggesting a movement from the disturbing recognition of the potential hollowness of sexual fidelity to a perception of the objective world as empty and meaningless or perhaps as complete and all-meaningful but at any rate as intractably and materially there. The petticoat and boot may in that sense be the precursors of the objects that litter *Ulysses*, the Dublin street furniture and other ephemera that so characterize Joyce's work.

Joyce was fascinated and disturbed by the theme of adultery; and, I have argued elsewhere, his fascination can be traced in his reading through a series of transformations in the literature that he knew, from *Madame Bovary* to Shakespeare (whose life and plays in Stephen's 'theory' of them in the library episode of *Ulysses* are a tissue of intra- and extra-marital relationships) to Homer, whose *Odyssey*, in Joyce's version of it, becomes a modern bourgeois 'problem' of marital separation and fidelity, and to the Gospels — since in Joyce's surviving library there are no less than four items which propose or refer to the hilariously and heretically literalist idea that Joseph was cuckolded by the Holy Ghost at the conception of Christ. The working notes for *Exiles* reveal a Joyce who was interested in the way that in *Madame Bovary* "the centre of sympathy appears to have been esthetically shifted from the lover or fancyman to the husband or cuckhold".[5] *Exiles* and *Ulysses* seemed to Joyce to be modern in precisely this regard, though many readers might wonder at this since traditionally in the literature of adultery the figure of the cuckold seems no less

5. *Exiles: A Play in Three Acts*, intr. Padraic Colum, London: Joh. Cape, 1977, p. 165.

widespread than that of the seducer; and in the modern fiction of adultery that most English readers may know best of all, Lawrence's *Lady Chatterley's Lover*, the attention is not so much on the crippled Chatterley as on Connie's sexual awakening and on the vigorous and "natural" gamekeeper Parkin (or Mellors as he appears in the final version), who frequently serves as a mouthpiece for Lawrence's own views, or at least the attitudes he is testing out in the novel.[6]

Lady Chatterley is, of course, an importantly "modern" book: modern in the sense that it, along with *Ulysses*, shattered the hypocritical censoriousness of English publishing law, and "modern" too in its courageously and expansively justified commitment to the kind of erotic fulfilment that has become central to modern liberal society. It is a novel with a modern social message, holding up the vital, energetic life of the lower classes against the emasculated and mechanical ruling class and ruling institutions; but it is just this kind of modernity that has sometimes made it seem didactic in a rather traditional way. Clifford, half man, half wheelchair, is presented as a representative deformity of the civilized world: all head and no body. He is a mechanical centaur but he is also, to the novel's possible detriment, a semiotic centaur, half character and half symbol in a way that arguably inhibits Lawrence's exploration, or our interpretation, of his situation.

Lawrence is a sexual radical but under the attack of modern sociology and feminism his sexual radicalism has sometimes seemed to be of a rather straightforward kind, posited on the belief that erotic love is "natural", endorsing rather than challenging traditional gender divisions and roles, offering what may seem a naïvely optimistic view of the potential for social change in cross-class exogamous sexual encounters and apparently content to interpret Connie's adulterous desire as the desire to change a poor mate for a better one, rather than investigating the potential fascinations of the adulterous situation itself.

6. D.H. Lawrence, *Lady Chatterley's Lover,* London: Penguin, 1960. I also refer to the two earlier versions published as *John Thomas and Lady Jane*, London: Penguin, 1977, and *The First Lady Chatterley*, London: Penguin, 1973.

According to Karl Marx in *The Communist Manifesto*, adultery is not the instrument to bring the bourgeois order to its knees. On the contrary, it is part and parcel of the capitalist world: "Our bourgeois", he observes, "take the greatest pleasure in seducing each other's wives".[7] The adulterous triangular relationship has, traditionally, been represented not as revolutionary but as an 'eternal' triangle, endlessly repeating itself. Examples are Schnitzler's recently revived *La Ronde*, the *Betrayal* of Harold Pinter, or, very interestingly, Beckett's *Play* where the skeleton cast of husband, wife, and other woman talk in cliché. With shattering Beckettian economy and force, the complete action is repeated identically as if it were a passage in a musical score.[8] In Lawrence's novel adulterous passions only go as far as the 'pleasure principle'; but there seems to be another mode of adultery in modern literature which, like the later Freud, confronts obsessive and problematic repetitions and goes beyond that principle to something else.

The sexual explicitness of *Lady Chatterley* is of a different kind from that of *Ulysses*, representing, in a form of continuity with some aspects of the novelistic tradition, a desire for things to be fully known and articulated. The implication, it seems, is that when we finally have faced up to things without shameful evasion we will, like Connie and Mellors, be completely satisfied. *Lady Chatterley*, as is well known, went through a series of revisions. The two previous versions have been in print for some years. The first version is not continuous but is punctuated by a series of gaps. According to Frieda, Lawrence left these spaces blank and he "always intended to go back fill them in".[9] This is what happened. The two further versions of the novel fill in supposed gaps in the story: not, in most cases, literally those gaps that are left in the first version but, among other things, working up and expanding those famous "passages" in the novel where Connie and Mellors "fucked

7. Karl Marx, *The Communist Manifesto*, in *Basic Writings*, ed. L. Feuer, London: Fontana, 1984, p. 67.

8. Samuel Beckett, *Play*, in *Collected Shorter Plays*, London: John Calder, 1984, pp. 145-60.

9. *The First Lady Chatterley*, p. 10.

a flame into being",[10] as if the hard thing for Lawrence to tolerate was any gap of incompletion in his knowledge of their repeated exploration of sex.

The textual history of *Ulysses* is also one of repeated rewriting and accretion. Yet the additions do nothing to "fill in the gap" caused by the refracted narration of the encounter between Molly and Boylan. Notwithstanding its deeper, more extensive and more learned "explicitness", or even obscenity, in writing about sex, *Ulysses* has a kind of tact or restraint, and a more profound tolerance of this kind of gap.

One of the things that happened between the first and second versions of *Lady Chatterley* seems to have been Lawrence's encounter with *Ulysses*; and he includes a brief conversation where Clifford's enthusiasm for the book is noted. For Connie, this is typical of his excessive intellectuality. *Ulysses* "wearies" her; she finds it no more than an amusing clever trick. "It is", for her and was for her author D.H. Lawrence, "a perverse activity of the will"[11]; but it is no less interesting for that. To return for a moment to the working notes for *Exiles*, Joyce refers there to what must be the key for any writer investigating the theme of adultery, *Othello*. "As a contribution to the study of jealousy", he wrote, "Othello is incomplete" (p. 163). He might have put it in the opposite terms, for *Othello* is a tragedy not of incompletion, like *Hamlet*, but of overcompletion, of doing too much. The popularity and significantly mistaken phrase from Act III where *Othello* conducts an interpretation of Iago's report of Cassio's dream is a case in point. Cassio's supposed cries suggest to Othello a "foregone conclusion": that is, in precise gloss of the phrase in its logical context, a consummation that has already taken place between Desdemona and him. But what the phrase has since come to mean — that is a conclusion made before the evidence on which it ought to be based has been heard — is equally, perhaps even more, relevant to Othello's cast of mind. Othello leaps to the conclusion, filling up or skipping over any gaps, uncertainties, or inconsistencies that there may be in the evidence before him. He has loved, or more to

10. *Lady Chatterley's Lover*, p. 316.
11. *John Thomas and Lady Jane*, p. 222.

the point, has interpreted "not wisely, but too well".

From Joyce's modern point of view there is insufficient doubt in *Othello*; insufficient doubt in Othello's own "free and open nature", but also insufficient doubt in the dramatic situation that is offered since we are sure throughout that Desdemona is entirely innocent and we may think (as apparently Joyce thought) her to be too naïve or too good to be true. To a modern audience what may seem tragic in the "morality" of *Othello* is not only Othello's inability to correctly determine whether Desdemona is guilty or not, but his, and the play's, apparent confidence that if she were guilty his actions would be more justifiable.

It is not difficult to see the historical changes that brought about this shift: the weakening of the economic importance of inheritance in mass society; the breaking of the necessary link between sexual pleasure and reproduction; and the growing equality between the sexes. These changes do indeed seem to have brought about a situation where the husband's situation need no longer be that of the jealous madman or ridiculous cuckold, but can in many cases be importantly emblematic of what we might call the modern intellectual situation.

We do not always recognize quite how familiar these situations of adultery are to Modernist literature. These situations play logically or effectively with the relationship of self and other, with the complex suspicions and fears that can characterize emotional relationships. One might think of the utter isolation of individuals in Conrad: of Verloc in *The Secret Agent* who fondly believes, in that desperately ironic phrase, that he was "loved for himself"[12] even as his wife murders him, or of the polite, aloof Axel Heyst in *Victory* and his tragic incomprehension of the girl Lena's final act of sacrifice for him. Moments of incomprehension may be tied up in modern features of narrative structure and effect. Examples are the naïve perspective of James's Maisie on the manoeuvres of the adults in *What Maisie Knew*, and the limitedness of Ford Madox

12. Joseph Conrad, *The Secret Agent*, London: Penguin, 1963; *Victory*, Oxford: Oxford, UP, 1986): Henry James, *What Maisie Knew*, London: Penguin, 1966; and Ford Madox Ford, *The Good Soldier*, London: The Bodley Head, 1961.

Ford's personalized narrator in *The Good Soldier* who only gradually begins to perceive that he is telling the story of his own cuckolding. In these cases Modernistic narrative device and the adultery topos are the one same thing. One work which takes the idea to a kind of logical extreme is Alain Robbe-Grillet's *Jealousy* where the jealous husband's obsessive desire to see and to know can be taken as a metaphor for the act of writing itself.[13]

A tragic failure of knowledge seems to be at stake in these works, but also a sceptical and stoical triumph. "We are only free once in our lives", says the cynical prison warder at the start of Wyndham Lewis's study of hollowness of emotional and political rhetoric, *The Revenge for Love*, "that is when we gaze into the bottom of the heart of our beloved and find that it is false — like everything else in the world".[14]

In Virginia Woolf's historical *jeu d'esprit* Orlando, dismissed by Elaine Showalter as "tedious high camp", there is another relevant and interesting case.[15] The novel begins with the narrator as a young male courtier in Elizabethan or Jacobean London, from whence he sets out on a Tiresian journey through history ending up in the present day of 1928. Orlando's curious Odyssey of sexual transgression and self-doubt begins significantly at a moment of adulterous deceit. He finds his lover, the Princess Sasha, *in flagrante* on the knee of a sailor in the hold of a ship. Evidence enough, one might think, to convince a court of law. But what is evidence? It is in the very nature of adulterous deceit (at least of the familiar, decorously private kind) that the deceived party can never really know what has taken place. Perhaps, Orlando thinks, she has been helping him to move a crate. There is a gap in the perceiving, narrating consciousness; a deadly sickness comes over Orlando and he falls into a swoon on the floor. The narrative of *Orlando* has several such gaps, most notably and literally, the gap in the supposed manuscript evidence that Woolf's narrator refers to at length, telling us that it is "big enough to put your finger

13. Alain Robbe-Grillet, *Jealousy*, trans. Richard Howard, London: John Calder,1965.

14. Wyndham Lewis, *The Revenge for Love*, London: Penguin, 1972.

15. Virginia Woolf, *Orlando*, London: Grafton Books, 1977. Elaine Showalter, *A Literature of their Own*, London: Virago, 1978, p. 291.

through". This is the gap that occurs at the crucial moment in the story where Orlando changes sex and becomes a woman. Just as in the passage from "The Dead", in *Orlando*, at the moment of registration of the adulterous deceit, the hollowness of truth is filled in by the appearance of material objects in all their materiality: "Faithless mutable, fickle he called her; devil, adulteress, deceiver, and the swirling waters took his words, and tossed at his feet a broken pot and a little straw" (p. 40). It is, of course, in Elizabethan/Jacobean London a performance of Othello that Orlando has been to see.

Orlando, like so many characters in modern literature is launched into a flight or quest for the other, the female other, the unknown. Transgression of the sexual divide lets Orlando into the secrets of the world of the other sex, but cannot supply the ultimate truth or answer to his or her quest. Life in general, and the sexual life in particular, remains a puzzle. In subsequent epochs Orlando, as a woman, finds herself drawn to the company of Pope, but also to an 18th-century London prostitute. As a Victorian woman she tries out marriage to a sailor — but is that really a marriage at all, she asks? "The kingfisher comes; the kingfisher comes not." The secret of desire remains a secret.

In "The Dead", by his careful manipulation of the single, fallible narrative point of view, Joyce is able to create for his readers a gap, an absence. We are able to participate in Gabriel's moment of doubt, his intimation of some knowledge of his wife's that is beyond his grasp. In *Ulysses* there is no single point of view and we are neither led nor can we be deliberately misled in this way. Yet structurally, by occluding Molly Bloom's perspective until the end of the book, Joyce creates a similar sense of lack or absence, obscuring the "truth" of Molly's adultery, separating male and female perspectives and sending Bloom into an encounter with the other, the unknown, even to the extent of having him, like Woolf's Orlando, cross the gender divide and become, for a moment, the "new womanly man". Joyce offers the tantalizing prospect of an end, an answer, a final female truth. But what kind of truth is it we get from the "Penelope" monologue when it comes? Famously and delightfully Molly's account is as fallible as that of any other source. We never know, no more than Bloom knows, exactly what went on during the afternoon's "deceptions":

whether, for instance, she and Boylan have enjoyed each others ardour 2 or 3 times (*U* 18.143), '4 or 5 times locked in each other's arms' (*U* 18.895) or '5 or 6 times handrunning' (*U* 18.1511-12).

Even the shared memory of past happiness between Bloom and Molly on Howth Head that offers one of the most unequivocally optimistic moments in *Ulysses*, shows this difference of perceiving consciousnesses. Bloom finds it a lyrical moment of shared sensuality; Molly meanwhile remembers her prudence and self-possession on what she calls "the day I got him to propose to me".

To make such observations may be to come dangerously close to repeating the critical cliché that modern or Modernist fiction focusses on the unknowability, the undecidability of human experience. Yet it has also been my intention to argue that the occasions of this recognition in moments of suspected or actual adulterous deceit cannot be forgotten, and are perhaps as important as this recognition itself. The moment of recognition is tied to an observable historical moment or configuration of moments: consisting in certain changes in the organisation of family life in mass society; changing patterns of sexual behaviour and changes in the social and economic condition of women. Passages like the end of "The Dead" have their effect partly because the linguistic "signifier" is not always necessarily attached to a given "signified", but partly also because it sometimes, however arbitrarily, is. Can one accept this historical argument whilst at the same time appreciating the full impact of the unknowable, the undecidable which includes, at least in recent deconstructive and other versions of the theme, an unknowability of history itself?

Leeds

MOLLY BLOOM AND MARY ANDERSON:
THE INSIDE STORY

MARY POWER

The basic assumption of this paper is that Molly's career as a singer is essential to the understanding of *Ulysses*. To view Molly's imminent concert tour simply as a ruse for running around with Blazes Boylan is to underestimate Molly, and calls the worst kind of sexism into play; yet, somehow, Joyce's worst characters lead the reader to do just that. Molly may well have combined business and pleasure in her choice of managers, but it is necessary to take a longer view of her career. She has been singing, as Bloom recalls in "Eumaeus", since she was sixteen. Many Dubliners consider her a star. Her voice, her beauty, and her presence set her apart from her contemporaries. Molly has transcended the domestic roles — daughter of Tweedy, wife of Bloom, mother of Milly — to become a public person. Many in *Ulysses*, including Bloom, cherish memories of that public Molly. Bloom reflects on Molly's performances at the Greystones concert, the Glencree dinner, Dolphin's Barn and the Coffee Palace.

If readers of *Ulysses* will grant Molly her career, then her actions on June 16th, 1904 take on a new meaning. First, being an *artiste* gives Molly license to languish in bed and about the house all day. The explanation is simple and standard. As the "Polite Notice" columns in *The Era* would have it, she is "resting between engagements". Secondly, if we view Molly as an *artiste*, her private life is given the added allure of keyhole revelation. Readers are catching a glimpse of Molly, not on stage, but on her day off. In reality, this sort of trivia fascinated readers at the turn of the century, if we can go by the countless articles in theatrical and music hall publications like *The Encore*, *The Sphere*, *The Era*

Almanac, with such titles as: "An Actress at Home", or "Sarah Bernhardt's Menagerie".

The next step entails comparing Molly to an actress or *artiste* who appears in *Ulysses*. Such a comparison would help determine what kind of a performer Molly Bloom was, and also establish a context for looking at an actress's career at the turn of the century realistically. By this I mean that the reader is curious about what constituted success, or popularity, or excellence at that period. The method, indeed, could be glorified by adding that it is probably what Molly Bloom herself wanted, because we know how she bristled at the mention of an amateur or rookie like Kathleen Kearney.

The historical women of the stage who appear in *Ulysses* like Mrs Kendal, Mary Anderson, and Mrs Bandmann Palmer, are all seasoned veterans whose careers were well established long before the turn of the century. They had all held forth in Dublin on previous occasions, and were, in fact, institutions. Joyce's choice of actresses must have originally increased reader recognition; it also gave Molly Bloom the advantage of appearing fresh and girlish at thirty-four. Of the group, Mary Anderson (1859-1940) seems the most likely candidate for comparison because outwardly the shape of her career seems most closely to resemble Molly's. While Mrs Bandmann Palmer and Mrs Kendal were real troupers, constantly and inexhaustibly in the public eye, Mary Anderson had made only three public appearances in the six months from December, 1903 to June, 1904. Within *Ulysses*, of course, Molly's scheduled tour is to follow Mary Anderson's appearance in Belfast.

Mary Anderson's career is helpful for bringing Molly's into focus because she, too, represents the triumph of the ordinary. There was no Gibraltar in Mary Anderson's childhood, she was born in Sacramento, California, and grew up in Louisville, Kentucky. She defines herself in her first set of memoirs, *A Few Memories*, as "coming ... so suddenly from obscurity into the dazzling light of public favour".[1]

1. Mary Anderson de Navarro, *A Few Memories*, London: Hutchinson, 1936.

In 1904, Mary Anderson was forty-five to Molly's thirty-four. Anderson had had a comparatively brief career on stage between 1875 and 1889; and it is baffling, if not incomprehensible to modern notions of stardom that public curiosity about her career persisted though she had lived in retirement for fifteen years! I looked through a file of newspaper clippings about her in the Harvard Theater Collection at Pusey Library for a clue to her popularity and her meteoric rise to fame. She was apparently very beautiful. One reviewer raved: "she was tall as a Grecian goddess, a sumptuous physical beauty with limbs marvellously long and as marvellously proportioned...." Another reviewer wrote: "she had all the charm of a direct unspoiled nature and a superb stage presence". Often the pleasing quality of her speaking voice was admired. She was best known for her Shakespearean roles — *Romeo and Juliet*, *Macbeth*, and *A Winter's Tale*. She was always a leading lady, as even her obituary in *The New York Times* noted, and such top billing at least helps to explain why she was so strongly remembered.

Her success tantalized theater critics. Some believed she had reached the heights by her youth and beauty alone; others compared her to Ellen Terry and Sarah Bernhardt. In 1884 Mrs Humphry Ward wrote a novel *Miss Bretherton* in which Mary Anderson served as a model for the heroine. Isabel Bretherton, an actress and *ingénue*, has the sensitivity and the humility to understand that tremendous public acclaim does not necessarily betoken true excellence of performance. She humbly sets herself the task of learning, and then, the pinnacle achieved, she steps down gracefully (one might say masochistically), and marries her severest critic.

In fact, the position and status of the actress in the last decades of the nineteenth century were so ephemeral that it is hard to know how to interpret the following comment on Anderson from the (N.Y.) *Saturday Evening Gazette* in 1888. It said: "she is not a great actress, but she is a charming young woman and she has done much to prove that the stage is not a hot bed of vice". Her career raises all the problems of essence and action, dancer and dance. Did the press seize upon Mary Anderson to convince the public that acting was really a proper career for a respectable woman?

Mary Anderson left the stage decisively in 1889 at the age of twenty-nine. She had been on a gruelling tour of American cities and in Washington D.C.; she was simply unable to go on. Physicians urged a complete rest. The surprising announcement that she had retired forever started an outburst of speculation in the press. Newspaper headlines boomed: "STAGE AGAIN — NEVER", and, more sensationally, "OUR MARY INSANE". While the truth was probably closer to complete exhaustion, cynics speculated that she had made a lot of money, and was simply quitting while she was ahead. Whatever the true reason, a mystique enshrouded her after that and curiosity about her life never waned.

Mary Anderson married a handsome, wealthy, foot-loose New Yorker with a Columbia law degree, Antonio de Navarro, shortly after she left the stage. His family had made a fortune in a solid American way — Portland Cement and Equitable Life Insurance. The marriage was romanticized beyond description in newspapers and women's magazines. The couple were apparently unctuously happy, and lived quietly in the English countryside — first in Tunbridge Wells, and later in Worcestershire. Anderson was forever refusing great sums of money to return to the stage. Instead, she had two children, took singing lessons, and was devout in her practice of Catholicism. Late in her life, Anderson reflected: "It was eight years after our first meeting before we were engaged. I gave up the stage and we were married. When Tony wanted anything, he never minded how long he waited for it. He often said that if the stage appealed to me, he would be happy if I returned to it. But the stage had lost its glamour. From our marriage until his death we were as any two mortals can be; we were of the same faith and our tastes very similar in people and things" (*A Few Memories*, p. 20).

In 1895-6 Mary Anderson's memoirs, *A Few Memories*, were serialized in *The Ladies' Home Journal*. The stated purpose of the autobiography was to dissuade stage-struck young women from following in her footsteps, but it would be hard to miss another important theme: Mary Anderson could never have arrived at such a grand life style had she not first been on stage. Celebrity had given her entrance into a charmed world of writers, artists and church dignitaries, from Longfellow and Henry James to Cardinal Manning and the Reverend Bernard Vaughan, S.J. Mary Anderson was before all else a devoted wife, mother and hostess — a latter day *chatelaine*. Her career gave her the opportunity to leave Kentucky, see the world, marry well, live among the landed gentry and mingle in distinguished company.

George Bernhard Shaw was not impressed by *A Few Memories*. In fact, in his review he railed, "I therefore say boldly that Mary Anderson was no actress. In no page of these *Memories* can you find any trace of the actress's temperament. Mary Anderson is essentially a woman of principle, which the actress essentially is not: the notion that all bravery, loyalty, and self-respect depend on a lawless and fearless following of the affectionate impulses which is the characteristic morality of the artist, especially the woman artist of the stage — is to her, simply immorality".[2]

At the urging of Father Vaughan, which seems an inescapably Joycean historical detail, Mary Anderson came out of retirement to perform for charity. She gave two shows at the People's Palace in London's East End in December, 1903 and the whole city was rumoured to have been present. Anderson re-enacted some great scenes from Shakespeare and then sang. The performance at the Ulster Hall in Belfast in June, 1904 aided the Catholic poor as well. After enthusiastic applause, Mary Anderson went back to Worcestershire to resume her effusively happy private life.

But how does this relate to Molly Bloom? On one level, Mary Anderson's success in filling the Ulster Hall in June, 1904 answers a nagging question about celebrity status and its persistence in the popular imagination. Anderson's career makes it altogether plausible to assume that Molly Bloom in Dublin, without driving ambition, but with a lovely voice, could very well have had a strong following and be part of a touring company with major bookings anywhere in Ireland. Secondly, the comparison of Molly Bloom and Mary Anderson is not without its ironic elements. Mary Anderson's career and life style recall the traditional order and aspirations of a bygone era. Molly, although she sings "Love's Old Sweet Song", breaks the rules and looks to the future. It is

Molly, not Mary, who in Shaw's terms and probably Joyce's is more the artist.

Univ. of New Mexico
Albuquerque

2. George Bernard Shaw, *Dramatic Opinions and Essays,* London: Constable and Co., 1896, I, 372.

JAMES JOYCE, WYNDHAM LEWIS, AND THE
MEDIATIZATION OF WORD AND IMAGE

PETER J. DE VOOGD

The fashionable term in my title caused me to consult several dictionaries. After ample thought I decided not to limit myself to either one possible root meaning ("mediate: to act as intermediary agent; to interpose to reconcile; to transmit") nor to another ("mediatize: to annex; take over; subdue"), but rather to attempt a mediatization, and bring the two basic meanings together, adding a third for good measure. In this paper, then, I will, perhaps rather perversely, take the term "mediatization" to mean "using different media so as to reconcile or supplant them". I will focus on the way in which the rivalry between Joyce and Lewis may illuminate an issue in media studies which used to be indicated by the Latin tag *ut pictura poesis*. Indeed, my title does almost naturally lead to the subject of the comparison of the Sister Arts of poetry, music, and painting: the main difference between James Joyce and Wyndham Lewis is, bluntly put, that the one sang, the other painted.

Sixty years ago Wyndham Lewis published *Time and Western Man*, a vast and complex philosophical work more quoted than read, in which his objection to romantic subjectivism is vented in a famous chapter called "An Analysis of the Mind of James Joyce". In this chapter abundant praise is unambiguously mixed with condemnation ("the rich, confused ferment of *Ulysses*"). But when all is said and done the chapter is an attack on Joyce's work, culminating in the description of *Ulysses* as "a gigantic victorian quilt or antimacassar ... eternally cathartic, a monument like a record diarrhoea ... an immense *nature morte*."[1] Tempting though this would be, I shall not go into the history of the Lewis-Joyce

---

1. Wyndham Lewis, *Time and Western Man*, London: Chatto & Windus, 1927, pp. 91-130.

controversy, which in a sense began in 1927, although the stylistic and narrative differences between James Joyce and Wyndham Lewis are part of my subject. Nor do I dare enter the field where Hugh Kenner has been prominent for the greater part of my lifetime (although I don't believe, as Kenner does, that Lewis failed to notice the ironies of Joyce's parodic games;[2] surely a great satirist like Lewis would recognize satire's favourite mode). I will, however, gratefully borrow from *Joyce's Voices* Hugh Kenner's epithet for Lewis as "the most helpful of devil's advocates" (p. 23), and add that most Lewisians consider Joyce to be equally helpful. After all, Joyce and Lewis are remarkably complementary.

The most basic difference between the arts — poetry (or music) on the one hand, and painting on the other — is hinted at in the second paragraph of the "Proteus" episode in *Ulysses* where Stephen Daedalus muses on the *nacheinander* and the *nebeneinander*, the audible and the visible, that is to say: time and space, or poetry/music and painting. The passage is often glossed as referring to Kantian philosophy, but can more satisfactorily be linked with a study which irritated Stephen Hero because of its "fanciful generalisations" (*SH* 33), namely Gotthold Ephraim Lessing's influential *Laokoon; oder, Über die Grenzen der Malerei und Poesie*. Like *Time and Western Man* this is a study unfortunately more summarised and partly quoted than actually read.

When Lessing challenged, in 1766, the neoclassical doctrine of the Sister Arts, he did not deny its central assumption, that painting and poetry are comparable. He objected to too literal an interpretation of the phrase "ut pictura poesis" and to the excesses of the doctrine, such as are found in Joseph Spence's popular *Polymetis*, which was (to quote its 1747 title-page) an "Enquiry concerning the Agreement between the Works of the Roman Poets, and the Remains of the ancient Artists, being an Attempt to illustrate them mutually from one another".[3] Lessing argued against such simple-minded comparisons between the arts, and made it clear that any comparison could only work provided

2. Hugh Kenner, *Joyce's Voices*, London: Faber & Faber, 1978, p. 69.
3. Joseph Spence, *Polymetis*, 10 vols, London: J. Dodsley, 1747.

careful distinctions were made. In a rather ponderous passage in chapter 16 of *Laokoon* he spells out how painting and poetry differ, the long and the short of which is, that the subject proper for painting is the visible object, as actions are for poetry.[4] This makes sense, as much of the eighteenth-century debate about these matters still does, and it may explain why Lewis's attempts to write painterly fictions were bound to be unsuccessful: the novel is indeed by nature if not by definition a temporal thing, to do with action (plot depending upon causation in time, development of narrative upon the depiction of character in action).

Indeed, all neoclassical theorists from John Dryden onward agreed on this perhaps obvious fact.[5] As Sir Joshua Reynolds has it in No. 45 of *The Idler* (1759): "It is not very easy to find an action or event that can be efficaciously represented by a painter ... for the time of a picture is a single moment." Similarly, Charles Lamotte in *An Essay upon Poetry and Painting* observed: "The Painter is generally confin'd within the narrow Bounds of a single Action ... Whereas the Poet can still start something new, still can shift the Scene from one Place to another."[6] I will come back to this, as the implications of what looks like a truism are not always realized.

But there is of course more in which painters and writers were

---

4. "*Gegenstände, die neben einander folgen... heissen Körper. Folglich sind Körper mit ihren sichtbaren Eigenschaften die eigentlichen Gegenstände der Malerei. Gegenstände, die auf einander ... folgen, heissen überhaupt Handlungen. Folglich sind Handlungen der eigentliche Gegenstand der Poesie.*" G.E. Lessing, *Werke, bd. II: Kritische und philosophische Schriften*, München: Winkler Verlag, 1969, p. 91. See also my *Henry Fielding and William Hogarth: The Correspondences of the Arts*, Amsterdam: Rodopi, 1981, esp. ch. 3; and, of course, J.H. Hagstrum, *The Sister Arts: The Tradition of Literary Pictorialism and English Poetry from Dryden to Gray*, Chicago: Univ. of Chicago Press, 1958; and H.J. Jensen, *The Muses' Concord: Literature, Music, and the Visual Arts in the Baroque Age*, Bloomington: Indiana U.P., 1976.

5. John Dryden, "A Parallel Betwixt Painting and Poetry" in *De Arte Graphica: The Art of Painting*, London: J. Tonson, 1695, pp. i-lxvi.

6. Charles Lamotte, *An Essay Upon Poetry and Painting*, London: F. Fayram, 1730, p. 25.

said to differ. In a few words, taken from *The Freethinker* of 1718: "The Painter is equally understood in all Nations"[7] (and of course ambitious poets have always tried to undo this disadvantage; hence perhaps Joyce's "cross-word polyglottony" as Lewis rather unkindly put it in his great novel *Childermass*).[8] Conversely, to "lay open the internal Constitution of Man" (James Harris's phrase in his 1744 treatise on the topic)[9] was held to be almost impossible for the painter who, after all, had but one moment and but one space to use. Indeed there's wisdom in the marvellous beginning of the Mookse and Gripes story in *Finnegans Wake*: "Eins within a space and a wearywide space it wast" (*FW* 152.18).

Lewis's major objection to Joyce's art in *Time and Western Man* — that it was temporal, in Bergsonian flux — was rather silly given the very nature of the novel. His own ambitious attempt in *The Human Age* to make the novel do what it almost by definition cannot do, namely become a purely spatial construct like a vast abstract canvas, was, I think, not unlike Joyce's attempt, for that same reason perhaps equally unsuccessful, in making the novel as wordlessly universal as music in *Finnegans Wake*. Joyce, as we know, was kind enough to grant Lewis his sublimity at the end of the Ondt and the Gracehoper episode, when he has his alter ego the Gracehoper sing to Ondt/Lewis: "Your genus is worldwide, your spacest sublime! / But, Holy Saltmartin, why can't you beat time?"[10] (*FW* 419.7-8). But just as Lewis could not beat time, Joyce could hardly hope to beat space, as the "ut pictura poesis" doctrine makes equally clear. And here I must come back to *Laokoon*.

Comparing Lewis and Joyce should never be a matter of seeing parallels (or even analogies) as to subject-matter: that is the sort of thing Joseph Spence did and Lessing, I think rightly, objected to. It will invariably lead either to the seeking of illustrations for a text, or vice versa — or to conclusions that can more easily and

7. *The Free-Thinker*, No. 63 (27 October 1718), 53.

8. Wyndham Lewis, *The Childermass*, London: Chatto & Windus, 1928, p. 175.

9. James Harris, *Three Treatises*, London: J. Nourse, 1744, p. 58.

10. It is tempting to think that Joyce in calling Lewis "Ondt" was also punning on Dutch "ont-" (the negative prefix, like English "un-").

better be explained by (simply put) the *Zeitgeist*. The comparison of the arts makes sense only in the realm of what art-historians call "expression", i.e. the way in which the artist conveys his subject by technical means. In neoclassical theory, too, the parallel between poetry and painting was felt to be most valid when it related to the expression of character and to the unity of composition. Expression in literature was seen as the result of plot and diction, in painting of design and colour; unity of composition was attained in literature through a principal idea or emotion, in painting through the principal figure. According to eighteenth-century aesthetics, a writer's and a painter's work could be compared on the basis of a kind of check-list that would at any rate include terms such as design, plot, composition, genre, register, diction, colouring, style, focalisation, and perspective. It is still an adequate check-list for determining whether the work of a painter and of a writer have features in common, and it has the advantage that chance similarities in content are cancelled out as evidence.

This is where the history of the rivalry that existed between Joyce and Lewis becomes truly instructive. Their conversation about the gothic architecture of Rouen Cathedral, reported by Lewis in his autobiographical *Rude Assignment* sums it all up in a way. Wyndham Lewis objected loudly to the cathedral's heavily encumbered façade, its "fussy multiplication of accents .... scholasticism in stone".[11] And, in an intriguing phrase later echoed in the last chapter of *Self Condemned*, he noted the cathedral's "dissolving of the solid shell — the spatial intemperance, the nervous multiplication of detail." Lewis continues his account as follows: "Joyce listened and then remarked that he, on the contrary, liked this multiplication of detail, adding that he himself, as a matter of fact, in words, did something of that sort" (p. 60). It is not hard to see how this amusing incident could be fully worked out in formal terms to yield the essence of the difference in Joycean and Lewisian "expression".

11. *Rude Assignment: An Intellectual Autobiography* first appeared in 1950. I quote from the recent edition by Toby Foshay, Santa Barbara: Black Sparrow Press, 1984, p. 60.

Lewis's formative years were spent in developing the vortex: time arrested, art frozen in non-representational primary form.[12] One can see why Lewis disliked *Dubliners* and *A Portrait* and didn't want to publish them in *Blast*: even in parodic form Naturalism is unacceptable to the true-blood Vorticist. The Lewisian description of Rouen's gothic architecture must be typically inverted to grasp his positive ideal. All one has to do is bear in mind the pencil portraits Lewis made of his subjects (the splendid line drawings of Joyce, Eliot and Pound) to understand Lewis in *Satire and Fiction* (1930) proudly saying of *The Apes of God*: "No book has ever been written that has paid more attention to the outside of people."[13] Surely this is the most immediately obvious difference between Joyce and Lewis: outside versus inside, or outline versus detail, contour versus content, moment versus action, space versus time.

Where Joyce creates circles and fluid streams, Lewis brutally curtails narratives, disrupts them by throwing up stylistic dams. Lewis segments circles, loves angles. In punctuation Joyce liked to make distinctions disappear — no quotation marks, the Sternean dash. Lewis began his writing-career by disfiguring the pages of *Tarr* with eye-stopping sentence-blocking bold-faced (in both senses) punctuation marks looking thus: ==.[14]

Also compare the external portraiture of, for instance, Lady Fredigonde in *The Apes of God* and Joyce's creation by indirection of Gretta Conroy. In Lewis we find an external third person narrator in absolute control, who observes gesture or notes dialogue in a series of expansive narrative tableaux: the cast is more often than not very large, and observed, as it were, in frames. We read his scenes as we read large history paintings. A typical passage in *Childermass* is not unlike Lewis's war paintings where the personages in the landscape, though by the looks of them in motion, cannot be said to move. Joyce's scenes in comparison, even in "Nausikaa", the art of which is painting, are like the stills of Joyce's favourite modern art, the motion picture ("tableau!").

12. See T. Materer's *Vortex: Pound, Eliot, and Lewis*, Ithaca: Cornell U.P., 1979, *passim*.
    13. Wyndham Lewis, *Satire and Fiction*, London: Arthur Press, 1930. The whole pamphlet is well worth reading.
    14. Wyndham Lewis, *Tarr*, London: Egoist Press, 1914, *passim*.

Related to this is something Arthur Calder-Marshall pointed out in 1935 in *The Arts To-Day*.[15] Lewis's metaphors, he writes "are sight metaphors. They leap before the eye as pictures. Lawrencian and Joycean metaphors are seldom visual in this way" but rather a matter of "an unconscious association" (p. 129). It is indeed quite typical of Lewis that in his description of Joyce in *Rude Assignment* he observes: "Odds and ends of words or phrases were always floating about in his pockets: he would put his hand in his pocket to take out a packet of cigarettes and bring out with them a scribbled scrap of conversation scratched on an envelope, or notes of the names of objects" (p. 60). The effect is intended for the reader's sight, the initial metaphor wholly pictorialized.

When all is said and done, a painting is not a poem, a poem not a speaking picture. Both Joyce and Lewis realized this and tried, in their own and different ways, to avoid pictorializing their writing or making their pictures pleasingly narrative in a nineteenth-century fashion. Their ways were different, but their purpose, I think, identical. In trying to go beyond the limits of their art, both overreached, both, in a sense, ultimately failed, and for a very similar reason: you just can't mediatize word and image.

Free University, Amsterdam

15. A. Calder-Marshall, "Fiction", *The Arts To-Day*, ed. G. Grigson, London: John Lane, 1935, pp. 113-54.

HISTORY AND MODERNITY IN JOYCE'S ULYSSES

MARIUS BUNING

It can be safely said that the problem of history — setting down the deeds of men — has been one of Joyce's life-long preoccupations. His scope is broadened from national, Irish history in the early works (*Dubliners* and *A Portrait*) to international and universal history in *Ulysses* and *Finnegans Wake*, and the method has developed over the years from incidental to inclusive, from history as a subject to history as structure, and from the mythical to the mystical. Although, like his alter ego Stephen in *A Portrait*, "he chronicled with patience what he saw, detaching himself from it and tasting [testing] its mortifying flavour in secret" (*P* 67), Joyce cannot be considered a historian. Nor was he a philosopher of history, in spite of the fact that he borrowed heavily from Giambattista Vico's theory of history, in particular the latter's concept of the rise, fall, and resurrection which seemed to him to underlie universal human history — a pattern that was to inform *Finnegans Wake* both structurally and conceptually.

Joyce was an artist devoted to recording human experience in imaginative form through the medium of language. What he realized already at an early age and brought to fruition in his mature works was that history — the historical process and its representation — was essentially a verbal artifact, and therefore subject to a particular point of view or a collection of such viewpoints. For this insight he found much support in Vico, who argued that particular types of figurative discourse dictate the fundamental forms of the historical data. Thus history like fiction is inseparable from its discourse, that is its verbal representation or mediation. Consequently, narrative style and fictional strategy (and their pluralizations) are the modern artist's primary concern,

as is borne out in the works of Franz Kafka, Robert Musil, Marcel
Proust, and Thomas Mann. Viewed from this angle, the novel
Ulysses can be seen as Joyce's experiment in how to write about
human history in a responsible artistic form — a form which
'modernizes' our view of history as well as 'revolutionizes' our
concept of literature. Therein lies his modernity in the first place.

The main portion of this essay will be devoted to a brief, though
inevitably non-exhaustive examination of the problem of history
and narrative discourse in *Ulysses*. I intend to do so in the light of
recent views in the philosophy of history, and by means of
borrowing some of its descriptive terminology.[1] This somewhat
unusual perspective is preferred because it would seem that the
age-old antithesis between history and literature is no longer as
obvious and natural as we have long thought. One may recall
Aristotle's famous dictum: "The poet's function is not to describe
the thing that has happened, but a kind of thing that might
happen, i.e. what is possible as being probable or necessary. The
distinction between historian and poet is not in the one writing
prose and the other verse ... its consists in this, that the one
describes the thing that has been, and the other a kind of thing that
might be. Hence poetry is something more philosophic and of
graver import than history, since its statements are of the nature of
universals, whereas those of history are singular."[2]

But such a clear-cut opposition is no longer tenable in the light
of recent philosophy of history. According to Hayden White, its

1. F.R. Ankersmit, *Narrative Logic: A Semantic Analysis of the Historian's Language*, Den Haag, Boston: Nijhoff, 1983. For some informative
articles on the subject, see F.L. Radford, 'King, Pope, and Hero-Martyr:
ULYSSES and the Nightmare of History' in *James Joyce Quarterly*, 15
(1977), 275-322; John M. Warner, 'Myth and History in Joyce's "Nausicaa" Episode' in *James Joyce Quarterly*, 24 (1986), pp. 19-31. At the
time of going to press I became acquainted with Ulrich Schneider's ' "An
Actuality of the possible as possible": Reflections on the theme of history
in 'Nestor' ' in G. Gaiser ed., *International Perspectives on Joyce*, New
York: Whitson, 1986, pp. 44-58, whose views on "Nestor" are close to my
own.
2. *The Basic Works of Aristotle: Poetics*, R. MacKeon ed., New York:
Random House, 1941, pp. 1463-64.

eminent spokesman, all historical texts are fundamentally literary artifacts. He considers Aristotle's long-cherished distinction as obscuring as much as its illuminates, as the following quotation illustrates: "If there is an element of the historical in all poetry, there is an element of poetry in every historical account of the world. And this because in our account of the historical world we are dependent, in ways perhaps that we are not in the natural sciences, on the techniques of *figurative language* both for our *characterization* of the objects of our narrative representations and for the *strategies* by which to constitute narrative accounts of the transformations of these objects in time. And this because history has no stipulatable subject matter uniquely its own; it is always written as part of a contest between contending poetic configurations of what the past *might* consist of."[3]

Hayden White's innovative views on the writing of history (which continue to be hotly debated among historians) are particularly attractive to Joyceans because they privilege, together with Northrop Frye's theory of fictions, a Viconian concept of figurative language which is used as a meta-language to describe the types of narrative tropes the historian employs, viz. metaphor, metonymy, synecdoche, and irony. This 'blurring' of genres and crossing of boundaries — not to be confused with the current notion of interdisciplinary studies — seems to me another sign of Joycean modernity: it implies a deconstructive critique of the traditional concepts and hierarchies which are our professional concern.

What allows us to connect Joyce's views on history with recent historiographic reflection is not, however, the links with Viconian theory, interesting though they are, but primarily the Joycean text itself, in particular the Nestor episode of *Ulysses*, which takes the art of history as its main topic, and the personal catechism,

3. Hayden White, 'The Historical Text As Literary Artifact' first published in *Clio*, 3 (1974) and reprinted in *The Tropics of Discourse: Essays in Cultural Criticism*, Baltimore: Johns Hopkins UP 1978; *Metahistory: The Historical Imagination in Nineteenth-Century Europe*, Baltimore, Johns Hopkins UP, 1973, esp. the introduction entitled "The Poetics of History", and "The Politics of Historical Interpretation: Discipline and De-Sublimation" in *Critical Inquiry*, 9 (1982), 113-38.

interspersed with flashes of interior monologue, as its overall narrative strategy. In point of fact, the subject of history makes its first appearance already in the opening chapter, where Stephen Dedalus in conversation with the Englishman Haines confesses to be the servant of two masters at the same time: imperialist England and the Holy Catholic and apostolic church. Haines' quasi-apologetic reply remains virtually unanswered, but the phrase "history is to blame" will recur as a *leitmotiv* in later chapters: "I can quite understand that, he said calmly. An Irishman must think like that, I daresay. We feel in England that we have treated you rather unfairly. It seems history is to blame". (*U* 1. 647-49)

Haines' answer can be interpreted as the result of a *deterministic* view of history, a poor form of historicism: if indeed history as an abstraction is responsible for injustice and oppression, it precludes the question of human reponsibility. Such a stance implies, in fact, a defense of the status quo, aptly epitomized in Aexander Pope's celebrated phrase: "Whatever is, is right".

In the Nestor episode history — concretely realized in the history lesson — is primarily presented as a chronicle of unreal facts and dead dates. For Stephen's pupils "history was a tale like any other too often heard, their land [being] a pawnshop" (*U* 2.46). Naturally, they prefer a story, preferably a ghost story; instead they are treated to a Miltonic passage, followed by a difficult riddle that has continued to puzzle even seasoned Joyce-ans. For Stephen too this form of history is problematic, as appears from his reflections after the lesson about the victory of the Greek general Pyrrhus over the Romans in the battle of Tarentum. In his eyes this victory is exemplary for history itself; via a pun on Pyrrhus/pier he concludes that history is a "disappointed bridge" (*U* 2.39): every victory entails defeat and disappointment, which is symbolized by the banal end of the story since the invincible general was eventually killed by a tile-throwing vixen. Later in the novel Pyrrhus is compared to Moses and Parnell whose victories were Phyrric in that they failed to lead their peoples into the promised land of independence. Even the great Caesar was knived to death, and important twelfth-century philosophers like Averroes and Maimonides — Aristotelians in their own way — were not recognized for their brilliance.

Stephen's historical scepticism goes much deeper than that,

however, as appears from his mental leap to William Blake's well-known description of Clio as "fabled by the daughters of memory", and not by "the daughters of inspiration" who are responsible for the arts and literature. This rich intertextual reference not only refers back to the classic Aristotelian passage cited earlier (and to the notorious distinction between fancy and the imagination, or allegory versus symbolism), but it also sheds light on Stephen's (and Joyce's) conception of literature. Via an allusion to Aristotle's definition of movement as "an actuality of the possible as possible" (*U* 2.67), that is the realization of one of the possibilities out of the total sum of possibilities, Stephen's deprecative view of history can be distilled: history is the realization of only one possibility in the past only and it is therefore necessarily reductive, concerned with dates and victors; on the other hand, the poet/novelist can imagine through his art the non-realized possibilities of man and he is thus more truthful to human experience. Moreover, historical discourse is a matter of phraseology (like Phyrrhus' reported phrase "Another victory like that and we are done for"), that results in "a dull ease of the mind" (*U* 2.15) instead of vibrating the imagination.

For this privileging of literature over history we find further support in Joyce's own essay on the Irish poet Mangan: "Poetry ... is always a revolt against artifice, a revolt in a sense against actuality. It speaks of what seems fantastic and unreal to those who have lost the simple intuitions which are the tests of reality; and, as it is often found at war with its age, so it makes no account of history, which is fabled by the daughters of memory.... [H]istory or the denial of reality, for they are two names for the same thing, may be said to be that which deceives the whole world" (*CW* 81). When applied to the Nestor fragment under discussion, it would mean that the pupils are right: the history lesson is divorced from their own situation because it denies the oppressive reality of the Irish situation in 1904.

The denial of Irish reality is personified in Mr Deasy, whose view of history can be called a fundamentalist variation on historical determinism. For this Protestant, pro-England Irishman things are simple since "All human history moves towards one great goal: the manifestation of God" (*U* 2.380-81). In his eyes it is the Jews who are to blame for history's imperfections: "Mark my words, Mr. Daedalus, he said. England is in the hands of the jews.

In all the highest places: her finance, her press. And they are the signs of a nation's decay. Wherever they gather they eat up the nation's vital strength. I have seen it coming these years. As sure as we are standing here the jew merchants are already at their work of destruction. Old England is dying". (*U* 2.346-51)

The other collective scapegoat is woman: "A woman brought sin into the world. For a woman who was no better than she should be, Helen, the runaway wife of Menelaus, ten years the Greeks made war on Troy. A faithless wife brought the strangers to our shore here, MacMurrough's wife and her leman, O'Rourke, prince of Breffni. A woman too brought Parnell low". (*U* 2.390-94)

Critics like R.A. Adams and Richard Ellmann have convincingly shown that Mr Deasy's view of history depends on a selective memory; it is a mixture of clichés and falsifications.[4] Stephen's own thoughts and the narrator's voice further emphasize his unreliability and his ideological *Weltanschauung*, epitomized in his anti-Home Rule slogan '*For Ulster will fight/And Ulster will be right*' (*U* 2.397-98) — a battle cry still used by Dr Paisley's followers in Northern Ireland today.

It is against this background that Stephen's famous pronouncement, "History ... is a nightmare from which I am trying to awake" (*U* 2.377) should be seen. His heartfelt cry not only refers to Mr Deasy, the personification of eight hundred years of troubled Irish history, but it expresses at the same time his profound ambivalence towards his mother, his motherland, and his mother church. His view of history can best be described as *subjectivistic*, with a strong *apocalyptic* slant (as appears later in the surrealistic history parade in the Circe episode).[5]

Although there is no demonstrable influence, Stephen's statement comes close to Karl Marx's view of history: "Men do make their own history, but they do not just make it as they please; they do not make it under circumstances chosen by themselves, but

4. R.M. Adams, *Surface and Symbol: The Consistency of James Joyce's ULYSSES*, New York: Oxford UP, 1962, pp. 18-26, and Richard Ellmann, *Ulysses on the Liffey*, London, Oxford UP, 1972, pp. 20.23.

5. Again Stephen's view is close to Joyce's own; according to his brother Stanislaus, Joyce 'looked upon history as chronicles riddled with falsehoods,' in *My Brother's Keeper*, New York: Viking, 1958, p. 170.

under circumstances directly encountered, given, and transmitted from the past. *The tradition of all the dead generations weighs like a nightmare on the brain of the living.* And just when they seem engaged in revolutionizing themselves and things, in creating something that has never yet existed, precisely in such periods of revolutionary crisis they anxiously conjure up the spirits from the past of their service and borrow from them names, battle cries, and costumes in order to present the new scene of world history in this time-honoured disguise and this borrowed language" (italics added).[6]

Stephen's sceptical and subjectivistic views of history are balanced by Leopold Bloom's philosophy, which gives *Ulysses* its truly international and even universal historiographic weight. This is due, first of all, to his Jewish origin which allows for dense references to Eastern Europe (Hungary) and Israel (Palestine), and to his marriage to Marion Tweedy, born in Gibraltar. More importantly, the importance of Bloom's function derives from the fact that he is both a historical character and a mythical one, and in that order. He is the product of Joyce as historian: an objective and detached recorder of diachronic reality, and of Joyce as a myth-maker, who subsumes history under the synchronic, timeless reality of his imagination. Bloom's dualistic nature (which reflects the dual structuring of the novel as both history and myth) does not invalidate his pronouncements on history. On the contrary, it gives them more truth-value.

Invoking Hayden White once more, we may conclude that history and myth are not polar opposites (as has long been thought, especially by historians), since historical consciousness conflates with mythic consciousness. There is, then, no writing of history possible without mythic plot structuring, be it romantic, comic, tragic, or ironic, nor without figurative mediation. As

6. Karl Marx, *Basic Writings on Politics and Philosophy*, L.S. Feuer ed., Toronto: Doubleday, 1959, p. 320. Joyce would have loved Marx's opening sentence: "Hegel remarks somewhere that all facts and personages of great importance in world history occur, as it were, twice. He forgot to add: the first time as tragedy, the second time as farce". The reference to Marx is not to suggest that Stephen had Marxist leanings, of course. Joyce's own political sympathies were with Bakunin's anarchism.

Nietzsche wrote in *The Use and Abuse of History* (1874), "history is the work of the dramatist". [His task is] to think one thing with another, and weave the elements into a single whole, with the presumption that the unity of plan must be put into the objects if it is not already there".[7] This antihistorical critique of the idea of history is echoed more than a hundred years later by Julian Barnes's narrator in *Flaubert's Parrot*, when he exclaims that "we can study files for decades, but every so often we are tempted to throw up our hands and declare that history is merely another literary genre: the past is autobiographical fiction pretending to be a parliamentary report".[8]

As for Bloom's philosophy of history, it appears most clearly and dramatically in the final passages of the Cyclops episode, which describe the altercation between the nameless Irish citizen -- a representative of a nationalistic, strait-jacketed view of history -- and Leopold Bloom. It is told by two narrators: an anonymous Dublinesque barfly and an omniscient narrative voice, employing the technique of "gigantism", an epic form of narration replete with exaggeration and hollow rhetoric, and thus an apt narrative strategy since politics is the chapter's central topic. After several offensive and antisemitic remarks by both the citizen and the barfly, a confrontation is inevitable:

> Bloom was talking and talking with John Wyse and he quite excited with his dunducketymudcoloured mug on him and his old plumeyes rolling about.
> —Persecution, says he, all the history of the world is full of it. Perpetuating national hatred among nations.
> —But do you know what a nation means? says John Wyse.
> —Yes, says Bloom.
> —What is it? says John Wyse.
> —A nation? says Bloom. A nation is the same people living in the same place.

7. Friedrich Nietzsche, *The Use and Abuse of History*, trans. Adrian Collins, Toronto: Doubleday, 1957, pp. 37-38. Hayden White concludes that Nietzsche liberated the historian "from having to say anything *about* the past; the past is only an occasion for his invention of ingenious 'melodies' " in *Metahistory*, p. 372.
8. Julian Barnes, *Flaubert's Parrot*, London: Knopf, 1984, p. 90.

135

—By God, then, says Ned, laughing, if that's so I'm a nation for
  I'm living in the same place for the past five years.
So of course everybody had the laugh at Bloom and says he,
trying to muck out of it:
—Or also living in different places.
—That covers my case, says Joe.
—What is your nation if I may ask? says the citizen.
—Ireland, says Bloom. I was born here. Ireland.
The citizen said nothing only cleared the spit out of his gullet
and, gob, he spat a Red bank oyster out of him in the corner. (*U*
12.1414-33)
The full force of Bloom's philosophy emerges in a dramatic
passage that deserves to be quoted in full:
—And I belong to a race too, says Bloom, that is hated and
  persecuted. Also now. This very moment. This very instant.
Gob, he near burnt his fingers with the butt of his old cigar.
—Robbed, says he. Plundered. Insulted. Persecuted. Taking
  what belongs to us by right. At this very moment, says he,
  putting up his fist, sold by auction in Morocco like slaves or
  cattle.
—Are you talking about the new Jerusalem? says the citizen.
—I'm taking about injustice, says Bloom.
—Right, says John Wyse. Stand up to it then with force like
  men.
. That's an almanac picture for you. Mark for a softnosed bullet.
Old lardyface standing up to the business end of a gun. Gob,
he'd adorn a sweepingbrush, so he would, if he only had a
nurse's apron on him. And then he collapses all of a sudden,
twisting around the opposite, as limp as a wet rag.
—But it's no use, says he. Force, hatred, history, all that. That's
  not life for men and women, insult and hatred. And everybody
  knows that it's the very opposite of that is really life.
—What? says Alf.
—Love, says Bloom. I mean the opposite of hatred.
  (*U* 12.1467-85)
It spite of Bloom's plea for non-violence and tolerance, the scene
almost ends in a fight:

And says he:

—Mendelssohn was a jew and Karl Marx and Mercadante and Spinoza. And the Saviour was a jew and his father was a jew. Your God.

—He had no father, says Martin. That'll do now. Drive ahead.

—Whose God? says the citizen.

—Well, his uncle was a jew, says he. Your God was a jew. Christ was a jew like me.

Gob, the citizen made a plunge back into the shop.

—By Jesus, says he, I'll brain that bloody jewman for using the holy name. By Jesus, I'll crucify him so I will. Give us that biscuit box here.

—Stop! Stop! says Joe. (*U* 12.1804-13)

The chapter is concluded, however, by the omniscient narrative voice, describing in a burlesque-heroic manner the imaginary ascension of "ben Bloom Elijah" amidst clouds of angels.

This magnificently rendered contrast between the nameless citizen and Bloom can be seen, in more than one way, as a counterpart to the exchange between Mr Deasy and Stephen: both the citizen and the schoolmaster claim to have a monopoly on historical truth which is perverted in their hands; and both are anti-semitic anti-feminists. Both also symbolize the nightmare of history — inimitably parodied in the long list of Irish heroes and heroines — from which Stephen is trying to escape but in which he is still trapped.

Bloom's philosophy of history as an apparently absurd cycle of violence, hatred, and persecution partly agrees with Stephen's sceptical view. But it transcends that of his youthful friend because it is an affirmative human vision which opposes love to hatred, non-violence to violence, and tolerance to nationalism. His philosophy can therefore be characterized as fundamentally humanistic.[9]

It comes as no surprise that this viewpoint is mocked by the bystanders: "A new apostle to the gentiles, says the citizen. Universal love. —Well, says John Wyse. Isn't that what we are

---

9. See Joyce's youthful essay (1898) "Force" (*CW* 17-24), and his "A Suave Philosophy", dealing with Buddhism and non-violence, (*CW* 93-95).

told. Love your neighbour. —That chap? says the citizen. Beggar my neighbour is his motto. Love, moya! He's a nice pattern of a Romeo and Juliet." (*U* 12.1489-92) Even the narrative voice comments by way of intertextual parody: "Love loves to love love.... You love a certain person. And this person loves that other person because everybody loves somebody but God loves everybody". (*U* 12.1493, 1499-1501) Nevertheless, the word has been spoken: "Love ... the opposite of hatred". It may be more than coincidental that "love" is also the key word in the restored passage in Hans Walter Gabler's 1984 corrected text: "Love, yes. Word known to all men." (*U* 9.429-30) In the preface to this edition Richard Ellmann writes that the theme of love pervades the whole novel. This may be so but, as Jean Kimball has reminded us, the dramatic nature of this textual change only highlights the juxtaposition of love and death.[10] Indeed love and death are the two great realities in *Ulysses*, as they are in history, that is in life itself.

Free University, Amsterdam

10. "The New Edition of *Ulysses*: An Assessment of Its Usefulness One Year Later", in Bonnie Kime Scott ed., *New Alliances in Joyce Studies*, Newark: U of Delaware P, 1988, p. 222.

Part III: Commentary

IT LOSES SOMETHING IN TRANSLATION:
ITALIAN AND FRENCH PROFANITY IN JOYCE'S *ULYSSES*

MARISA GATTI-TAYLOR

The 1974 publication of *Notes for Joyce*: *An Annotation of James Joyce's Ulysses* has greatly simplified the reader's task of deciphering most of the arcane passages in the novel, including foreign language phrases.[1] However, the authors of this indispensable compendium deliberately omit any interpretive remarks on Joyce's use of foreign phrases, and give only translations and sources, when relevant.[2] Their primary intention is to provide the raw material on which critical studies can be based. This is particularly true in the case of foreign phrases where the authors' translations purport to be verbatim. Unfortunately, most of the passages which I will analyse here have been translated inaccurately in *Notes for Joyce*. Nevertheless, the literal meaning is essential to a critical appraisal, although meaning alone does not reveal the role of these phrases in context.

A selected number of foreign expressions in *Ulysses* convey increasingly complex connotations each time they recur. They serve, in fact, as variations on a theme. This paper examines the meaning and function of several Italian and French phrases found in *Ulysses*, and will also demonstrate how they have been mistranslated in *Notes for Joyce*.

Stephen Dedalus first learns Italian from "the plump round-

1. Don Gifford and Robert J. Seidman, *Notes for Joyce*: *An Annotation of James Joyce's Ulysses*, New York: E.P. Dutton, 1974.
2. Gifford and Seidman, pp. xi-xiii. In this article, I provide my own translations of the Italian and French phrases cited, which are often at variance with the versions given in *Notes for Joyce*.

headed professor of Italian with his rogue's eyes",[3] and later maintains a student-teacher relationship with Maestro Almidano Artifoni,[4] another stout, round-faced Italian with heavy hands and "human eyes".[5] Yet, in spite of his academic associations with the Italian language, Stephen uses it several times as a medium for blasphemy and obscenities. While criticizing this "best of all possible worlds", Stephen declares that 'vthe lord of things as they are whom the most Roman of catholics call *dio boia*, hangman god, is doubtless all in all in all of us, ostler and butcher...." (*U* p. 213). When committed to writing, this expression elicits shock among most Italians.

The same holds true of phrases quoted in a passage included in the Eumaeus episode, where Bloom and Stephen "perceived an ice-cream car round which a group of presumably Italians in heated altercation were getting rid of voluble expressions in their vivacious language in a particularly animated way, there being some little difference between the parties. —*Putana madonna, che ci dia i quattrini! Ho ragione? Culo rotto!* [Whore of a Blessed Virgin, let him give us the money! Am I right? Degenerate opportunist, literally, broken arse!] —*Intendiamoci. Mezzo sovrano più* ... [Let's understand each other. Half a sovereign more ...] —*Dice lui, pero.* [So he says, however.] —*Farabutto! Mortacci sui!* [Scoundrel! Damn his dead! literally, His evil dead ones!] .... Mr Bloom ... remarked to his *protégé* in an audible tone of voice, apropos of the battle royal in the street which was still raging fast and furious: — A beautiful language. I mean for singing purposes.

3. James Joyce, *A Portrait of the Artist as a Young Man*, London: Heinemann Educational Books Ltd., 1964, p. 178. All quotations from this work are documented within parentheses in the text, using the letter P.

4. This resonant name belonged to a Berlitz instructor who helped Joyce locate teaching positions during the author's stay in Trieste and in Zurich. See Angela Bianchini, "James Joyce e l'Italia", *Tempo Presente*, 9 (1964), p. 54.

5. James Joyce, *Ulysses*, New York: The Modern Library, New Edition, Random House, 1961, p. 228. All subsequent quotations from this volume are documented within parentheses in the text, using the letter *U*.

Why do you not write your poetry in that language? *Bella Poetria!...*" [Beautiful Poesy!] (*U* pp. 621-22).

Gifford and Seidman give the following somewhat inaccurate translation of this passage: "—Whore of a Blessed Virgin, who gives us these half-farthings! Am I right? It breaks your arse!/ —We understand each other. No longer his own boss ..../ —So *he* says, however./ —The rascal! Death to him!'"

There are several linguistic points to discuss here. The translator for Gifford and Seidman has mistaken the "*che*" which introduces the subjunctive mode "*dia*", for the relative pronoun "who", causing a mistranslation of the verb mode as indicative [*dà*], rather than subjunctive [*dia*]. "*Culo rotto*", literally "broken arse", is an insult whose strict application refers to a homosexual prostitute. In a broad sense, it refers to someone who will do anything for money. By placing the pronoun at the end of the verb "*intendiamo*", Joyce has made the verb imperative [Let's understand each other], rather than indicative [We understand each other], which in Italian would be "*c'intendiamo*". The translation "No longer his own boss ..." is a classic case of *traduttore traditore*, since it interprets "*sovrano*" as "ruler" instead of the British coin "sovereign", which in proper Italian is "*sterlina*". Furthermore, the word "*sovrano*", belonging to courtly or ecclesiastical usage, would not be used to mean "boss", or "*padrone*". Likewise, the word "*più*" cannot be considered a negation when it is used without a negative particle such as "*non*" or "*mai*". "*Mortacci sui*", a curse heard in Central and Southern Italy, applies to the man's dead relatives, and is not a wish for *his* death. Finally, it is interesting to note that Bloom's use of the word "*Poetria*" does not really constitute incorrect Italian, as Gifford and Seidman state. "*Poetria*", an archaic term for "*poesia*", is equivalent to the English word "*poesy*". While Bloom may not have been aware of this subtlety, surely Joyce was! Consequently, we find here several levels of language at play.

The passage also has a twofold ironic intent: on the one hand, it expresses the Italian immigrants' financial plight shared also by Stephen ("They were haggling over money" p. 622); on the other, it reveals Bloom's conception of Italian as a language to be sung, an association based on his day-long preoccupation with Mozart's *Don Giovanni*.

Italian was the language spoken in the Joyce household during its stay in Trieste as well as the idiom of Joyce's intimate correspondence.[6] Furthermore, as a tenor of uncommon talent, Joyce might have been expected to link Italian with its artistic lyrical art form. However, with the exception of Bloom, the characters' use of Italian in *Ulysses* does not generally conform to its stereotyped role as a medium for passionate sentimentality. It functions rather as an outlet for banal venality. A closer analysis of Stephen's meeting with Almidano Artifoni will further illustrate this statement. The stocky, mustachioed, round-faced Maestro attempts to persuade Stephen to pursue a musical career. He argues mainly from the financial standpoint: "*Perchè la sua voce ... sarebbe un cespite di rendita, via*" [Because your voice ... would be an easy source of income, that's why]. He cannot bear to see Stephen sacrifice himself to a seemingly unprofitable literary career, although, he too, at Stephen's age, had similar ideals. "*Eppoi mi sono convinto che il mondo è una bestia. E peccato*" [And then I realized that it's a beastly world. It's a shame]. Signor Artifoni applies his powers of persuasion to try to prevent Stephen from continuing his self-sacrifice, but Stephen assures him that it is a "bloodless one", quoting the Italian expression synonymous with the Holy Sacrifice of the Mass: "*—Sacrifizio incruento*, Stephen said smiling, swaying his ashplant" (*U* p. 228). True to his namesake Dedalus, he has consecrated himself to the mission of his "Old father, old artificer" (*P* p. 235), a mission which at times also parodies that of Christ.

Like Jesus, Stephen here faces a temptation to abandon his calling. His Satan takes the form of a heavy-set "human eyed" Mammon, whose corpulence reflects enjoyment of the good things in life. Even the Maestro's name is suggestive of his role as seducer: "Almidano" sounds like macaronic Latin, "*anima*" and "*damnum*" [soul and damnation], while "Artifoni" could be a play on the words "art" and "phoney". To the promise of financial success, however, Stephen prefers the bloodless sacrifice of a literary vocation. The "tempter" leaves, excusing himself, wishing the obstinate artist "*tante belle cose*" [many lovely things] and vanishes, ironically enough, in the direction of the Trinity Gates. In the above instances, Joyce associates Italian with blasphemy and earthy practicality, a connection that may very well reflect his personal attitude, because after ten years in Trieste and a brief stay in Rome, Joyce claimed to have become "outrageously, illogically sick" of Italy, Italian and Italians.[7]

French, on the other hand, is linked with sensuality and religion, as illustrated by the motif of the *sacré pigeon* [damned pigeon]. This irreverent reference to the Holy Spirit first occurs to Stephen in the Proteus episode, when he is walking along the beach toward the Dublin electricity and power station known as the Pigeon-house. The name reminds him of a French joke based on the Virgin Birth of Christ: "—*Qui vous a mis dans cette fichue position*? — *C'est le pigeon, Joseph*" [—Who got you into this wretched condition? —It was the pigeon, Joseph] (*U* p. 41). This reference recurs in the Oxen of the Sun episode, which takes place in the hospital. This time the bird motif is amply explicated. Stephen leads a discussion on conception and childbearing, rendered more relevant by the cries caused by labour pains from Mrs Purefoy or "Pure faith", who is suffering the consequences of her credulity. He observes that man is guilty of a grave sin against the Holy Ghost, the Lord and Giver of Life, through his nightly "impossibilising" of those "Godpossibled" souls (*U* p. 389). In this context, the pigeon phrase conveys the paradoxical nature of the dogma of Christ's Virgin Birth: "But here is the matter now. Or she knew him, that second I say, and was but creature of her creature, *vergine madre di tuo figlio* [virgin mother of your son] or she knew him not and then stands she in the one denial or ignorance with Peter Piscator who lives in the house that Jack built and with Joseph the Joiner patron of the happy demise of all unhappy marriages *parce que M. Léo Taxil nous a dit que qui l'avait mise dans cette fichue position c'était le sacré pigeon, ventre de Dieu!*" [because Mr Léo Taxil told us that the one who got her into that wretched condition was the damned pigeon, God's belly!] (*U* p. 391).[8]

---

7. Chester G. Anderson, *James Joyce and His World*, New York: The Viking Press, 1967, p. 65.

8. Gifford and Seidman, p. 37, cite the source of this reference: *La vie*

For Stephen, these allusions to Mary's "pregnancy without joy" (*U* p. 391), relate indirectly to his role as a pseudo-Christ figure. That is, the pigeon motif adds a mock-religious quality to Stephen's reference to his namesake, Dedalus — "My father's a bird" (*U* p. 41) — a quality later brought into sharper focus by his parody of Christ in the exchange with Maestro Artifoni, and by Stephen's claim to be "the eternal son and ever virgin" (*U* p. 392). The bird motif reappears in Stephen's allegorical journey to the land called Believe-on-Me, or religious faith, which he never reaches because of a certain bird, here reminiscent not of Catholic dogma, but, in my opinion, of the "nightingale" in the Fourth Tale, Fifth Day, of the *Decameron*. Boccaccio's delightful account describing a young lady's desire to sleep on the balcony in order to hear the nightingale, culminates with her and her lover being discovered in a compromising pose, "her left hand holding the thing you are ashamed to mention among men",[9] after which the girl's father judiciously concludes that since she was so fond of the "nightingale" as to catch it, it shall be hers. In his tale, Stephen also cleverly and graphically exploits a proverb about birds: "Yes, Pious had told him of the land and Chaste had pointed him to the way but the reason was that on the way he fell in with a certain whore of an eyepleasing exterior whose name, she said, is Bird-in-the-Hand and she beguiled him wrongways from the true path by her flatteries that she said to him as, Ho, you pretty man, turn aside hither and I will show you a brave place, and she lay at him so flatteringly that she had him in her grot which is named Two-in-the-Bush or, by some learned, Carnal Concupiscence" (*U* pp. 397-98).

Likewise, in the Nighttown episode, the bird motif surfaces first

---

de Jésus, Paris: 1884, by Léo Taxil (pseud. of Gabriel Jogand-Pages, 1854-1907), adding that "the tone of Jogand-Pages's book is not angry denunciation but a chaffing and humorous one in the attempt to develop absurdities in traditional Christian versions of the life of Jesus". The translation of *sacré* in the expression *sacré pigeon* should not be "sacred", as Gifford and Seidman provide, but "damned, cursed, or bloody", because it precedes rather than follows the noun.

9. Giovanni Boccaccio, *The Decameron*, trans. Richard Aldington, New York: Dell Publishing Co., Inc., 1962, pp. 330-31.

in the guise of a moth, whose ditty can be viewed as yet another derisive allusion to the Holy Spirit, since the Feast of the Annunciation is traditionally commemorated in the spring: "I'm a tiny tiny thing/ Ever flying in the spring/ Round and round a ringaring/ Long ago I was a king,/ Now I do this kind of thing/ On the wing, on the wing!/ Ring!" (*U* p. 517).

Stephen's own quotation, "Spirit is willing but the flesh is weak" (*U* p. 519), can also be read in relation to the bird motif as a further stab at the Holy Ghost.

The French version of the pigeon motif recurs immediately after Kitty's account of "Mary Shortall", whose last name also alludes to the paradox of the Virgin Birth: "And Mary Shortall that was in the lock with the pox she got from Jimmy Pidgeon in the blue caps had a child off him that couldn't swallow and was smothered with the convulsions in the mattress and we all subscribed for the funeral" (*U* p. 520). (Presuming that Mary Shortall and Jimmy Pidgeon's child is Christ, the "funeral" could be the ceremony of the Mass). At this point, Philip Drunk and Philip Sober,[10] the Siamese Twins representing yet another personification of the paradox, dramatize the pidgeon pasquinade:

PHILIP DRUNK
(*Gravely.*) *Qui vous a mis dans cette fichue position, Philippe?*

PHILIP SOBER
(*Gaily.*) *C'était le sacré pigeon, Philippe* (*U* p. 521).

This bizarre caricature gives way to a grotesque image which culminates the pigeon motif and its double allusion to dogma and perverse sex. Still in the brothel, Zoe asks Stephen to give the group "some parleyvoo", so Stephen complies, describing with marionette jerks the "Perfectly shocking terrific of religion's things

---

10. Gifford and Seidman, p. 407. This representation is based on "the story of the woman who, upon receiving a bad judgment from Philip of Macedon when he was drunk, appealed to him sober and had the initial judgment reversed". It therefore means asking for reconsideration of a matter that has been hastily decided. Again, the implication is that the Virgin Birth was a matter decided upon in haste.

mockery seen in universal world. All chic womans which arrive full of modesty then disrobe and squeal loud to see vampire man debauch nun very fresh young with *dessous troublants* [disturbing lower parts]. (*He clacks his tongue loudly.*) *Ho, la la! Ce pif qu'il a!*" [My oh my! What a snout he's got!] (*U* p. 570). The pigeon has undergone a nightmarish metamorphosis: "*Vive le vampire!*" [Long live the vampire!] (*U* p. 570).

My translations again differ from Gifford and Seidman's, which give "disordered underthings" for "*dessous troublants*", and "The bang that it has!" for "Ce pif qu'il a!" (p. 421). "*Dessous*" means "underthings" only in the expression "*vêtements de dessous*", literally "underclothing", while the adjective "*troublants*" does not translate as "disordere*d*" (in French: "*déréglés*"), but as "disturbing". *Pif* means "bang" only as an interjection. As a noun, which it clearly is in Stephen's expression, it is a slang term for "large nose, bottle nose, or conk".[11]

The Virgin Birth is thus transformed into a semi-public act of seduction which brings pleasure to spectators and performers. Stephen himself is an enthusiastic reporter of this blood-thirsty unholy ghost's descent intended to shock and mock believers. The various manifestations of the pigeon or bird motif reveal Stephen's hostility against The Lord and Giver of Life, by making clever, imaginative use of a few French phrases which ridicule one of the most important tenets of Christian doctrine.

In conclusion, the text of *Ulysses* is studded with foreign phrases, many of which are spoken by persons who have neither traveled out of Ireland nor studied languages. In Bloom's case, for example, these expressions often indicate a frustrated desire for travel and adventure, as well as a pathetic attempt to refine his conversation. Stephen's use of foreign phrases, on the contrary, originates from familiarity and knowledge. His thought pattern has the richness and the variety of the polyglot, and his uses of Italian and French are not purely gratuitous: in translating his obsessive arguments regarding theology, Stephen multiplies them, at the same time suggesting connotations and adding an exotic

11. See Harrap's *New Standard French and English Dictionary*, 3 vols., London: Harrap, 1972, for all details on translations.

touch to the English version. Furthermore, his use of foreign languages in these matters serves to create a distance as far as he is concerned. It is as though an *alter ego* makes the pronouncements in Italian and French, since "*Dieu* was the French for God and that was God's name too; ... still God remained always the same God and God's real name was God" (*P* p. 12). Thus, the foreign phrases constitute a significant part of "the violent or luxurious language in which Stephen escaped from the cold silence of intellectual revolt" (*P* p. 168). They contribute more than occasional graffiti on the walls of the verbal labyrinth which is *Ulysses*.

Univ. of Wisconsin
Milwaukee

PROTEAN INGLOSSABILITIES
"To No End Gathered"

Fritz Senn

Readers of Joyce depend on the mediators of background information, the commentators, annotators, source tracers, scholiasts. Reading Joyce is, in part, to play such roles. But no matter how superior we may comport ourselves, we need co-operation; no single reader knows enough. Group readings, pooled experience, are one antidote, printed notes or glosses another. They also invade the class room when the teacher supplies comments, and as soon as "Any questions?" becomes the question. The mediation of background and intertextual sources — whether the results are called "Annotation", "Notes for Joyce", "Allusions", "glosses", "scholia", "commentaries" or whatever — is both necessary and problematic. We may not give much thought to what kind of notes, exactly, we need for which occasion. Once we stop assuming that all a student/novice needs to be told is the sum total of the notes that happen to be in main stream existence, the misgivings become intriguing. The following remarks will take cautious common sense looks at some of the issues.

No doubt, we want our glosses to be accurate, correct, reliable. Not all of the ones in circulation are. If a note for "Schwanzenbad-Hodenthaler" (*U* 12.560) reads: "German: 'Idle-about-bath-Inhabitant-of-the-valley-of-testicles'"[1] then it is unreliable, incorrect,

---

1. The note (never mind where) is quite on target, except that it misses a German vulgarism "*Schwanz*" (penis) to match the testicles in "*Hoden*", and that "Idle-about-the-bath" is entirely unfounded: "*Schwanzen*" is not a verb, the suffix "*-en*" links composite nouns [there is however a verb, one with a morphemic difference, "*schwänzen*" (what's in an umlaut?), which indeed means "play truant, shirk" (a dictionary may give

and not accurate, and one might wishfully imagine such sloppiness to be a rare exception. No matter what the practice is, at least we have an ideal of "correctness" against which to measure short-comings. Correctness in itself is already quite a tall order, requiring serial safeguards of double-checking. For certain occasions, say for a very advanced level, we might even want commentaries to be reasonably complete — more of an aspiration than a possible achievement, already beyond the reach of any one expert or small team. Ideally we should all collaborate in the supremely con-sequential task. Which, in a scattered sort of way, we do, but then the editorial and organisational problems become formidable.

Beyond correctness and inclusiveness we want notes to be relevant. Relevance is a less objective notion even than accuracy; it already belongs to the realm of interpretation. Notes should enable interpretations, not predispose them; but in incommodious vicious recirculation they are already part of what they help to bring about. Every item in a note is interpretation by its tacit assumption of deserving a place there; every note is also, by nature, a meddlesome intermediary. Readers, Joycean ones in particular, are note-creating beings. All these dilemmas are certain to remain Protean insolubilities. Meddlesome interpretation will inevitably lead to disagreement. No wonder, Joyce's works are essentially also *about* this problem — the mind interpreting the world and words. An interior monologue or a nationalist harangue or a Circean phantasy or an Ithacan list are abristle with running notes and comments. Our notes are (sorry!) meta-notes.

In the following queries particular stress will be put, further-more — and principally — on a didactic aspect: At what time is what kind of information profitable — or can information be, on occasion premature and detrimental? Notes, in other words, should also be expedient (should, etymologically, "free our feet" for exercises of our own), and be stimulating not blunting. They

---

an intransitive "idle about") and has blatantly nothing to do with the name], and that note is insufficient also since it does not tell us that the whole matrix "the Archjoker Leopold Rudolph von Schwanzenbad-Hodenthaler" is a common one for the old Austrian aristocracy (Archduke).

should open, not close. This has to do with time, the appropriate moment, *kairos*, and the time devoted to our own, unaided, primary interaction with the text. Notes deceptively posit the simultaneous availability of all their information.

Questions of this kind could be tackled systematically. Principles could be established, perhaps; but they might either be too rigidly cramping, or else too vaguely flexible for precise application. Principles usually have the advantage of revealing more about their own metaphysics than the perennial uniqueness of each individual item. The approach taken here is purely pragmatic: what has been done, and what might be done in specific cases (all cases are specific) and exemplified frustrations. A few inductive non-generalizations will be tried. The trial runs are selected from the chapter which above all others acts out mutability, the elusive "Proteus" chapter of *Ulysses*. This suitably highlights the problems at hand. Implicit in all will be the overall concern of *how* to gloss the most pervasive drive, change itself, not just its single manifestations. Notes have a way of securing and fastening their objects, treating them *as* objects. Such fixation is often betrayed in the wording of a note: "this is an allusion, a reference to ...." We entangle ourselves in an inherent contradiction. "Put a pin in that chap, will you" (*U* 3.399), Stephen addresses himself when he tries to fix fleeting thoughts, ideas, inspiration, into the stability of letters. (How, by the way, would we gloss the odd word "chap"?) Pins are, or were, proverbially put into butterflies for their exposition. What gets lost in doing this is the flying, the flutter, the motion, whatever characterizes butterflies. In trying to put pins in the chapter we may lose nothing but its "proteity".

Ineluctable Dilemma

What words in *Ulysses* should be glossed in the first place? Surely words like "diaphane" or "*Frauenzimmer*" (which has been wrongly glossed as meaning "midwife", an annotation that has sporadically survived lexical truth). Perhaps "modality" in the first line; and already this would not be too easy to pin down in a manner that is both precise and intelligible. What about "Ineluctable"? It means, we know and sometimes read, unavoidable, inevitable. Should we tell those who might pass by heedlessly that

154

an appropriate image is hidden in the rare adjective — that which cannot be struggled out of: "*in-e-luct-abilis*"; the verbal form *luctari* actually means "to wrestle". "Ineluctable" is what you cannot get out by wrestling.[2] It was Proteus, the versatile wise man of the sea, who wrestled out of anyone's grip by changing his form into such volatile things as fire or a running stream. How can you hold, or, as Leopold Bloom puts it, "own water really"? (*U* 8.95). Joyce began with the right word, which has a way of becoming alive beyond its merely epistemological niceties once its inherent metaphor is brought to light. And should any note indicate that for an older generation, brought up on the classics, "ineluctable" would have had two strong possible echoes? It was Virgil who used the adjective in a prominent position. It became a winged word, part of our heritage. Aeneas is told that the fall of Troy is imminent, in fact has already occurred, in these portentous words: "*Venit summa dies et ineluctabile tempus/ Dardaniae. Fuimus Troes, fuit Illium ...*" (*Aen*. 2:324-5) At this point Troy (Dardania) has become a matter of the past, the ultimate day (as prophesied in the *Iliad*) has arrived. There is no struggling out of it (the struggle about the city has at this moment become nearly pointless). Time is in fact ineluctable, it always is. Another part of the passage cited will turn up later in *Ulysses*: "Fuit Ilium!" (*U* 7.910). Elsewhere in the *Aeneid* it is destiny that cannot be wrestled against: "*fortuna omnipotens et ineluctabile fatum*" (*Aen* 8:334: "almighty fortune and ineluctable fate"). In such radiation the first word in "Proteus" calls up Fate and Time.[3]

All very well, but is it mandatory to force these classical ghosts on an unsuspecting reader who wants to go on with a rebarbative chapter and is content enough, at a first reading, to figure out what Stephen has in his complex mind? Certainly not, and certainly not too soon. If the above suggestions were to be condensed into a

2. A swamp can be *ineluctabilis*, or serfdom, and literally so. Out of a certain type of soil, Virgil instructs us, water may have to "force its way out": "**aqua eluctabitur omnis**" (*Georgica* II, 244).

3. Time and Fate are at least implied in "That lies in space which I in time must come to ineluctably" and "Self which it itself was ineluctably preconditioned to become" (*U* 9.1200, 15.2120).

short annotative entry, some dim-witted user might come along and claim: "Ineluctable" is an allusion to Virgil; or to Swinburne.[4] It is not, really, an allusion or reference, or even a "quotation", but perhaps the effective part of an aura. The word, unusual enough, has its own karma: in a former incarnation it served a Roman poet to designate momentous turning points. Some words too "remember their past lives" (*U* 4.365). It is wrong and heavy-footed to insert Virgilian ineluctability in a canon of comment; it is equally not quite right to leave it out and not to give readers a chance to tax its vibrations, or simply to appreciate the vividness of "wrestling out of". It may be worth knowing that the first word of the chapter has potential associations with Time and with Fate. Previous literary uses of a word conduce to our understanding of, or at least feel for, the context. Or else, this may lead us astray and clog our minds with gratuitous trivialities.

We have not even yet done with the first word in the chapter of change: the beginning is also a contrast: "ineluctable" is a word that has remained stable with the passing of time. For practical purposes it is still identical in shape with its Latin ancestor. Scholars took it over as it was from the classics. As a bookish term it did not have to undergo the metamorphoses that just before Joyce's age were being traced and reconstructed. The last word in the first Proteus sentence, "eyes", would be aligned by etymologists with German "*Auge*", Latin "*oculus*" or Greek "*ossomai*" —forms that do not appear to have much in common with each other. Etymology is the unveiling of past Protean shapes. Yet it should not therefore clutter the entries of notes even in a chapter whose "Art" is philology, or should it?

Potential Virgilian ("SAYS PEDAGOGUE", *U* 7.1053) echoes are definitely not allusions in any narrower sense. They are not part of the primary equipment we need to struggle with the chapter's opening. They are not quotations like "*maestro di color che sanno*" (*U* 3.6) soon to follow, which clearly derives from

---

4. "With all strong wrath of all sheer winds that blew, / All glories of all storms of the air that fell / Prone, ineluctable, / With roar from heaven of revel...." These lines are from a sea poem "Thalassius" (220-3). Swinburne, alias "Algy" (*U* 3.31) is all over the first chapters, many thematic relations might be listed.

Dante's *Inferno* and would be obscure without knowledge of that source. The original context determines, identifies, fixes the person referred to, Aristotle, a professional knower. This we accept, as Hugh Kenner reminded us[5], through a concatenation of commentaries that have come down through the centuries: Aristotle is not named in the *Divinia Comedia* either. Ironically, a reader has to be master of a little knowing (or to be informed by one). None of the presiding thinkers in the first paragraph — Aristotle, Berkeley, Jakob Boehme — are nominally present. One thing the Dantean line does is play with knowledge (personified by the arch-philosopher, "master of those who know") and with our ignorance (most of us do not recognize a line we never saw before). Among other things, *"maestro di color che sanno"* is a comment on commentaries and their tradition.

In that line, which a commentator will translate and put within a pertinent framework, at least one word other than *"maestro"* is tricky — *"color"*. It is our natural reflex to connect it with a preceding thought: "Then he was aware of them bodies before of them coloured?" Colour, of course; but no, the Italian *"color"* is — or rather: was — a demonstrative pronoun, merely pointing forward: "those". "Colour" is wrong, and yet it is hard to resist the idea that the antecedent "coloured" — and, of course, the fact that Stephen is meditating on colour which is an Aristotelian *accidens* (and not substance) — helped to call up the Dantean phrase in which the shape, body, appearance, *color* may be as effective as the actual (purely grammatical and hardly noticed) meaning. Proteus is about the treacherous relation between appearance and essence, semblance and reality. The wrong sense of *"color"* seems to be more vital than the essential one. What kind of shape is one grappling with by finding in the correct reading of *"color"* (a demonstrative, something you can point out to be seen) and the false one just once again the opposition Stephen is thinking about? Paradoxically in *"color"* we may be aware of the erroneous colour before (we are aware of) the functional body (*U*

5. "Who's He When He's at Home?" in Heyward Ehrlich ed., *Light Rays: James Joyce and Modernism*, New York: New Horizon Press, 1984, p. 60.

3.5). Such dynamic intricacies would exceed the requirements or feasibilities of annotation. Practically speaking, can we imagine, or accept, a gloss that would say that *"color"* does not mean colour but energetically calls up the misleading vision all the same? *"Color =* colour" is not a favourite, but a throwaway.

Notes, whose essence it is to be functionally brief, moreover, if they truly attempt to struggle with the text, become unwieldy and cumbersome, laborious to digest, an obstacle rather than an impetus. With all the necessary speculation and hedging, they tend to get too long for convenience; but it is again a Joycean fact that micro-notes strive towards comprehensive exhaustion. A few further proliferations of that sort will now document the inherent impossibility of solidifying metamorphoses. Examples are easy to find, they are everywhere.

Common Searches

Stephen imagines his uncle, Richie Goulding, whom he might visit: "He lays aside his lapboard whereon he drafts his bills of costs for the eyes of master Goff and master Shapland Tandy, filing consents and common searches and a writ of *Duces Tecum"*.[6] (*U* 3.80) Whole, are masters Goff and Shapland Tandy? Goff, Tandy, Shapland — uncommon, striking names. There is something quaint, antiquarian, memorable about them; we can understand that they would occur to Stephen. So we look around and might find, antiquarians ourselves, for example, one "Matthew Goffe" in Shakespeare's *2 Henry VI* who would help nothing. Our existing reference works and annotations offer items like this: "Goulding was a law clerk with Messrs Goff and Tandy" (*Norton Anthology of English Literature*, p. 224) — a possible explanation, except that we know that Richard Goulding is employed by Messrs Collis and Ward, solicitors, 31 Dame street. John Vandenbergh, the Dutch translator of *Ulysses*, who compiled a volume of annotation, expands this non-fact into a corrective gloss: "In reality the

---

6. The misleading nature of *"Duces"* (*ducere*: Latin for the lead, guide) has been dealt with in *Joyce's Dislocutions* ed. John Paul Riquelme, Baltimore: Johns Hopkins University Press, 1984, p. 31.

solicitor's office of Collis and Ward" (my rendering of *Aanteke-ningen bij James Joyce's ULYSSES*, De Bezige Bij, Amsterdam, 1969, p. 35). This still leaves Goff and Tandy unaccounted for. Most Joyceans turn to the *Notes for Joyce* by Gifford & Seidman: "Goff — one who is akward, stupid, a clown, an oaf. Master Shapland Tandy — combines Irish revolutionary Napper Tandy (1740-1803) (see 45:2-3n) and Laurence Sterne's eccentric hero from *Tristram Shandy* (1760-1767)". (p. 35) All such information consists of, no doubt, true facts, reflections or possible associations, but the commentaries amount to no more than guesses of some probability: Napper Tandy, for instance, takes us by the hand soon after (*U* 3.260). Sterne's Shandy is a bit removed from Tandy, however, but then Shandy's tale is at least proteanly confusing in perhaps fitting analogy. "Shapland", by the way, is still left dangling.

We would be on more solid ground consulting the entries on Goff and Tandy in the factually oriented *Thom's Dublin Directory* for 1904: "Goff, James, esq., taxing master, Supreme Court Judicature — res. 29 Leeson street, lower". (p. 1882); "Tandy, Shapland Morrie, taxing master, Supreme Court Judicature, and com. for affidavits — res. Clarinda park house, Kingstown". (p. 2022) We also find them under Supreme Court Judicature (Chancery Division) as members of the "Consolidated Taxing Office": "Taxing Masters, Jehu Mathews, esq. J.P.; Shapland Morris Tandy[7], esq.; James Goff, esq." (p. 898) So these two are real civil servants, taxing masters ("master" or "*maestro*" at this stage in the book is already a reverberating complex, a word of apprehension for Stephen Dedalus). We will in fact see "Richie Goulding carrying the costbag of Goulding, Collis and Ward" — most likely in a professional pursuit — "pass from the consolidated taxing office to Nisi Prius court" (*U* 10.470).[8] Appearance led most of us to believe the names belonged to fiction or

---

7. The discrepancy between the two entries: (Morrie — Morris), due to typographical chance, adds a minor Protean touch to the identifications.

8. Perhaps a shade of master Goff of the Nisi Prius court appears in *Finnegans Wake*: "growing the goff and his twinger read out by the Nazi Priers" (*FW* 375.17).

history, now they turn out to be part of existing legal institutions — Dublin surface, not historical embroidery. Goulding in a manner of speaking does work for master Goff and master Shapland Tandy, in the sense that the two are part of a supervisory board. We might now even detect Goulding's own voice as a reading possibility: just as he calls the firm he works for "Goulding, Collis, and Ward" (we learn later: *U* 6.56), he might facetiously claim to be working "for the eyes of master Goff and master Shapland Tandy", his superiors somewhere in the hierarchy; or else, such might be a scathing remark passed by Simon Dedalus on his brother-in-law.

The "correct" information would derive from a source like *Thom's Directory*. The correct information is trivial, but to the point. It clarifies something, not everything (how exactly do these taxing masters affect Goulding's work?, would Dublin folklore of 1904 have something worth while about them?, whose voice is being echoed?). If we do not know the identities of Goff and Tandy, as most readers obviously did not, not much is lost. Our understanding of *Ulysses* does not — *must not* — depend on it. In such a case the question mainly turns on *when* should such correct annotation be thrust on novice readers? If *Notes for Joyce* informed us right away in civil service terms (as it no doubt will in a future revised edition), it might also instantly lay all those ghosts from the past: Napper Tandy, the Goffs of yesteryear, and all sorts of maybe vague tentative overtones. The right information might lull the explorative urge which, especially in Proteus, is as much part of the active meaning as the correct factual answer — which *does* belong in a note. Instant facts may curtail the richness of associations in — mind you — the "interior monologue" which consists *of* associations. Associations are never wrong, but notes, even notes of associations, may be.

The struggle for meaning is more than a terminative gloss of resolution may seize. To put it differently, even when the local Dublin habitation of master Shapland Tandy has been determined, when we solve that little puzzle for good, that taste of that "Shapland" should linger disturbingly — for it is evidently also some such pulsation that made Stephen evoke it. "Tandy" will be redefined by the recall of a stereotyped consciousness of 1798 nationalism, the legendary Napper Tandy. "Napper" and "Shapland" are at least introspectively connected. The legendary rebel of a hundred years ago might be disheartened to see a Sassenach namesake firmly instituted in the levying of taxes and the dispensation of justice. So the entries above that actually were associative shots in the dark do add their quota, they lend *"color"* to the passage, they provide literary reverberations. But even the factually appropriate gloss may lead us into tangential by-paths: Stephen Dedalus seems to be beset by masters that are taxing him. Joyce, of course, is a taxing master for annotators.

The point is that even undoubtedly correct, that is verifiable information, notwithstanding its indispensability, may be hermeneutically ill-timed. A gloss has a levelling effect: it puts all its consumers in the same position. It enduces a state of knowledge which would precisely not have been identical for, say, Richie Goulding himself, or Stephen (who may never give any thought to the legal institution), or an ordinary Dublin citizen of 1904. Meanings change, and ought to, with the accidental state of our knowledge. New knowledge does not automatically replace former guessing. In *Finnegans Wake* a residual and often dominant element of guessing remains.

Stephen conjures up Dean Swift, "his mane foaming in the moon, his eyeballs stars". This leads to "Houyhnhnm, horsenostrilled" and then to "The oval equine faces, Temple, Buck Mulligan, Foxy Campbell, Lanternjaws". (*U* 3.111)[9]

The meaning we get out of this list differs according to what we bring to it. Every reader of *Ulysses* will recall Mulligan and may, but already less likely, remember one of Stephen's creditors, out of a given list of ten: "Temple, two lunches" (*U* 2.257). In *A Portrait* (which no reader is obliged to know, or memorize) a fellow student Temple featured often in the fifth chapter, so the reader of the previous novel will be at an advantage. A very attentive one may call to mind "eyeless faces" and: "Was it not a mental spectre of the face of one of the jesuits whom some of the boys called lantern Jaws and others Foxy Campbell?" (*P* 161-25) So the sum of four names refers to three people, all summoned from Stephen's past.

9. Pre-Gabler editions were further confusing by an intrusive period: "... Campbell. Lantern jaws."

"Lanternjaws" and "Foxy Campbell" are alternative appellations for the same person, a priest. If we did not know all this, if it were not served up ready-made as it is here, we might be more likely to wonder about "Lanternjaws". If it is not recognized as a nickname, it might be many things, as is borne out by the two translations Joyce was alleged to have supervised: "Têtes chevalines, Temple, Buck Mulligan, Foxy Campbell, lames de couteaux".[10] "Die ovalen Pferdegesichter, Temple, Buck Mulligan, Foxy Campbell, hohle Gesichter".[11] In both renderings the last item is not treated as a name at all. Once the correct designations are revealed to us, lanterns and foxiness subside, and may well be overlooked. One need not inspect what is familiar. If the list is still partly cryptic, there seem to be at least four interwoven clusters worth our attention: 1 and primarily) **persons** that have impinged on Stephen at one time or another; 2) there are **priestly** traits: one person is a jesuit, Mulligan played the role in mockery, Temple's name is sacerdotal; 3) description of **faces**: equine, lantern (=hollow) jaws, temple; 4) there are **animal** features: equine, foxy, buck. The Protean role of an item like "Temple" is more vital at the speculative stage. A certain amount of guessing, before the nominal identification brings it to an end, may be aptly fruitful. External complications may play their part: a textual corruption formerly separated "Lantern jaws" into a sentence all of its own, turned the passage into a more Protean one than its author may have contrived. But Joyce on the whole tended to push names back towards their primordial meaning by often putting them in lower case. The Dublin district called "Liberties" is invested with more original freedom in "From the liberties, out for a day" (*U* 3.33); the lower case letters at least make us stop and wonder. The text takes liberties with names like "the dead sea" (*U* 4.219); this is a bit of water that by its spelling becomes deader than an orthodox Dead Sea would have been.

What deserves inclusion? When a trite French "*Bonjour*" follows

10. James Joyce, *Ulysse, traduction intégrale d'Auguste Morel, revue par Valery Larbaud, Stuart Gilbert et l'auteur*; first published 1929; Paris: Gallimard, 1948, p. 42.

11. James Joyce, *Ulysses, vom Verfasser autorisierte Übersetzung*; first published 1927; Zürich: Rhein-Verlag AG, 1956, p. 48.

right upon *"Et vidit Deus. Et erant valde bona.* Hlo!" (*U* 3.440), does the *Bon* in the salutation echo *bona* from Genesis? Is *"Bonjour!"* supposed to be spoken not (only) by or to Kevin Egan, perhaps, in Paris, but by God in prophetic French, God who after all first created the day and certainly found it good? Would such ripples be part of the commentator's job? Most likely not.

Patient Groans

Beware of foreign languages, they may be traps; and make sure which languages *are* foreign. German *"Frauenzimmer"* (*U* 3.30) is not a room, *"Zimmer"*, but, oddly, a woman irrespective of where she happens to be. Before the Critical and Synoptic Edition of *Ulysses* settled for "Los *demiurgos"* (*U* 3.18) a phantom Spanish configuration (*"Los Demiurgos"*) added some congruous trickery to the phrase. On the other hand the bride in "Bride street" (*U* 3.34) is spurious[12] but psychologically effective; this is Irish saint Brigid turned into a location. "Romeville" (*U* 3.375) does not contain Rome, but a variant of "rum lingo" (*U* 3.378), not to be confused with the one in "rum tum tiddledy tum" (*U* 3.392), and again distinct from "mulled rum" or even "Rum idea" (*U* 8.196, 5.352). Beware of wrong *colors*. Beware of translations. It is fitting that Stephen's exploits in Paris should be observed and mocked by Irish missionaries to Europe: "Columbanus. Fiacre and Scotus on their creepystools" (*U* 3.193). Especially St. Fiacre, a vehicular saint, for in France he has become, by a series of random transversals, a hackney coach. A protean fate. Is it significant enough for acknowledgement in Ulyssean glosses that "navel" and *"omphalos"* — only a few lines apart (*U* 3.36,38), two words that share but one single letter — are akin, derived from the same ancestor, linked by etymological navelcords between them?

Annotation should not, presumably, take care of non-meanings: if *"ponton"* were French (it is Homeric Greek), it would mean something else, something that floats *on* the "winedark sea" — *"oinopa ponton"* (*U* 3.394); if "Algy" (*algae?*) or "mare" (*U*

---

12. Or, to put it differently, a disguise, just as "the head centre got away.... Got up as a young bride" (*U* 3.241).

3.31,22) were Latin, illegitimate overtones would accrue, not to be accepted or perputuated, but somehow in line. *"Prix de Paris"* (*U* 3.483, recalling *U* 2.302) is undoubtedly French but has a way of seducing us towards the unfaithful Helen, who was offered as a prize to Paris of Troy in a mythological French triangle (Helen is the wife of Menelaos, who tells of his encounter with Proteus in book IV of the *Odyssey*). When "Faces of Paris men go by, ... curled conquistadores" (*U* 3.215), we may think of the capital of France and of the Trojan beau. In other words, "Proteus" is also about selecting and refusing meanings, about semantic weavings and undoings. According to location, an identical verbal shape, or sound, can have different significance. Joyce's next work, *Finnegans Wake*, will brazenly exploit allotopical non-meanings of this sort.

No language is said to be more precise than Latin, one reason why students once had to learn it as a mental discipline. So nothing should be more facile than to clarify the significance of a short Latin passage, Late Latin at that, marked, indirectly, as a quotation of Saint Ambrose who heard the "sigh of leaves and waves, waiting, awaiting the fullness of their times: *"diebus ac noctibus inurias patiens ingemiscit"*. (*U* 3.466) As it happens, several English renderings exist in print, not all of them agree with the others. The views given differ: *Who* is groaning/sighing? *What* is *"inurias"* the object of? What is the determination of *"patiens."* etc:

A — Night and day he patiently groaned forth his wrongs (St. Ambrose)[13]

B — Days and nights it patiently groans over wrongs.[14]

C — He who suffers injuries complains day and night.[15]

13. David Daiches, *The Norton Anthology of English Literature*, New York: W.W. Norton & Co., 1968, p. 2454.

14. Weldon Thornton, *Allusions in Ulysses*, Chapel Hill: University of North Carolina Press, 1968, p. 65.

15. I. Arnold and N. Diakanova, *Three Centuries of English Prose*, Moscow, 1967, p. 267. Bernard Benstock compares several glosses of the Latin sentence in "Redhoising JJ: USSR/II", *James Joyce Quarterly* 6, 2 (Winter 1969), 177-80.

D — Day and night it [the Creation] groans over wrongs.[16]
E — Suffering injustice days and nights it sighs.[17]
F — Suffering wrongs by days and by nights it sighs.[18]

Not all of these paraphrases can be equally correct, though there seems to be a vague consensus (D, E, F). It is the departures that are interesting. A and B seem to construe *iniurias* as dependent on *ingemiscit*; *patiens* has naïvely created its English surface semblance "patiently", which all the other glosses think of, rightly, as an active participle: "suffering wrongs". A and C have a personal subject for the verb, the other versions a neutre "it". Most interestingly, C stands aloof as an autonomous and sententious rendering.

Most commentators take account of the patristic context (already indicated by "Saint Ambrose"): Stephen calls to mind a fragment from the saint's *Commentary on Romans* 8:22: "*Scimus enim quod omnia creatura ingemiscit et parturit usque adhuc*" ("For we know that the whole creation groaneth and travaileth in pain together until now"). The subject of the Latin clause is, therefore, "it" ("*creatura*", the result of creation), certainly not "he". But in ignorance of the original background we may naturally assume a personal agent, all the more so since the preceding specifications of "*creatura*", "weeds, fonds, leaves and waves", are all in the plural.

The transformations give evidence of "*diebus ac noctibus inurias patiens ingemiscit*" as a very Protean appearance. Six Latin words with their inflexion produce various English forms, grammatical relationships, differences of word order, alternatives like groan or sigh, wrongs, injustice, injuries, etc. Taken by itself, the sentence might mean something like version C: "He who suffers injuries complains day and night". There is some psychological veridity in this; and somehow it might apply to Stephen. It might co-explain why this particular echo and no other occurs to him now. His own

16. Don Gifford with Robert Seidman, *Notes for Joyce: An Annotation of James Joyce's ULYSSES*, New York: E.P. Dutton, 1974, p. 46.

17. Harry Vreeswijk, *Notes on Joyce's ULYSSES*, Part I, Amsterdam: Van Gennep, 1971, p. 190.

18. Brendan O Hehir and John Dillon, *A Classical Lexicon for Finnegans Wake*, Berkeley: University of California Press, 1977, p. 538.

mood is reflected, and the erroneous translation emphasizes this. Actually Saint Paul will continue: "And not only they, but ourselves also ... even we ourselves groan within ourselves...." (Rom. 8:23). Stephen groans/sighs and projects this onto creation: "they sigh" (*U* 3.464). The Latin must have some meaning taken by itself, in its newly transferred context.

It is part of the trickiness that two of Saint Ambrose's Latin shapes, *iniurias* and *patiens*, have English equivalents; so the text teases and misleads us with the phantoms *injuries* and *patient(ly)*, untrustworthy appearances. Paradoxically, the wrong, ignorant translations are the most Proteanly revelatory ones.

For the conscientious commentator a few questions arise. We know the source of Stephen's echo: how profitable is it? The late Father Noon, S.J., who traced the phrase, speculated that "Joyce probably came across this in some choir manual or sodality manual", and not in Migne's voluminous *Patrologia Latina* (*Allusions*, p. 65). At the same time the source is "written into" the passage by way of an intertextual link. Not knowing whether the author ever set eyes on it, should we revert to the fountainhead? For the sake of the experiment, it shall be given here, from *Commentaria in Epistolam ad Romanos*:

Scimus enim quod omnia creatura ingemiscit et parturit usque adhuc. Parturire dolere est. Ipse sensus est, quia omnis creatura per quotidianum laborem ingemiscit et dolet usque modo. Usque modo tamdiu significat, quamdiu legitur. Ipsa enim elementa cum sollicitudine operas suas exhibent, quia et sol et luna non sine labore statuta sibi implent spatia, et spiritus animalium magno gemitu artatur ad exhibenda servitia; nam videmus illa gementia cogi invita ad laborem. Haec ergo omnia exspectant requiem, ut a servili opere liberentur. Si autem haec esset servitus, quae ad Deum proficeret promerendum, gauderet, non doleret creatura; sed quia nostri causa subjecta est servituti corruptionis, dolet. Videt enim quotitie opera sua interire; quotidie enim oritur et occidit opus ejus. Recte ero dolet, cujus operatio non ad aeaternitatem pertinet, sed ad corruptionem. Quantum ergo datur intelligi, satis de nostra salute sollicita sunt, scientes ad liberationem suam proficere maturius, si modo nos citius agnoscamus auctorem. Haec itaque scientes, omni cura diligentiaque dignos nos praebeamus, aliis quoque ut exemplo simus, non nostra solum miseratione commoti, sed et ejus causa quae diebus ac noctibus injurias patiens ingemiscit; solemus enim in alienis causis propensius vigilare.

For we know that the whole creation moans and is giving birth up to this moment. To give birth is to suffer; the exact sense is that all creation, in its daily labour, is moaning and suffering up until now. "Until now" means however long as the moment in which this is being read. The elements themselves perform their works in anxiety: not without effort do sun and moon occupy the room assigned to them; and the breath of life must be forced to do its duty with a loud moan, for we see it driven to work unwillingly, with a cry. So all these things are awaiting their surcease, when they may be freed from their servile toil. Yet were this a service directed toward winning to God, the creation would be glad in it, not suffer: the reason it suffers is that it is in servitude for our own sake. For every day it sees its works perish: daily its work is born, daily dies. It has a just complaint, having its labour directed not towards eternity but decay. So far, then, as is given us to understand, they [the elements, the creation] are quite deeply concerned with our welfare, knowing as they do they can the sooner attain their own freedom the sooner we are brought to acknowledge our creator. And we ourselves, knowing this same, ought to use every care and pain to become examples to others, not only out of compassion for our own kind, but for the sake of what which "moans", bearing its harms day and night; for it is normal for us to pay more attention to others's troubles [than our own].

This *is* the context. Is it enlightening as a note, or just pedantic dead weight? Who will actually read — and not skip — it in the first place? If all glosses were thus laboriously detailed, any commentary would swell to unpractical proportions. What might we gain? The Ambrosian passage happens to contain coincidental echoes: "*Et vidit Deus*" (*U* 3.440); the creator's satisfied look contrasts with its opposite, after the fall: "*Videt enim quotidie opera sua interire*"; Ambrose's "*Occidit*" may be in some relation to a subsequent quote: "*Lucifer, dico, qui nescit occasum*" (*U* 3.486).

Anyone interpreting, that is to say, trying to make out "exact sense", might find many motives in the theological sources that surface in the *Ulysses* chapter. Stephen thought the weeds were swaying "reluctant arms" (*U* 3.462); Ambrose finds nature driven to work "unwillingly" (*invita*). In a later patristic recall, Stephen will think of "corruption" (*U* 7.843). That all is "*labor*", toil, is immediately taken up in Stephen's "loom of the moon" with a "toil of waters" (*U* 3.469, whether "toil" does duty as labour or as texture). The groaning connected with parturition (for which in English the Latin "labour" now does multiple duty) is connectable with Bloom's empathy with women's lot: "groaning on a bed ... her belly swollen out.... Life with hard labour. Mina Purefoy swollen belly on a bed groaning to have a child tugged out of her", (*U* 8.373, 378, 480). The saint points out several times that these things happen every day: "*quotidie*."

Professor Alan Brown of Ohio State University, who kindly supplied the translation and background information, suggests the relevance of a passage immediately following, one of Saint Ambrose's most famous metaphors or similes:

> Post creaturam mundanam adjecit etiam nos hoc exspectare, et ingemiscere ad Deum, ut hinc liberemur cuncti destinati ad vitam; quia christianis mundus his pelagus est. Sicut enim mare adversis excitatur procellis, insilit, et tempestatem navigantibus facit; ita et saeculum perfidorum conspiratione commotum, perturbat fidelium mentes: et tanta diversitate hoc agit inimicus, ut quid prius evitandum sit, ignoretur.

> Following the universal creation, [Saint Paul] adds that we ourselves await this event and bemoan to God that we may be set loose hence, all of us who are ordained to life. For to Christians the world is the deep sea. For as the sea is whipped up by contrary winds and rises and storms upon sailors, so the world, stirred about by the councils of faithless men, tosses the minds of the faithful, and the Enemy brings it all upon us to turn and turn about that one cannot tell which way to flee first.

Saint Ambrose's simile seems in part to derive from the *Odyssey* itself and its (also) symbolical adventures on the sea, at the mercy of contrary winds. (Conversely this remote part of a potential gloss belongs to the noxious councils that toss and agitate the minds of the faithful.) The original context potentially contributes (or we co-creatively make it contribute) to the imagery or atmosphere. The whole Ambrosian passage is in itself an interpretation. In cultural transformations we find an apostle commenting in Greek on the world's sufferings in the light of a new belief, which in part is based on Hebrew scriptures. A fourth century theologian interprets Saint Paul's commentary in Latin. Stephen Dedalus in turn meditates upon it, and ultimately it is up to us to find out what, as St Ambrose puts it, "*Ipse sensus est*". The results of such processes are always arbitrary and selective. Commentaries offer verdicts and, as the illustrative groanings here show, it may be hard to decide which of them are pertinent and valuable — and to whom, at which stage.

Interpretation — or minds tossed, like the sea, by contrary winds — does not naturally stop at any given place. A phrase like "*iniurias patiens*" has its own scriptural history, layers to be uncovered: we find it inflected in Acts 7:24, or in the Psalms (145:7, for example). The psalms also provide a precedent for Stephen's "Lord, they are weary" (*U* 3.464): "I am weary with my groaning" ("*Laboravi in gemitu meo*", Ps. 6:7). The New Testament re-circulates and recontextualizes material from the Old.

The sum total of all possible glosses is not to be confused with the "meaning" of any passage, a platitude that practically all Joyceans and certainly most recent theorists would pay lip service to. In practice, however, texts are still reduced to what happens to be conspicuous in print about them. Every gloss tends to be too much and yet not enough. Apart from the wealth of directly adducible commentary, with the ever intriguing problem of relevance, there are the possible refractions. Everything in the mind is refracted: Stephen's interior shorthand is not exact quotation ("to no end gathered"); thoughts are transformed into new shapes. Evidently the sighing over wrongs touches a chord in Stephen. The first chapter has displayed injuries to his self-esteem, grievances; one such indignity was afflicted in painful protraction by Buck Mulligan: "Stephen suffered him to pull out and hold up on show by its corner a dirty crumpled handkerchief" (*U* 1.70) — this is suffering: "*patiens inurias*". In *Ulysses*, however, it is mainly Leopold Bloom who suffers wrongs. Bloom indeed "sighs" several times in the next chapter; he is a "muchinjured but on the whole eventempered person" (*U* 16.1081). These epithets are Homeric: "**polytlas**" (*Od.* 5:171, and *passim*) and, perhaps, "**echephrôn**" (*Od.* 13:332). Transversal links are part of the reading experience, though these particular connections, being at best anticipations, looking ahead into territories yet to come, should emphatically not be put into a running commentary.

The Proteus episode in the *Odyssey* tells us about the fate of distant Odysseus. The sea god Proteus, once caught in a firm grip, reveals that he saw Odysseus on Kalypso's island shedding tears (*Od.* 4:555 ff.). Structurally, book 4 of the *Odyssey* is also in dramatic preparation for the appearance of Odysseus in person, in the next book, where indeed he is called "*polytlas*" (*Od.* 5:171, 354, 486). When we first meet him in person, he is groaning: "*dakrysi kai stonachêsi kai algesi thymon erechthôn*"; "[with] tears & groans & pains [his] soul racking" (*Od.* 5.83). A Latin translation says "*lachrymis et gemitibus et doloribus animum macerans*".[19] The Greek for groans ("*stonachê*") is the same root Saint Paul used in Romans 8:22, "*ingemiscit*" translates "*systenazei*" from "*stena-chein*". These are not relations Joyce ever knew or cared about; they just occur in the reshaping of similar themes. But even so it is obvious that *iniurias patiens* would well render what we learn about Odysseus right from the start and in many formulaic repetitions: he is introduced as suffering many wrongs: "**polla ... pathen algea**" (*Od.* 1:4; "*plurima ... passus est dolores*" in Clarke's Latin).[20] There are tantalizing coincidences. Menelaos who reports the encounter with Proteus, was approached by Eidothea, daughter of the unerring old man of the sea, and addressed like this: Are you foolish or "do you take pleasure in suffering woes" — "**terpeai algea paschôn**"? (*Od.* 4.372). She hints at a masochistic indulgence. Then again there is the recognition scene between father and son in the *Odyssey*, where much-enduring ("**polytlas**") Odysseus says to Telemachus: "I am your father, for whose sake you suffer many

19. *Homeri Odyssea Graece et Latine, edidit Samuele Clarke, editio sexta*, London: Longman & Co, 1827, p. 174.
20. Alexander Pope: "On stormy seas unnumber'd toils he bore"; Thomas Hobbes: "suffer'd grievous pains"; William Cowper: "He num'rous woes on Ocean toss'd, endured."

griefs with groaning". This is Telemachos himself *"iniurias pa-tiens"*; several motives come together: "**sy stenachizôn pascheis algea polla**" (*Od.* 16:188-9; Clarke: *"suspirans ... dolores multos, injurias sustinens"*, vol. II, p. 86).

What such philological evidence would show, once more, is the strandentwining of Judaeo-Christian and Hellenic chords, and the inexhaustibility of affiliations — irrespective of what the author may ever have had in mind. No reasonable and appropriate completeness could be achieved; just to gather all potential interlinkings would be a laborious accumulation of groans. Again our efforts mirror those under discussion: saint Ambrose (whose name means "immortal" and remains in fact the same Indo-european shape in merely a different transformation) tried to determine the meaning of words in scripture.

Extensive glossing can be intimated in exemplary selection only, as has been done here; one consequence is that it instantly becomes its own parody. Negative examples could be cited as well. In no matter how thorough a Homeric commentary on the Proteus chapter, an important figure like Eidothea, Proteus's daughter who advises and helps Menelaos, in the role that Athene plays to Odysseus,[21] may never register at all. There are no "allusions" to her, it is her attitude only that can be felt. It is she who says that her father will "try to assume all manner of shapes of all things that move upon the earth, and of water, and of wondrous blazing fire" (*Od.* 4:417-8). It is she who counteracts the stench of the seals under whose skins the Greeks lay in ambush with ambrosia (*Od.* 4:445). There is stench in the chapter, but no such sweet fragrance; but there is, as seen before, a saint who bears the name Ambrose, unrelated, and unrelated also to Homer's "immortal night" — *"ambrosiê nyx"* (*Od.* 4:429). There is, strictly annotating, no need to mention her, and yet her function pervades the episode. She outsmarts her father, she teaches not to be misled by appearances, to persist in the attempt. She is the goddess (*thea*) of appearance: *eidos* is outward form, shape, that which is seen: her name could

21. This happens when Menelaos, like Stephen Dedalus, is walking on the beach, alone, "as I wandered alone apart from my company" (*Od.* 4:367).

also be read, as it has been, as meaning "the goddess who sees, or knows". The Proteus chapter opens on that note, the "visible", "thought through my eyes". The root that spawned "visible" and Latin *"videre"*, generated Greek *"idein"*, to see, and *"eidos"*; but also — in words like *"idea"*, or *"wit"*, German *"wissen"* — the thought that arrived through the eyes, for "to have seen" has become "to know" in some languages.

To change to other shapes, is it worth taking up "a maze of dark cunning nets"[22] that Stephen observes in Ringsend (*U* 3.154) and to gloss the obvious? Stephen Dedalus aimed to fly by nets, using "cunning" and two other weapons; Daedalus the artificer built a maze or labyrinth: Stephen's past seems to meet him once more. So far, so trite (commentators are afraid to spell out what everyone would notice unaided). But why should — against English usage —nets be "cunning"? Well, in Greek *"daidalos"* could mean (and did in Homer) "cunningly wrought", and be applied to artifacts; *"daidalos"* of course is "cunning" and therefore became the name for the mythological craftsman. Allusions to Daidalos-Daedalus-Dedalus? No. Dynamisms perhaps.

The enemies of the heresiarch Arius attributed a disgraceful end to him: "In a Greek watercloset he breathed his last: *euthanasia*" (*U* 3.52). Does the ironic comment *"euthanasia"* (a happy, good, death) somehow also suggest the name of the principal opponent of Arius — Athanasius, a notable Greek Father of the Church, after whom one of the Creeds was named, but whose name is not in the text? Prefixes have to be shifted: a bad death is euphemistically turned into its opposite ("good-death") and may turn associatively to no-death ("*athanasia*"). The point is that such possibilities can very well be flashed in discursive equivocation (the purpose of this exercise), but that annotation has to be more responsibly decisive, with a responsibility, however, that is more towards the tradition of glossing than to Ulyssean polymorphism. In any case there will always remain a limbo area of mere potentiality. Some possibilities may be so vigorous that they too are "not to be thought away" (*U* 2.49); it may be hard ever after to unthink that "euthanasia" insinuates (or does *not* insinuate) Athanasius.

22. Compare "A darktongues kunning" (*FW* 223.28).

a maze of dark cunning nets

put a pin in that chap, will you? (*U* 3.399)

The preceding examples were all taken from the third chapter, the one that compounds the problems, as its thematic concern *is* Protean change. How can change be fixed? The preceding remarks are less a sweeping complaint against existing annotations or future attempts, than exemplars of an inherent predicament. It is difficult — in some essential way impossible — to handle processes, transformations, becoming. Proteus of many shapes, true to his nature, keeps eluding us.

Parenthetically again: Proteus is not limited to the *Odyssey*. Ovid proposes a changeful or ambiguous sea-god: "*Protea ambiguum* (*Met.* 2:9), he adds a few transient shapes of his own to Homer's, enumerating a youth, a lion, a raging boar, a serpent (and prefiguring a Wakean dichotomy: a stone or a tree, flowing water, a stream, fire (*Met.* 8:731-6)). Virgil's list includes a tiger, a scaly dragon ("*squamosusque draco*"), a lio*ness* with a mane (*Georgica* IV: 406-10). Horace has a "scoundrelly Proteus" who is, as Stephen Dedalus once wanted to be, not confined by nets or ties: "slipping through all those nets" — "*effugiet ... haec sceleratus vincula Proteus*" (*Satires* II, iii, 71). Proteus was developed long before Joyce, and again one might ask if these post-Homeric elaborations ought to be part of a commentary on the third chapter of *Ulysses*.

If the Protean dynamisms, not any particular situational "parallel", are of value — and they seem to be ubiquitous — then it is good to take Homer at the words he gives to his characters. Eidothea, daughter of Proteus, cautioned Menelaos that her father, when seized, "*panta ginomenos peiresetai*" (*Od.* 4.418), would "try to become everything", including fire and water; and when it happened, he did become a bearded lion, a snake, a pard, a boar, then running water, and a tree (see above, and *Od.* 4.456-8). The emphasis is here not on the various incarnations (corresponding, as they would, to the single identifications in our Glosses), but to the inconclusive actions of becoming and trying ("*peiresetai*").[23]

23. Even the verb forms change: they *become* different (which is easy in

The verb *peiraein* (related to "em*pir*ical" and to "ex*peri*ence") is one of the key activities in the *Odyssey*: to find out, examine, get information, to test, to make a trial of ("to try conclusions"[24]), to endeavour.

Proteus *can* be caught, by diligence and perseverance, but even then only for a short while, he answers a few questions (usually only those that are put to him), then he plunges out of sight. Information provided by him is important, reliable, but inevitably partial. Notes are such information, selected for pertinence. As long as we know that their finality (having to stop somewhere) is treacherous, no harm is done, as long as they are not taken, as in fact they often are, for conclusive truths.

Notes are what is known, "*(g)nota*" the results of knowing. Paradoxically, knowledge is ongoing: one can always know more, and better, and differently in widening or changing contexts. New theories, for one, add new questions, new answers, and new mysteries. The ancients were aware of this; it was reflected in their language. Verbs for knowing are inchoative, inceptive (a form marked by a *sk/sc*-suffix), that is to say they denote a beginning: Latin "*co-gnoscere*" or Greek "*gi-gnôskein*". The meaning in the present tense is not "to know" but "get to know". The Greek verb "*gi-gnô-skein*" is furthermore reduplicated in its initial consonant: "*gi-gno*", as though in imitation of the process, which demands a repeated effort (an effort that in Greek would take at least three syllables). One single attempt, the shape of the verb itself seems to imply, is not sufficient. The German verb "*erkennen*" (with its derivation "*Erkenntnis*", so all-important in philosophy) has a

---

Greek and may often be also metrically determined): "*ginomenos – genet' – gineto*", in three lines. Interestingly the lion becomes bearded: "*genet' eügéneios*" (4.456). This form has nothing to do with "*gen-*" becoming; "*geneion*", beard, is related to "*genys*" (=chin), it is merely a similar, deceptive, shape. See in this context my speculations on Protean features in the *Odyssey* in "Remodelling Homer", Heyward Ehrlich ed., *Light Rays: James Joyce and Modernism*, New York: New Horizon Press, 1984, pp. 81-2.

24. Significantly, these "conclusions" are not the final judgements of logic, but "experiments", the outcome of which is not yet certain (*Hamlet* III, iv, 194).

prefix that suggests a forward or outward motion, something in progress, a way rather than a goal. Notes have an air of finality which belies the inchoative process.

Perhaps that early Joycean signpost in *Dubliners* which has so often been critically discussed fits in here, "*gnomon*" (D 9), a Euclidian form which, however, is marked by a trace of a cognescent activity. A *gnomon* is one who knows, judges, interprets, discriminates. It may be one who can read oracles — a skill the chorus in an Aeschylus play pointedly disclaims: "*ou kompasaim' an thesphatôn gnômôn akros / einai*";" I do not boast to be an acute interpreter of oracles" (*Agamemnon*, 1130-1)[25], Joyce began his prose with a story in which we tentatively learn something and fail to learn as much as we need for our comfort. The agent of the story himself gets to know more and more by cautious deduction from observation or from questionable utterances, but never enough. His and our efforts are, at best, "cognoscent"; we still argue our findings. That same story exposes "*gnomon*" as a strange and fearful word which in the exact science of geometry has been redefined to mean something highly specific and exact: a form characterized by incompletion.

Reading and interpreting are in essence *cognoscent*; notes in contrast are fixed with a semblance of determinacy. What is by nature cognoscent is replaced by specific *cognita*, things now known. This is unavoidable. A pin *has* to be put in that chap if fleeting verbal inspiration is to be noted down (*U* 3.399).[26] For catching hold of processes, or associations, notes are a contradiction in term.

This inchoative nature of knowledge, its cognoscent quality, is at the pulsating core of what has been vaguely termed the "uncertainty principle"; it is not some stable principle or discovery

25. Why work in Aeschylus? *Gnomon* is not an "allusion" to *Agamemnon*. The word is, however, part of a literary heritage. Clearly such a lexicographical antecedent of Euclid's term ought not be part of annotations to "The Sisters". Yet not to go beyond the merely geometrical range would arbitrarily curtail the potential radiation of the sign.

26. As it turns out when the poem, temporarily fixed in Stephen's mind, is made known (*U* 7.522), it is in a form that we could not possibly know from the thoughts out of which it arose.

once hit upon by Joyce or anyone else. Uncertainty is an epistemological condition, as well as a humanistic stock-in-trade, to which we all, and Joyceans in particular, pay lip service and which we easily lose sight of when our interpretations and annotations, in their dazzling splendour, are to be revealed to the world.

The dilemma can be phrased in variable ways. It is the function of notes to abbreviate, condense, summarize, give the gist — this is what they are paid for, to save us all the preparatory labour. They are products, conclusions, outcomes. They emphasize the goal, often assume it has been reached, and must neglect the evolution. Notes are resultative, not processive. The "Result of Gold Cup races!" (U 13.1174) is not identical with the actual race, its waverings, developments, the ingenuity of its prophets, the tensions and expectations, the chanciness of what eventually took place.

Notes and glosses tend to freeze, fix, make static and factual. They offer things, facts, data, substances. They lose their edge if they are hedged in discursive qualifications, such as are possible in an essayistic probe. They tend to concentrate on WHAT and let go of HOW. The least we can do to counteract the inherent falsification of putting a pin into Proteus is to indicate from time to time, by whatever signals, that our offerings are stages or phases at best, that the results are discretionary, arbitrary, the semblance of chimerical relevance. It is true, presumably, that St. Ambrose lived "c. 340-397" or "340?-397" but it is false to assume that these dates are in any way more to the point than the many data that might have been adduced with equal justification. Notes tend to become canonical material, solidified into spurious truths by routine transmission.

Readers have to de-reify the glosses, and annotators should help this process along more than has been usual up to now. We need commentaries and glosses. No single reader knows enough, who knows, to take the chapter at hand, about the controversies of the Fathers of the Church, the Old and the New Testament, Shakespeare, Ovid, Virgil, Homer, Dante, Blake, Aristotle, Berkeley, Jakob Boehme (and commentaries on all these), Joachim Abbas, Thomas Traherne, Thom's Directory of Dublin, Latin, legal terminology, heraldry, and all the abstruse rest? So we depend badly on the experts and their mediators. But what Joyce also teaches us in

Ulysses — and diffusively in the *Wake* — is that you can never trust any messenger, no matter how well-disposed, even when the messenger is doing his of her best, seems ideally equipped (no-one is), and has no axe to grind (all communication is a grinding of axes). We cannot rely on the experts and messengers we need so desperately.

A serious drawback of even ideal annotation, a perfect compromise of conflicting demands, would still be that time is taken away from the reading process. It is possible to know too much too soon, before our minds have begun to revolve the possibilities of the text. None of the above suggestions, for example, should ever be proffered to novice readers of the "Proteus" chapter. Not only might it confuse them, it would litter their minds. What is even worse, it might make them imagine that the proposed intertextual echoes could replace their own essential, incubational, Odyssean explorations, searches and adventures. Even the most optimal note is wrong when it stifles curiosity and puts a stop to further inquiry.

All Notes are liars — useful, incomplete, overdone, misconceived, partly irrelevant, and unseasonable liars. The previous sentence is a note. So is the whole of this essay.

Zürich

THE TERTIUM COMPARATIONIS IS THE MESSAGE MEDIATION AND EUROPEAN JOYCE STUDIES

GEERT LERNOUT

When I first read Joyce, my discovery was embedded in a specific context of undergraduate *hubris* and post-structuralist theory. I read *Ulysses* and *Finnegans Wake* through what I had read of Hélène Cixous' *L'Exil de James Joyce* (especially its Derridian "postface"), through Stephen Heath's "Ambiviolences", and Philippe Sollers's "Joyce & Cie".[1] We had been taught courses on Lacan, Barthes, and Kristeva, and had organized our own seminars to read Deleuze, Guattari and Derrida. My way of approaching Joyce's two last works was miles away from what I found in the books and articles by the, mostly American, critics of the "Joyce Industry"; and it had even less to do with what I heard and read about Joyce in Dublin where I spent the academic year 1978-1979. I read John Garvin's *James Joyce's Disunited Kingdom*[2] because its title sounded vaguely Derridian and I found a very parochial and de-Europeanized Joyce, which I would encounter again and again in U.C.D. and Environs. When I next did my graduate course work at the University of Toronto, I was exposed to the North-American Joyce and to "theory"; and at that point the American and British Joyceans had begun to take notice of developments in French theory. It seemed only natural that in my doctoral dissertation I should attempt to bridge the gap separating

1. Cixous, *L'Exil de James Joyce: ou L'Act de Remplacement*, Paris: Grasset, 1968; Heath, "Ambiviolences", *Tel Quel* 50 (1972) 22-43 and 51 (1972) 64-76; Sollers, "Joyce et Cie", *Tel Quel* 64 (1975), 3-24.
2. Garvin, *James Joyce: Disunited Kingdom and the Irish Dimension*, New York: Barnes and Noble, 1976.

the different Joyces by thoroughly investigating one of them.

In order to describe one particular group of Joyce interpretations we must first place it in its context, and before we can do that, we have to defend the idea that there are different interpretations and that some of them can be grouped together. Nobody who has read or heard anything about Joyce will dispute the existence of different interpretations of Joyce's works: one of the distinct advantages of having regular conferences is precisely the realization that there is very little about him and his works we can all agree on. The cataloguing of these different idiolects into different dialects and languages is much more problematic, since that presupposes a general perspective on the ways Joyce has been and still is read today — a perspective nobody can still claim to possess. Who can honestly say that he/she keeps up with everything that is published on Joyce? Yet we all use these groupings constantly to praise or to diminish or simply to identify. Some of our terms misrepresent reality by the wideness of their scope; one of these is "Joyce Industry". Another is "American Joyceans" as used by Europeans, or "French Joyce" as used by Americans. The last two terms may well be polemically effective because they are vague, but there is no single American Joyce and neither is there one French Joyce, at least not in the sense of a monolithic poststructuralist interpretation of his work. Maybe deep down we all realize the falsity of these labels; and that explains why we hear them more often during coffee-breaks at conferences than we see them appear in print.

Just as the "American Joyce" or the "Joyce Industry" are convenient terms to dismiss a number of diverse phenomena such as excessive symbol searching or the biographical fallacy, so does the term "French Joyce" conveniently sum up all that is radical and progressive. Although, as I implied, we cannot altogether discount the polemic efficacy of the terms, they must be challenged. Any existing survey of Joyce criticism can be used to distinguish radically different kinds of American Joyce interpretations, since the vast majority of the texts discussed there will be American (See, for instance, Staley 1976; Benstock 1976; Feshbach and Herman 1984).[3] The criticism by Europeans, on the other

3. Thomas S. Staley, "James Joyce", in: Richard J. Finneran ed.,

hand, is largely uncharted territory and the role of the British critics seems to me crucial. The British academic critics have not been overly enthusiastic in recognizing Joyce's importance in Modernist literature. F.R. Leavis's refusal to include Joyce in his great tradition has often been mentioned, and we need only look at the very first reviews of *Ulysses* to find that Joyce's "European-ism" was a central issue in the debate. Larbaud had written in the *Nouvelle Revue Française* that with *Ulysses* Ireland had made "a sensational re-entrance into high European literature"; and John Murry in *Nation & Athenaeum* replied that Joyce's anarchism was un-European.[4] Other reviewers stressed Joyce's Frenchness, espe-cially the supposed naturalist quality of his works. After the war, the publication of more and more American Joyce studies only helped to reinforce the British distrust of Joyce's writing; and even a Joycean such as Anthony Burgess managed in 1964 to summa-rize that attitude in his review of four books on Joyce: "The four books I have in front of me are all American and all recent. They confirm my belief that all American English departments have two main activities that amount to industries: one is the plucking of the Joyce-bird, now down to the more microscopic feathers; the other is the amassing of European literary holographs, drafts, toilet-paper jottings against the coming of Cisantlatic Domesday. These preoccupations are, of course, cognate: they both need time and money, of which (and American business has told us they are the same thing) American universities must possess a great deal".[5]

This latent anti-Americanism is still alive today, although it only rarely surfaces in print. Roland McHugh's *A Finnegans Wake*

Anglo-Irish Literature: *A Review of Research*, New York: Modern Language Association, 1976, pp. 366-435: Bernard Benstock, "The James Joyce Industry: A Reassessment", in: Kathleen McGrory et al. eds., *Yeats, Joyce, and Beckett*: *New Light on Three Modern Irish Writers*, Lewisburg: Bucknell Univ. Press, 1976, pp. 118-32; Sidney Feshbach and William Herman eds., "The History of Joyce Criticism and Scholarship", in Zack Bowen and James F. Carens eds., *A Companion to Joyce Studies*, Westport: Greenwood Press, 1984, pp. 727-80.

4. See Robert H. Deming ed., *James Joyce: The Critical Heritage*, Vol. 1, 1902-1927, London: Routledge & Kegan Paul, 1970, p. 253 ff.

5. From: *Urgent Copy*, Harmondsworth: Penguin, 1973, p. 83.

Experience[6] is one of these exceptions; McHugh clearly thinks little of the American Joyce critics; and they in their turn have objected (rightly it seems to me) against their absence in the "Acknowledgments" of *Annotations to Finnegans Wake*,[7] in which McHugh does include an older generation of American Joyceans such as Glasheen, Campbell, Dalton, and Thornton, but not Kenner, Hayman, Benstock, or Litz. The Irish too, and it is not clear whether we should think of McHugh as an adopted Irishman in this context, have mixed feelings about Joyce and about American Joyceans stalking through Dublin looking for the ghost of Poldy Bloom. Like Burgess, the Irish critics seem to prefer a distinctly Dublin Joyce and they tend to dismiss symbolic or "fancy" interpretations in favour of the simple and humane ones — which boils down to Burgess's rallying cry: take Joyce from the professors and give him back to the people.

But the most powerful and effective juxtaposition in contemporary criticism is that between the French and American versions, especially in the parlance of those who belong to the latter context and have sympathies with the former. In their introduction to *Post-Structuralist Joyce: Essays from the French*, Derek Attridge and Daniel Ferrer claim that fantasies about May 1968 in Paris "helped to strengthen British and American conservatism; and fantasies about the intellectual movements in Paris in the 1970s helped to keep Anglo-American literary criticism on its straight and narrow path".[8] This is misleading on two counts: first it suggests a continuity between May 1968 and the intellectual movements of the seventies that cannot be upheld unless we exclude a large number of these movements; and, secondly, one cannot possibly describe American criticism as following (or setting) a straight and narrow path. No other culture, no other academy is so receptive as the American one to all kinds of influence, and especially to French ideas[9] — so receptive even that the author of a recent review of Derrida's last book wrote in *Le*

6. Dublin: Irish Academic Press, 1981.
7. Baltimore: Johns Hopkins U.P., 1980.
8. Cambridge: Cambridge U.P., 1984, p. 2.
9. See William C. Booth, *Critical Understanding: The Power and Limits of Pluralism*, Chicago: U. of Chicago P. 1979, p. 327.

Monde of the need to follow in France the Americans' appreciation of this vastly underrated philosopher.

While Ferrer and Attridge are certainly correct in pointing to the lateness of the American appropriation of "French" ideas in Joyce studies, it seems to me that since the Frankfurt symposium, and especially since Copenhagen, we cannot any longer accuse the American critics of having refused to read Lacan and Derrida. Even in Britain things are changing: in the last few years we have seen crucial "new" readings of Joyce and other classic authors, in series such as Basil Blackwell's "Rereading Literature" edited by Terry Eagleton, Methuen's "New Accents" edited by Terence Hawkes, and Harvester's "Feminist Readings" edited by Sue Roe. A brief look at the catalogues of Methuen, Harvester, or Blackwell's reveals how central literary theory and feminist literary theory have become: "New Accents" has just celebrated its tenth anniversary.

But what is most upsetting about the introduction to *Post-Structuralist Joyce* is the facile use of the term "continent" when clearly France is meant. This is a Napoleonic misconception that the French themselves have not really tried to remedy: when Jack Lang, the former minister of Culture, spoke of the importance of European culture as opposed to the American media invasion, there was never any doubt that what he meant was *French* culture. The British and the Irish too equate "Europe" and "Continent" (even more since they have joined the Common Market), and, when it concerns culture or philosophy, with France or, more precisely, with Paris. But just as there is more to France than Paris, there is more to Europe than France, even in Joyce studies. A brief look at Thomas Jackson Rice's *James Joyce: A Guide to Research*[10] teaches us that among the "Major Foreign-Language Studies" the French do lead in the "Book-Length Critical Studies and Essay Collections" section, closely followed by the Italians, but that there are more German books on *Ulysses* than French.

One of the reasons of the great American interest in the French Joyce is undoubtedly, as Ferrer and Attridge point out, the fact that Lacan and Derrida both considered Joyce's writing "crucial

10. New York: Garland, 1982.

to their enterprise" (p. 9), but in both cases this accolade involves a distinctly revisionist gesture: Lacan only started to talk of Joyce in the mid-seventies at the very end of his career when his thought had been fully developed. The movement is even more clear in Derrida who had made brief and often crypic references to Joyce literally in the margins of his texts (mottos, footnotes, epilogues) until "Deux mots pour Joyce", which dates from 1982 when all of his major and most influential works had already been published for at least a decade. In this text, first published in *Les Cahiers de l'Herne*, and later in English in *Post-Structuralist Joyce*, Derrida stresses the continuing presence of the Irish writer in his own texts, "even in the most academic pieces of work, Joyce's ghost is always coming on board" (p. 149). The truth is that before 1982, no real reading of Joyce is offered by Derrida himself, whereas it is equally clear that Hélène Cixous built her "Thoth et l'écriture" entirely on Derrida's seventeenth footnote in the first part of "La Pharmacie de Platon". The work of Jean-Michel Rabaté, Stephen Heath, Philippe Sollers and other critics is clearly marked by a Lacanian and/or Derridian influence, it is true, but most of their work precedes 1975 and 1982 respectively; and it seems, therefore, that the psychoanalist and the philosopher have clearly benefited from the work done by Joyce critics: Lacan refers to Sollers and Jacques Aubert, Derrida to Rabaté in "Scribbledehobble" and to Cixous in "Deux Mots".

The impact of "French" thought on British and American Joyceans came not from the French *anglistes* but from the pre-Joycean writings of Derrida and Lacan. In Britain Colin MacCabe may well represent the most notorious case of a "new" reading of Joyce and the adverse reaction of the establishment; but if we look closely at *James Joyce and the Revolution of the Word*[11], we will note a number of remarkable features, the first of which is its openly Maoist sympathies. In the bibliography we find works such as Lenin's *Collected Works* in 45 vols, Mao Tse-Tung's "On Contradiction", and Stalin's *Collected Work* Vol. 1-13 (unfinished). Not only does MacCabe attempt to show the truly revolutionary effect of Joyce's *écriture*, he goes one step beyond *Tel Quel* in

11. London: MacMillan, 1978.

trying to prove that Joyce's real-life politics were analogous to the radical impact of his work. The final irony is that by the time *James Joyce and the Revolution of the Word* was published, *Tel Quel* has already changed its politics in the wake of the *nouveaux philosophes*. MacCabe's polemic, directed against the logocentric criticism he considered prevalent in Britain, uses terms that closely resemble those of Roland Barthes' attack on the academic critics in his *Critique et Vérité* of more than a decade earlier. In fact, the parameters of MacCabe's argument were already contained in the much earlier essays that Stephen Heath published in the early seventies in *Tel Quel* and *Discours Sociale*.

It cannot come as a surprise that when Jean-Michel Rabaté reviewed the book in *Critique*, he called MacCabe's work not a "French" but a "continental reading of Joyce"[12], another instance of the France-Europe equation since he does not explain the difference between the two, and since he praises MacCabe for quoting Lacan in French and then translating him, instead of working with an English translation like Margot Norris. In Ireland , too, MacCabe found support in an essay by the Heideggerian professor of metaphysics Richard Kearney who wrote in *Screen* that the book represents to the " 'Anglo-Saxon' industry of literary criticism".[13] Finally, Terry Eagleton reviewed MacCabe's book with Hugh Kenner's *Joyce's Voices*, and he seriously underestimated the liberalism of the British academy by suggesting that MacCabe's book was not the kind of criticism likely to enhance one's chances of obtaining a chair of English.[14]

In the homeland of the "Anglo-Saxon" industry, critics were fairly late in taking note of the developments in French criticism. While Robert Scholes had been active both in Joyce-studies and in the introduction of a formalist-structuralist narratology for a number of years, subscribers to the *James Joyce Quarterly* had to wait until 1979 before they could read about structuralism. Most writers on recent developments in the field of literary criticism agree that the conference in 1966 on "The Languages of Criticism

12. *Critique* 36 (1980), 433-5, 434.
13. "Joyce on Language, Women and Politics", *Screen* 20 (1979-80), 124-34, 124.
14. See: *New Statesman*, 19 Sept. 1980, 21.

184

and the Sciences of Man" at Johns Hopkins marked the beginning of the influence of the new structuralism and Jonathan Culler's *Structuralist Poetics* (1975) its domestication.[15] The first large scale confrontation between Joyceans and the new French critics also occurred in 1975 at the Paris Symposium; and the impact must have been considerable since traces of the animosity between the Americans and the French even surface in the proceedings and since, as Jennifer Levine pointed out four years later, the *James Joyce Quarterly* had only published pictures of the symposium, no comments. The double issue of the *Quarterly* on "Structuralism and Reader Response", in which Levine's article on *Tel Quel* appeared, only managed to miss the mark: apart from an essay by Brook Thomas on Iser, most of the contributions refer to the narratological structuralism of Brémond, Genette, Todorov and the early Barthes.

If a "French" Joyce has caught on in the States it is the post-structuralist Lacanian or Derridian Joyce first introduced by Margot Norris in her *The Decentered Universe of Finnegans Wake*,[16] which was based first on Lévi-Strauss, Lacan, and Derrida, and beyond them on Freud and Heidegger. The major defect of the book is the narrowness of its theoretical base: Norris describes her own book as "a structuralist analysis" and seems to see no break between an American linguistic structuralism and the anthropo-logical structuralism of Lévi-Strauss, or between Lévi-Strauss and Derrida, or Derrida and Lacan. Also, as Jean-Michel Rabaté has pointed out, she refers only to Anthony Wilden's translation (with commentary) of Lacan's "Discours de Rome" and to "The Insistence of the Letter in the Unconscious" in Macksey and Donato's *The Languages of Criticism and the Sciences of Man*, in which the proceedings of the Johns Hopkins conference were published. Wilden's book is not as bad a guide as Rabaté seems to imply; after all, Lacan himself seems to have liked it. The problem is that Norris's reading of Derrida is even more limited. She only refers to his "Structure, Sign and Play" in Macksey and Donato —

15. See: Frank Lentricchia, *After the New Criticism*, Chicago: U of Chicago P, 1980, p. 104.
16. Baltimore: Johns Hopkins Univ. Press, 1976.

although I think she can lay claim to the first recorded use of the term "deconstruction" in American Joyce studies.

Implicit in the above comments is a movement away from a study of Joyce's texts to a study of his readers; and before we can move back to the texts we must first look at what is involved in such a shift. Basically, I believe, it is a question of paradigms, of the different ways of perceiving the world, or those parts of it that the scientist has chosen to investigate. Thomas Kuhn has shown that perception is never immediate, that the isolation of phenomena, the kinds of questions a scientist asks, are determined by the set of beliefs prevalent in the social group he or she belongs to. Although I believe that Kuhn's theory has had a number of rather painful effects in the field of literary theory and criticism, such as the hailing of each new theoretical novelty as the advent of a new paradigm, and although I am firmly convinced that literary theory is still pre-paradigmatic, Kuhn has at least made it clear that no serious scientist or critic can afford not to investigate the presuppositions on which his approach is based. Secondly, Kuhn and other historians and sociologists of science such as Pierre Bourdieu have shown what is really at stake when one defends or attacks a paradigm; and it is clear that in our discipline similar forces are at work. Readings of texts or theoretical positions also function as commodities in a specifically academic part of the market of symbolic goods in which stocks can fall or rise, and the Joyce industry is no exception, on the contrary.

There are two dimensions to the structure of power and prestige in Joyce studies, one within the community of Joyceans, and one in the wider field of literary studies. It is obvious, I think, that to be a Joycean entails a considerable amount of prestige in most English departments (Joyce is the most difficult of modern writers), especially in the States and in most European countries with the possible exception of the United Kingdom. A Joycean is supposed to have mastered at least six languages and is therefore often cross-appointed to the comparative literature department. Judging from the number of books and essays published each year, Joyceans do not seem to encounter too many difficulties in publishing. In fact, European journals that specialize in Irish literature even tend to stay away from essays on Joyce because they can easily be published elsewhere. Joyce is one of the few writers who have an entire journal devoted to their work, and in his case there are even four: the *James Joyce Quarterly*, the *James Joyce Broadsheet*, the *James Joyce Literary Supplement*, and *A Finnegans Wake Circular*. The proceedings of all international symposia have found a publisher, and the present series of *European Studies* is yet another outlet.

But there is also a structure of power and prestige within the community of Joyce readers and critics, which I will here, against better judgment, suppose to be identical with the members of the James Joyce Foundation, the readers of the Joycean journals, and the participants at the different Joyce symposia. Within that community there is another matrix of power and prestige based largely, but not exclusively, on scholarly reputation: some Joyceans are asked to deliver a major address, others participate in workshops or paper-sessions. I have already gone on record as claiming that of all the primal hordes I know, the Joycean one is the one most open and most democratic; and I do not intend to take it back now. Yet it cannot be denied that, although the statutes of the Foundation make such a hegemony seemingly impossible, many European Joyceans resent the "Americanism" of the Foundation. I am convinced that the reasons for this attitude have less to do with politics or ideology, than with the general European inability to come to terms with America to which George Steiner refers in the first issue of 1988 of the *Times Literary Supplement*; and it is therefore up to the Europeans to do something about it.

One of the difficulties often quoted by European critics as explanation for the lack of a European branch of the Industry is the comparative lack of funds available from European universities to establish centers, to organize symposia, or to publish Joyce material. While it is true that almost all of the manuscripts and Joyceana that have come up for sale since the war have moved to the States, one should not overlook the fact that the same financial advantage has made it possible for Garland to publish all that material in the *James Joyce Archive*. Thus these texts become available again to all the larger university libraries. However, the last ten years have seen only a marginal increase in studies based on the *Archive*, and it seems safe to argue that we should first blame ourselves for the failure to create the circumstances in which an interest in Joyce's work can yield productive results. The establishment of the Zürich centre, the Gabler edition of *Ulysses*, and these *Studies* can only be first steps in that direction.

One of the major reasons for the relative lack of operative Joyce centres is not the lack of finances or the limited scale of our English departments (the French have shown that scholars from different universities can easily cooperate), it may well be due to an attitude that is still prevalent among older colleagues: the idea that non-native spakers of English have no business in criticism, that they should confine their attention to translations, general surveys, introductions, bibliographies, or essays of the "Joyce in the literature of Liechtenstein" type. This is an attitude we cannot avoid answering. Can a person who is not a native speaker of the language ever acquire the passive fluency to address Joyce's texts on their own terms? I cannot think of a critic who can honestly say that he or she has never used a dictionary in reading Joyce; and anybody who has attempted to translate more than a single sentence of *Ulysses* into his own language will certainly know what I mean. Yet I know of only one instance in which this argument was ever used against an interpretation offered by a non-native speaker: at the Monaco symposium somebody claimed that maybe a native speaker should have headed the team that edited the new *Ulysses*, and Roland McHugh expressed an even more uncompromising position when claiming that one needs to live in Dublin in order to understand *Finnegans Wake*, an opinion shared by many Dubliners.

The general tendency of these comments is one of the exclusion of mediation and of an implicit valorization of the immediacy of understanding. The ideal reader of Joyce is a Catholic and polyglot Dubliner who has spent several years in Trieste, Rome, Zürich, and Paris. Everything that distinguishes this reader from Joyce himself puts him at one more remove from the possibility of understanding his work: if he was born a protestant e.g., or if he grew up in the Bronx, or if he is a she. The problem with this is, of course, that even if such a reader ever existed he died some thirty-seven years ago. Since that date we have left the paradise of unmediated perception and have entered the world of glossaries, annotations, concordances, and gazetteers.

This Edenic or Pauline fallacy is based on the assumption that Joyce wrote in English, which is, especially in the case of *Finnegans*

Wake, not so obvious as it may sound; neither is this suggestion, however, just an attempt by a continental European to get a share of the market — as when Philippe Sollers claimed that the English language has been dead since 1939. One should not take Sollers all that seriously, after all; in 1982 the French language ceased to exist when Philippe Lavergne published his translation of *Finnegans Wake*. A native speaker, Strother B. Purdy, has even written that Joyce's last book "is strongly deviant from English. Although it uses the syntax of other languages, it is probably closer to English than to any other language, and therefore it cannot be considered to be written in any real, or natural language, in the speech of any group".[17] Purdy's is, I would argue, the most productive position to hold: as far as *Ulysses* and *Finnegans Wake* are concerned, we are all foreigner; there are no native speakers of Djoytsch. The dynamic of Joyce's last two books is based on the resistance to meaning and without any kind of mediation it loses its whole *raison d'être*.

17. "Mind Your Genderous: Toward a *Wake* Grammar", in: Fritz Senn ed., *New Light on Joyce from the Dublin Symposium*, Bloomington: U of Indiana P, 1972, pp. 74-5.

THE MEDIATIZATION OF JOYCE

ALAN ROUGHLEY

Mediatize ..., v. 1818. [ad. F. *médiatiser*, f. *médiat*; see MEDIATE a. ...] 1. *trans. Hist.* In Germany under the Holy Roman Empire: To reduce (a prince or state) from the position of an immediate vassal of the Empire to that of a mediate vassal. Hence, later: To annex (a principality) to another state, leaving to its former sovereign his title, and (usually) some rights of government. Also *fig. 2. intr.* To mediate (*mod.*). (*OED*)

The process of mediatization thus entails a reduction in political power and perhaps also a concomitant distancing in terms of presence. As we know, Joyce annexes titles, the names of characters and places, and literary styles. These are set to work in such a way that their conventional signifying play is subordinated to their signifying play in Joyce's text. How many of us still think immediately of a traditional Irish folk song when we hear the title *Finnegans Wake*; or of Homer when we hear "*Ulysses*"? The sovereign of a realm that is annexed to another state may retain his title, but his immediate political power is limited to the role of mediating between the annexing state and the principality, or realm, over which he rules. The title no longer signifies the full control of its signified over the economy of which it was the ruling head; nor does it, as a capitalized proper name, guarantee the presence of immediate political control. How is a new reader of *Finnegans Wake* to begin? With the text? With the text and a copy of *Annotations to Finnegans Wake*? What happens to the signifiers "Joyce", or "Joyce's meaning", when our students take out copies of Burgess's *A Shorter Finnegans Wake* from their libraries and leave Joyce's text on the shelf?

My title "The Mediatization of Joyce" can signify at least two sets of textual operations: (1) Joyce's mediatization of the literary styles and textual fragments absorbed by his writing, and (2) the responses to Joyce's writing that we make as readers and critics who must attempt to annex our experiences of Joyce's writing to what is presumably a larger understanding of language and writing in general. In order to consider the former it might help us to examine Joyce's texts in relationship to what Jacques Derrida has defined as the "event" whose exterior form consists of a "*rupture and a redoubling*".¹ Derrida is referring to that moment of historical change when the Enlightenment subjugation of language by reason (that allowed the idea of Man as *homo cogitans* to function as the centre of knowledge and the storehouse of values) was displaced, and "language invaded the universal problematic". I will touch on this relationship a little later in considering *Finnegans Wake*'s mediatization of a certain book title; but first I should like to turn to the second set of textual operations, which is not as remote from the first set as it may appear.

Examining the mediatization of Joyce's writing by his critics requires that we pay attention to the various ideological and theoretical formations that have been set to work in critics' readings of Joyce's texts and then passed into the canon of received critical proclamations which determines subsequent readings of Joyce's writings. For those of us who weary of new-fangled critical jargon and question its necessity for a reading of Joyce's text, this solicitation of the theoretical procedures that constitute the history of Joyce criticism may seem like yet another distraction from Joyce's writing, but this inquiry cannot be avoided. Joyce's writings continually demand it. They insist that we look at the ways in which we read those writings and re-think the *theoria*, the process of looking, that constitutes the *praxis* of our reading. None of this is new, yet I do not think it is necessary to apologize for my simple re-citation of what has been said elsewhere with much more elegance. Now that we can cite Joyce's name — along with those of

---

1. "Structure, Sign and Play in the Discourse of the Human Sciences", in *Writing and Difference*, trans. Alan Bass, Chicago: U of Chicago P, 1978, pp. 278-80.

Nietzsche, Freud, and Heidegger — as referring to an author whose discourse participates in the decentering and displacing reformation of language into a limitless "domain or play of signification" (Derrida, p. 281), now that we can begin to approach Joyce's annexing of literary, philosophical, historical, and psychological formulations to the play of a writing that splits away from the term "literature", perhaps we can also learn the "doubling", "doubleview" reading, and "raiding" that will enable us to submit our *theoria* to Joyce's writing and see what happens to it.

I want to establish, at this point, a hinge on which we might hang our considerations of Joyce's and his critics' respective practices of mediatization. The writings of the Marquis De Sade provide us with just such a hinge. On the one hand, they can serve as a prototype of the sort of subversive mediatization of the neo-classical, scientific, linear, models of reason that *Finnegans Wake* repeats in ALP's 'Anna-logical' (and according to ALP's or Anna's logic) articulation of "Yet is no body present here which was not there before. Only is order othered" (*FW* 613.13-14). De Sade's response to the French classical modernist[2] formulation of *la raison* that is exemplified by Boileau, Arnauld, and Descartes, applies the systematic rational classification of classical discourse to the very thing which reason could not systematically classify: irrational human passion. Casting perverse sexuality in the "crypto-arithmetic forms" of rational categorization, De Sade inverted the hierarchy of classical reason to produce a parodic discourse that may well remind us of the efforts at founding encyclopedias, dictionaries, and universal grammars on the premise that language is rational. This parodic discourse gives human passions a positive value that the reasonable, classical discourse reserved for distinct ideas. As Peter Ackroyd explains, for De Sade: "Nature is a malevolent and destructive force; belief in the socialised truths of Man is a crime and the supreme belief, in the absolute presence of God, is the supreme crime. Even specific acts of evil smear, by

2. "French modernism" refers to the post-Renaissance period in Western history. The term "Modernism" is used to refer to the twentieth-century literary-historical movement.

making local and visible the transcendent Nothing, that complete annihilation of 'values', of which De Sade's figures are the saints".[3]

Of course, we now recognize De Sade as the progenitor in a genealogy of French modernism that includes the revolutionary and self-annihilatory impulses shared by Lautréamont, Rimbaud, and Baudelaire; the concept of literature that emerges from Flaubert's desire for a writing about nothing; and Mallarmé's mediation of *Le Néant* within a writing in which the author disappears so that words may come into being. Joyce's name has been added to this list for some time. As Derek Attridge and Daniel Ferrer remind us, it was fashionable to mention Joyce's name in such a context as early as the sixties, and serious studies of the affinities between Joyce's writing and the French theory of the subject and textuality are no doubt likely to continue for some time.[4] What I wish to acknowledge here, however, is not only Joyce's participation in the tradition of French modernism but also the similarities between De Sade's mediatization of the forms of classical discourse and Joyce's articulation of order as the other.

However, the work of De Sade also enables us to better comprehend the similarities between De Sade's practice and the mediatization of Joyce's writings by the kind of critic who attempts to rationalize the analogical structures of these works, and who hopes to determine and stabilize the meaning of Joyce's texts by subjecting them to the quasi-scientific modes of inquiry that constitute humanism's inheritance from the neo-classical elevation of reason. If, as many readers claim, Joyce's writing is the site of an opaque language in which the subject disappears in a continual play of difference, might it not be possible to see the critical project of converting Joyce's writing into a vast cataloguing array of manuscript drafts, lexicons, and directories of characters, of places, of themes, and of allusions, a reversing mirror image of the procedure by which De Sade invented a

---

3. "*Notes for a New Culture: An Essay on Modernism*", London: Vision P, 1976, pp. 17-18.

4. Derek Attridge and Daniel Ferrer, *Post-structuralist* Joyce, Cambridge: Cambridge UP, 1984, p. 8.

paradoxical discourse from the classical forms which he inherited? De Sade wrenched writing free from rationality by making it articulate the irrational. Could we be following the reverse procedure when we subject Joyce's texts to the rationality of our scientific humanism?

The difference, of course, is that De Sade's revolutionary discourse operates by using the surface effects of classical technical discourse to displace both the reason that guides and dominates that discourse and the concept of Man (capital M, capital Male) as *homo cogitans*, the absolute presence at the centre of the universe that neo-classical reason subjects to scientific inquiry. Numbered classifications, persuasive examples and arguments, and careful observations of the minute details of sexual activity constitute the ironically objective mode of De Sade's analysis of human passion, but all of these techniques remain precisely at a surface level beneath which we discover the irrational patterns of human desire operating in a universe of nothingness. Beneath the list of Joyce's characters, the so-called literary allusions in his texts, the re-creations of Joyce's compositional techniques, the lists of Dublin place names, and the stabilizing recitation of the literary themes, we find access to the meaning of Joyce's meaning — or do we?

The mediatization of Joyce's writing by scholars and critics is an international process, but because Joyce wrote primarily in English — even the multilingual puns of the *Wake* are, of course, grounded in that text's base language of English — many of the methods that came to dictate the ways in which students approach Joyce have historical roots in Anglo schools of English studies. These schools are the inheritors of the moralistic and aesthetic humanism that Arnold inherited from Coleridge, a humanism which sustains the neo-classical view of Man's importance and an unquestioning confidence in Man as a moral agent wielding the tool of reason in a spirit of progressive and beneficial scientific inquiry. The relationship between the concept of the narrative "I" and the being of language which is problematized by Mallarmé, by Nietzsche, and, of course, by Joyce, receives little or no interrogation in England. Language is viewed by and large as a medium to serve the purpose of a poetic self proclaiming and celebrating its own existence.

The orthodoxies of all practical criticism, and, to a certain extent, of the so-called "New" criticism, are grounded in such a view. The focal point for the study of literature derives from literature's social and moral values and from a permanent and secure view of the artistic personality that the European Dadaists and Futurists (and De Sade, though for different reasons) would doubtless have found laughable. In the year before Joyce finally managed to get *Dubliners* in print, Sir Arthur Quiller-Couch stated in his inaugural address to the English Cambridge School that: "literature is a nurse of noble natures", and "it improves our sensibility" by conveying the moral values embodied within the individual. We should read literature "with minds intent on discovering just what the author's mind intended". In contrast to the French view of language's autonomy, Quiller-Couch saw literature as "so personal a thing [that] you cannot understand it until you have some personal understanding of the men who wrote it".[5] Perhaps it is more than a simple historical accident that one of the greatest contributions to Joyce Scholarship that has emerged from England is Richard Ellmann's monumental biography.

The second generation of the Cambridge English School sustained the view that the meaning of literature was to be sought in the mind of the author and in the moral values embodied within the relatively transparent, if ornamentally decorative, language of his work; and it is surely a very similar attitude that would identify the young and immature Stephen's theories — theories that Joyce has Lynch dismiss as "prating" about the "luminous silent stasis" of aesthetics — with those of Joyce himself. Literature is valuable only in so far as it performs the familiar, reasonable, and religious function of making "reason and the will of God prevail". Here we also find a concomitant refusal to submit "so-called literary texts" to theoretical or philosophical investigation that is echoed by those of us who would like to see terms like theory, discourse, and textuality removed from our discussions of Joyce's work. Quiller-Couch expressed this refusal in stating: "Our investigations will deal largely with style ... aiming at the concrete, eschewing all general definitions and theories". (Ackroyd, p. 45)

F.R. Leavis shared Quiller-Couch's anti-theoretical position and

5. "On a School of English", *On the Art of Reading*, Cambridge: Cambridge UP, 1928, p. 103.

expressed this in *Scrutiny*. Two years before Joyce published *Finnegans Wake*, René Wellek's "Literary Criticism and Philosophy" invited Leavis to provide a theoretical defence of some of his critical discriminations and judgements.[6] Leavis refused, arguing that philosophy and literary criticism were "distinct and different kinds of disciplines". He saw no purpose in "queering one discipline with the habits of another", and claimed that while he "could not see what would be gained" by subjecting literary criticism to philosophical inquiry, he could "see what is lost by it".[7] While Leavis is never very clear about what will get lost if we subject literary criticism to the rigours of philosophical logic, it is presumably something connected with "the living principle, Leavis's touchstone for assessing the ultimate value of a literary work. If a work embodies this principle and imbues language with a living spirit, then it is good literature; if it fails to do so then it is bad literature. Leavis's mediatization of Joyce was quite in keeping with his ideology. He excluded Joyce from the "great tradition" of English novelists on the grounds that *Ulysses* lacked the "organic principle" necessary for "determining, informing and controlling into a vital whole, the elaborate analogical structure, the extraordinary variety of technical devices, the attempt at an exhaustive rendering of consciousness for which *Ulysses* is remarkable". In short, Leavis thought the work a good try at depicting consciousness but bad literature, or to use his own words, a "dead end" and a "pointer to disintegration".[8] Leavis thought *Finnegans Wake* only strengthened this point of view.

Given the importance of philosophy in the formulation of practical and new critical principles, the exclusion of philosophy from literary criticism seems curious to say the least. Yet this exclusion was sustained even by I.A. Richards, who later wrote the *The Philosophy of Literary Form*. In the work which he co-authored with C.K. Ogden, philosophers were to be excluded not only from literary criticism, but also from any investigation of meaning in language. Examining the "meaning of philosophers", Richards

6. *Scrutiny* 5 (1937) 4, 375-83.

7. "Literary Criticism and Philosophy: A Reply", *Scrutiny* 6 (1937) 1, 59-70, 61.

8. *The Great Tradition*, London: Chatto & Windus, 1979, pp. 25-26.

and Ogden stated that their "study of the utterances of Philosophers suggests that they are not to be trusted in their dealings with Meaning".[9] It is of course the title of this study, *The Meaning of Meaning*, that Joyce mediatized in *Finnegans Wake's* articulation of "Mimosa Multimetica, the maymeaminning of maimoomeining!" (*FW* 267.2-3).

Edmund Wilson's *Axel's Castle*, a study that explicitly acknowledges its indebtedness to English criticism, provides an example of one of the first major American attempts at mediatizing Joyce's writing. Wilson proceeds very much in the same vein as Leavis as he assesses the merits of what he terms the "symbolistic monologues" and "technical devices" of *Ulysses* and the "dream-literature" and "realistic framework" of the *Wake*. Besides detailing *Ulysses'* Homeric correspondences, Wilson offers a short plot summary of the characters, and discusses the similarities between the work of Proust, *Ulysses'* "Naturalistic foundations", and Joyce's direct representation of "the minds of his different characters".[10] Of the vast variety of linguistic styles which Joyce annexed during the course of his writing Wilson says only that "as we get further along in 'Ulysses', we find the realistic setting oddly distorting itself and deliquescing, and we are astonished at the introduction of voices which seem to belong neither to the characters nor to the author". (p. 206)

While Wilson's astonishment is understandable — who is not astonished in their first encounter with *Ulysses*? — his evaluation of both *Ulysses* and *Finnegans Wake* reveals a critical practice similar to that shared by Leavis and Richards. This practice hinges on the evaluation of literature through an assessment of its organic form and the appropriateness of this form to a content that is judged from the narrow perspectives of the realistic psychological depiction of characters and the creation of a realistic, naturalistic, or symbolic setting. Such criteria are, of course, incapable of

---

9. *The Meaning of Meaning: A Study of the Influence of Language upon Thought and of the Science of Symbolism*, London: Routledge & Kegan Paul, 1960, p. 185.

10. *Axel's Castle: A Study in the Imaginative Literature of 1870-1930*, New York: Scribner's, 1931, pp. 204-05; and "The Dream of H.C. Earwicker", *The Wound and the Bow*, Boston: Houghton, 1941, pp. 243-71.

dealing with Joyce's linguistic achievements, and it comes as no surprise that Wilson tempers his admiration of Joyce's work with comments like: "I do not think Joyce has been equally successful with all these technical devices" (p. 209); "beyond the ostensible subject ... beneath the surface of the narrative, too many other subjects and too many different orders of subjects were being proposed to our attention"; and Joyce elaborated "Ulysses too much ... he tried to put too many things in it" (p. 214).

Only about half of *Finnegans Wake* was available to Wilson when he wrote *Axel's Castle* — he later continued his study with articles like "The Dream of H.C. Earwicker" — but even in this early study we find critical assumptions that determined, and are still determining, the ways in which Joyce's text was, and is, read by many English and Anglo-American readers. The two major assumptions are that *Finnegans Wake* has a "realistic framework" that "holds it firm" and a "subject" that is given a "poetic freedom of significance" by a "machinery of history and myth" (p. 235). This subject is a dream, specifically the dream of "H.C. Earwicker, a Norwegian, or descendant of Norwegians, living in Dublin, who is married and has children, but has apparently been carrying on a flirtation with a girl named Anna Livia" (pp. 229-30). Of course, these assumptions would probably not be so simply articulated today; but we are still getting plot summaries along the same lines as Anthony Burgess's *A Shorter Finnegans Wake*, and even John Bishop's admirable and sophisticated *Joyce's Book of the Dark: Finnegans Wake*.[11] Unable, or unwilling, to examine the *theoria* determining the *praxis* of our reading, we persist in our attempts at mediatizing Joyce's writings by subjecting them to a critical scrutiny dominated by the *arche* of reason and the principles of *mimesis*, and directed towards a *telos* of converting the analogical to the logical and the unreadable to the readable.

But consider Joyce's mediatization of the title "The Meaning of Meaning", assuming (please note the danger of this assumption) that "the maymeaminning of maimoomeining" is a simultaneously decapitalizing and expanding recitation of the title of the book by

11. Burgers, *A Shorter Finnegans Wake*, London: Faber & Faber, 1966; Bishop, *Joyce's Book of the Dark: Finnegans Wake*, Madison: U of Wisconsin P, 1986.

C.K. Ogden and I.A. Richards. In order to accept Roland McHugh's assertion that this is an allusion[12] — a term, incidentally, that in English was once synonymous with both the word 'play' and 'illusion' — it is necessary to create an identity between the two sets of terms by ignoring precisely those operations of decapitalizing and grafting that Joyce performed in order to destroy the identity created by the repetition of "meaning", and to introduce a play of difference into the repetition of the decapitalized as Joyce sets it to work within the play of *Finnegans Wake*.

Decapitalizing and grafting, decapitalizing and annexing, for annexing is a sort of grafting: two steps of mediatization. Consider how letters and spaces are used to mediatize "The Meaning of Meaning". There is at least a double decapitalizing that replaces the capital M's with those in a lower case. Then letters are inserted that open up the two "meanings" and convert them into a sequence of sememes that can be read as "ma", "may", "ay", "mea", "am", "minn(e)", "in", "inn", "inning", and "ma", "mai", "maim", "aim", "oo", "om", "me", "mein", "ein", "in", "in". Roughly, in English: mother, permission, yes, me, mine, am, love, in, (double) inn, inning, and mother, but, maim, aim, (double) oo, om, me, mine, one, dublin (double, or two times [2 x], "in"). Is this taking too much liberty with the meaning of Joyce's meaning? Is this being too free with his text? Remember *Finnegans Wake*'s frequent assertion of the primacy of the letter in all senses of the word, and consider two questions that the *Wake* poses. 1) "So why, pray, sign anything as long as every word, letter, penstroke, paperspace is a perfect signature of its own?" (*FW* 115.6-8). 2) How are we to enter into the language that constitutes the double, publication/"*Publocation*", or get "Inn [the] Inn" (*FW* 262.26) except by a decapitalizing, cap-severing cut: "Whom will comes over. Who the caps ever .... howelse do we hook our hike to find that pint of porter place?" (*FW* 260.4-6).

Are we not frequently reminded that *Finnegans Wake* offers us a double writing in which Dublin doubles, and is doubled, in a "doubleviewed" (*FW* 296.01), "doubleyous" ((*FW* 120.28), "double-

---

12. *Annotations to Finnegans Wake*, Baltimore: Johns Hopkins UP, 1980.

face" (*FW* 363.21), "doublejoynted" (*FW* 27.02), "Doublends" (*FW* 20.16), and "bisexycle" (*FW* 115.16) text? Is not ALP's position the first position that is no longer a single position but a "doublefirst" (*FW* 450.34) position, the double position of a "daughterwife" (*FW* 627.2) who is the 'she' that is 'it' in the place of the 'here' that is also 'there'? Consider, for example, the fusing together of questions and assertions in "As we there are where are we are we there" (*FW* 260.1) ('we there are'/'where are we'/'we are'/'are we there'). The double "maymeaminning of maimoomeining" re-cites at the level of the letter and the "paperspace" precisely the double ALP, maternal/filial, permitting/denying assertion of the love given-to/claimed-by the self in relation to the other and the double experience of the loving/maiming that constitute the functions of oscillating desire on psychic cathexis. The double positions of the twins, of the "daughterwife", "sonhusband", progenitor/offspring, creator/creature are inscribed within this double, maternal, textual position from which they emerge in order to become the desiring/desired displacers of the paternal desired and de-sired *objet à* of the other. Of course the "maymeaminning of maimoomeining" in such a fashion does not re-produce the meaning of Joyce's meaning but the results of reading operations that are performed upon it.

I conclude in a somewhat unorthodox manner, by reciting some informal "gossiple so delivered" in my "epistolear" at the 1986 International James Joyce Symposium in Copenhagen, for this "gossiple" seems to point towards what happens when we unthinkingly stop our ears to theories or ideas about Joyce with which we might disagree: "these feminists who talk about 'Joyce as Woman Writer' are trying to pervert Joyce. They are all Lesbians, you know". The term "gossiple" seems appropriate to this declaration for at least two reasons: firstly, my recitation like most gossip, can provide only an imprecise account of the exact words that were spoken; secondly, the words express a sort of reactionary gospel, an opinion that only a firmly committed, unquestioning, and unreasonable belief could sustain. To emphasize what is at stake when we mediatize Joyce's writing, I double this "gossiple" with a statement that exemplifies the anxiety about Joyce's writing which post-structuralist criticism frequently seems to create: "Life is too short for all of this Derridean and Lacanian nonsense. We don't want theory; we want Joyce's meaning". While it might be possible to sympathize, to a certain extent, with the naïve longing in the second of these statements — reading Joyce would certainly be easier if *Finnegans Wake* were a Victorian, or Edwardian, realistic novel — we should realize that both statements express a reactionary and potentially dangerous attitude towards reading and interpreting Joyce that could lead to the sort of literary and cultural hegemony which would deny, or at least suppress, the fundamentally radical and revolutionary nature of Joyce's art.

York

"BEYOND THE VEIL":
ULYSSES, FEMINISM, AND THE FIGURE OF WOMAN

JERI JOHNSON

But what exigency of life might compel men to ask
themselves the woman question and find some 'solution' for
it? Does not the 'vital exigency' here require both that man
try to respond to such an enigma and at the same time be
unable to respond 'truly', so that he cannot help finding
false solutions...?

Sarah Kofman, *The Enigma of Woman*[1]

The enigma is the structure of the veil suspended between
two contraries.

Jacques Derrida, *Glass*[2]

Now where the blue hell am I bringing her beyond the veil?
Into the ineluctable modality of the ineluctable visuality.
She, she, she. What she?

Stephen Dedalus (*U* 3.425-26)

Within the international community of Joyce studies recent
conferences and publications have shown a marked increase in
critical analyses using feminism, in its various Anglo-American and
more theoretically inclined French permutations.[3] I say increase

---

1. Sarah Kofman, *The Enigma of Woman: Woman in Freud's Writings*,
trans. Catherine Porter, Ithaca: Cornell U.P., 1985, p. 68.
2. Jacques Derrida, *Glas*, Paris: 1974, 284, quoted in Kofman, p. 9.
3. I am working with the distinction between what Toril Moi has called

because the questions have been there, and have been addressed, from the beginning in, for example, Mary Colum's assessment of Molly as "an exhibition of the mind of a female gorilla"[4] or Carl Jungs's countering comment that Molly's monologue contained a "string of veritable psychological peaches ... about the real psychology of women".[5] But the current situation differs in both the degree of attention paid and the underlying, but very real, hostility it has generated.

At the International James Joyce Symposium in Copenhagen in 1986, feminism burst onto the scene with all the force of the "return

---

variously Anglo-American feminist or "female" literary criticism and French feminist or "feminine" literary theory. (The geographical names are misleading: "French" theoretical criticism is currently practiced in England and America as well as Europe; however, for simplicity's sake I shall use these handy misnomers so as not to confuse the reader with endlessly proliferating 'females", "feminines", "feminists". The distinction between the two hinges on how they view "Woman", Anglo-American criticism assumes "Woman" to be the equivalent of biological female and does not generally distinguish it from gender (the social construction of patterns of sexuality and behaviour through the imposition of cultural and social norms — the "feminine"); nor does it, generally, give an account of writing or language as implicated in or actually producing and re-inforcing gender. French feminist theory, on the other hand, sees the term "Woman" as in itself problematic; distinguishes between females and the feminine and does give an account through the critique produced by such post-structuralist and psychoanalytic theorists as Jacques Derrida and Lacan of language as implicated in the production of gender. In doing so, however, it has been charged with ignoring the specificity of woman's position within this psycholinguistic order. See Toril Moi, *Sexual/Textual Politics; Feminist Literary Theory,* London: Methuen 1985; Toril Moi, "Feminist Literary Theory", *Modern Literary Theory: A Comparative Introduction,* ed. Ann Jefferson and David Robey, 2nd ed., London: Batsford, 1986, pp. 204-21.

4. Mary Colum to Joyce in conversation, quoted in Marvin Magalaner and Richard M. Kain, eds., *Joyce: The Man, the Work, the Reputation,* New York: Little Brown, 1962, p. 185.

5. Carl G. Jung, letter to James Joyce, Aug. 1932, *Letters of James Joyce,* 3 vols., ed. Stuart Gilbert (vol. 1) and Richard Ellmann (vols. 2 & 3), New York: Viking, 1957, 1966, 3: p. 253.

of the repressed". Everywhere one looked women were talking —talking about Joyce through feminism. In the summer of 1987 in Leeds, a subtle counterattack was launched.[6] It came not in the form of masculinist panels asserting Joyce's clear misogyny, but rather as a number of attacks on theory generally, and a careful comment or two dropped in question sessions or worked into conversations over coffee that feminism was wrong-headed to go searching in Joyce's work for anything which might be of interest or support. At the 1988 Venice Symposium, the debate continued.

Outside the domain of specialist Joyce studies, the paradigm is repeated, this time in the larger community of feminism. As feminist criticism addresses Modernism, Joyce frequently stands in as the misogynist author against whom particular female writers' feminism can be seen more clearly. Take, for example, Jane Marcus's feminist centenary volume on Virginia Woolf and Bloomsbury. Here Sandra Gilbert, American feminist critic, writes on "Woman's Sentence, Man's Sentencing: Linguistic Fantasies in Woolf and Joyce".[7] While we might wonder what the Irish exile is doing in Bloomsbury, his presence in an essay on literary Modernism's linguistic experimentation needs no explanation. But this pun is plied against Joyce: while Gilbert reads Woolf as spinning linguistic fantasies, writing a liberating "woman's sentence", she condemns Joyce for practising a restrictive sentencing of woman to her mindless body: "In all cases ... what marks these women's words is a kind of essential emptiness, a vacancy which expresses the world and the flesh to which Joyce sentences them".[8] Feminist Gilbert joins ranks with the anti-feminist Joyceans.

6. See Jeri Johnson, *"Finnegans Wake*: Contexts", Leeds Symposium, 13-17 July 1987, *James Joyce Broadsheet*, 24 (Oct. 1987), 1., 1.

7. Sandra M. Gilbert, "Woman's Sentence, Man's Sentencing: Linguistic Fantasies in Woolf and Joyce", *Virginia Woolf and Bloomsbury: A Centenary Celebration*, ed. Jane Marcus, London: Macmillan, 1987, pp. 208-24; another version of this piece is printed as Chapter 5, "Sexual Linguistics: Woman's Sentence, Men's Sentencing", of Sandra M. Gilbert and Susan Gubar, *No Man's Land: The Place of Woman in the Twentieth Century, Volume 1: The War of the Words*, New Haven: Yale U.P., 1988, pp. 227-71.

8. Gilbert, p. 214.

French theoretical feminism, on the other hand, seems to have found some useful project in Joyce. Here, examples proliferate, from among which I select the work of Julia Kristeva. While Kristeva has herself refused the appellation "feminist", her work with language through a post-structuralist psychoanalytic model has been adopted by many feminists, because it suggests that a potentially revolutionary force which disrupts and displaces phallogocentric discourse can be detected in modernist or avant garde writing.[9] Such a force, exploited, might eventually produce a language beyond patriarchy. Such a force, if it could be located within Joyce's writing (and Kristeva suggests it can), might just turn the old misogynist into a radical feminist.

So, the mirror inverts, and where before feminism divided Joyceans, now Joyce divides feminists. What is it about the conjunction Joyce and Woman that engenders such discord? A closer examination of these two critiques might enlighten us.

In her comparison of Woolf and Joyce, Gilbert describes Woolf as exploring the possibilities of a radically new writing, one that would undermine the traditional means of representation, first by providing a new referential lexicon (new "images" of, or "fantasies" for, women — specifically the "fantasy" of women wresting possession and command of language from men) and further, by re-thinking and reshaping language at the syntactic and semantic level. Her discussion of Joyce, however, remains at the lexical (or "representational") level. The question asked of Joyce is not "How does this writer change language?" but simply "What (images of) women does he give us?" In attempting to locate Woman (read "female") in Joyce's texts, she is restricted to an examination of his representations of the female. And what are these females like? Intellectually shallow or impoverished, even rendered irrational,

9. If, as such theorists suggest, it is language which produces us as subjects (which structures and genders us, which elides sex and gender —male is "masculine"; female is "feminine" — and so bears the burden of having produced woman's marginal position within society), there is a very real, political justification for wanting to disrupt and displace such a phallogocentric discourse. A writing which did so might justifiably be called feminist. See, e.g., Julia Kristeva, *Revolution in Poetic Language*, trans. Margaret Waller, (New York: Columbia U.P., 1984.

they are condemned, says Gilbert, simply to be, or, at the very best, to utter inanities ("met-him-pike-hoses"). It is as if she were complaining that Molly doesn't speak the way Woolf writes. No longer a linguistic effect, Molly has become real. Gilbert may claim that these women are *sentenced* to flesh, embodied in *language*, but those sentences, that language, are invisible to her. No longer the sign of physicality, Joyce's Woman is physicality. Only by ignoring that words are not flesh nor ever shall be can she say, wholly without irony, that "what marks these women's words is a kind of *essential emptiness*".[10]

Gilbert will inevitably produce such anomalies because of the assumptions on which her reading rests: that is, that an adequate representation of women is possible; mimesis is not a problem because to her an *a priori* real exists (e.g., a real woman's experience unmediated by patriarchal ideology) which can be adequately represented in a language which in turn remains undisturbed by figurality. But to fail to account for the disturbance of writing or for the rhetoricity of language is to fail to account for Joyce, whose uniqueness consists largely of his flagrant violations of linguistic norms, his flaunting and exposing of the disturbances of mimesis by the rhetoricity of language. If we ignore that writing, we might as well admit defeat as feminists right now on the issue of Joyce, a man who clearly had pretty offensive ideas about women.[11] If we ignore that writing, Molly becomes an archetypal, fleshly woman, the sexist stereotype of the good-hearted whore, that "perfectly sane

10. Gilbert, p. 214.

11. See, e.g., Joyce's comment to Mary Colum: "I hate intellectual women" in: Richard Ellmann, *James Joyce*, 2nd ed., 1982; New York: Oxford U.P., 1983, p. 259. Frank Budgen claims that, in conversation with him, Joyce railed bitterly against "woman's invasiveness and in general her perpetual urge to usurp all the functions of the male — all save that one which is biologically pre-empted, and even on that they cast jealous threatening eyes". " 'Women write books and paint pictures and compose and perform music. ... And there are others who have attained eminence in the field of scientific research. But ... you have never heard of a woman who was author of a complete philosophic system. No, and I don't think you ever will' ". Frank Budgen, *James Joyce and the Making of Ulysses*, Bloomington: Indiana U.P., 1960, pp. 318-19.

full amoral fertilisable untrustworthy engaging shrewd limited prudent indifferent *Weib. Ich bin das Fleisch das stets bejaht*".[12]

These assumptions would be anathema to Julia Kristeva who, not surprisingly therefore, sees Joyce's Woman quite differently. Within Kristeva's linguistic/psychoanalytic paradigm, Woman has no essence, no substance; "she" merely signifies "the invisible secret of feminity which ... [is] the inaccessible part of both sexes' personality". "She" is the very sign of the inaccessible. In her 1984 lecture "Joyce 'The Gracehoper' or the Return of Orpheus", Kristeva suggested that narrative fictions re-enact the very processes by which, in psychoanalytic terms, the subject's individual identity is initially formed (through the pre-Oedipal recognition by the child, in the mirror stage, of the mother as mother whom the child wishes to ingest/devour and with whom the child is locked in a dynamic of love). Joyce's particular genius, claims Kristeva, lies in his possessing "the formidable superiority of having explored, mimed, known and brought to light, through a knowledge perhaps ignorant of itself as such but nonetheless assuredly at work, the details of identification's mechanism".[13] She sees identification's topoi, most particularly in the transformation of orality and amorous fusion into linguistic tropes, everywhere at work in *Ulysses*. For Kristeva, Woman (or the "feminine") within *Ulysses*, can not be located in any representation of women or even of feminine sexuality, but in a rhetorical trope of the Other, there only to be of service to masculine identity formation. "She" finds

12. "I am the flesh that affirms", or technically, "I am the flesh that answers in the affirmative". Actually, Joyce wrote "*Ich bin der Fleisch der stets bejaht*", and so made the neuter term "flesh", masculine. A little disturbance from the realm of language? This, I would argue, is a classic example of parapraxis. Here, a compromiseformation appears in which the masculine desire to distance the self from the body/flesh by designating it female (i.e., Molly is flesh) is subverted by the unconscious threat or fear of one's self being too, too fleshly (hence, the "gender" is mistranscribed as masculine). Joyce in a letter to Frank Budgen. 16. Aug. 1921, *Letters*, 1, p. 170.

13. Julia Kristeva, "Joyce 'The Gracehoper' or the Return of Orpheus," International James Joyce Symposium, Frankfurt, June 1984, unpub. translation by Louise Burchill.

meaning only in the "assimilation, in the final monologue, of the character of Molly by the [male] narrator". "It has been a mistake to search in this ending of *Ulysses* for a recognition or, on the contrary, a censuring of feminine sexuality. More correctly, it concerns the male-artist who sated with a final appropriation-identification ... [a]nd achieving the plenitude of his text-body, can, at last, release his text to us, as though his body, his transubstantiation". We as readers then partake of this textual body and re-enact a seemingly endless string of identifications to the furtherance of our own health and pleasure.

What has happened to the revolution? Why are Joyce's texts not merely normative if they result only in an increased health and pleasure of the reader? Elsewhere, Kristeva has made it clear that "The moment of transgression is the key moment in [signifying] practice ... a transgression of systematicity, i.e., a transgression of the unity proper to the *transcendental ego*".[14] Every signifying practice threatens the stability of the self. In some writers (and she names Joyce) this trangression is so radical that it "rocks the foundations of sociality", and "renew[s] and reshap[es] the status of meaning within social exchanges to a point where the very order of language is renewed" (p. 32). This transgressive practice must remain (just barely) intelligible, socialized, if it is to facilitate change, and not simply annihilate the (reading) subject. Joyce's writing ensures that its reader, no mere passive consumer, will enact newly available subject positions and experience a radically altered signifying system, while remaining sane.

The truth or falsity of this model is not of interest to me here, but rather the use to which Woman is put within it. For Kristeva, Woman is rhetorical trope functioning within a narrative economy as means to the end of a revolutionary textual formation and a radically altered reader whose pleasure is not simply egocentric. The price one pays for such a reading is the disappearance of any signifying practice immediately relevant to women within culture, society or history. For Gilbert, Woman in Joyce is too, too solid

14. Julia Kristeva, "The System and the Speaking Subject", *Times Literary Supplement*, 12 Oct. 1973, 1249-52, rpt. in *The Kristeva Reader*, ed. Toril Moi, Oxford: Basil Blackwell, 1986, p. 29.

flesh; for Kristeva, "she" has resolved herself into a do.

In the debate between feminisms about Joyce, the "figure of Woman" mediates. What I would like to argue here is that Gilbert and Kristeva, anti-Joyce and pro-Joyce feminists, enact a debate which is repeated by anti-feminist and feminist Joyceans, even by feminist and post-feminist Joyceans. I would argue further that in so doing they replicate a debate already conducted within *Ulysses*, a debate presided over, and rendered undecidable by, the "figure of Woman". In becoming the ground of the struggle, "she" becomes the sign of divided, irresolvable meaning.

I would like to examine the problem more closely by looking at the "figure of Woman" as it functions in *Ulysses* specifically in the textual economy marked by "Stephen Dedalus". The seeming naturalness of Joyce's "characters", the facility with which the text moves to produce the illusion of being in the presence of an individual mind, or as Joyce says an "individuating rhythm",[15] has been discussed elsewhere, most recently perhaps by Cheryl Herr.[16] What I would argue here is that the "articulation" of "Stephen Dedalus" consitutes itself repeatedly on the textual terrain of a misogynistic aesthetic itself grounded in a dextrous manipulation of the "figure of Woman". I would argue further, however, that this aesthetic demands a control of language, signification and figuration precisely at the site of Woman, a control which can not be maintained. Thus, this aesthetic is both woven and unravelled through the figure of Woman. Fundamental to my argument, therefore, is the recognition that the text produces the illusion of presence, of a rational mind meditating, in its articulation of Stephen Dedalus (though I would not want to limit this textual effect to that locus except for the specific purposes of this essay). I would obviously distinguish a particular discourse articulated in the specific textual economy "Stephen" from the more general textual

15. James Joyce, "A Portrait of the Artist", *The Workshop of Daedalus: James Joyce and the Raw Materials for A Portrait of the Artist as a Young Man*, ed. Robert Scholes and Richard M. Kain, Evanston: Northwestern UP, 1965, p. 60.

16. Cheryl Herr, "Art and Life, Nature and Culture, *Ulysses*", *Joyce's Ulysses: The Larger Perspective*, ed. Robert D. Newman and Weldon Thornton, Newark: U of Delaware P, 1987, pp. 19-38.

economy "Joyce" — a distinction too seldom made in the rush to concede that the definite article in the full title of *A Portrait* provides the authority necessary to merge the two.

Let us begin with the "Scylla and Charybdis" episode. Here Stephen Dedalus expounds his theory of artistic creation through the mediation of Shakespeare and by means of continual recourse to the "figure of Woman". Central to the Dedalean argument is Stephen's exegesis of the structures of paternity and maternity and by extension their relevance to the creation of art[17]: "Fatherhood, in the sense of conscious begetting, is unknown to man. It is a mystical estate, an apostolic succession, from only begetter to only begotten. On that mystery and not on the madonna which the cunning Italian intellect flung to the mob of Europe the church is founded and founded irremovably because founded, like the world, macro and microcosm, upon the void. Upon incertitude, upon unlikelihood. *Amor matris*, subjective and objective genitive, may be the only true thing in life. Paternity may be a legal fiction" (*U* 9.837-44). Stephen's logic is clear: maternity, clearly verifiable as fact through the senses, and therefore linked to the body, birth, and empirical knowledge, is certitude; paternity, impossible to prove, and linked therefore to mentality, rationality, and the imagination, is in-certitude. This characterization leads to a question which has focused the attentions of feminist and post-feminist Joyceans alike. The question: is Joyce, in acknowledging the truth of maternity, admitting the necessity of including or inscribing this truth in his art, or is he asserting this truth only to distinguish and exclude it from art which, like paternity, is fictive? Does Joyce give voice to the maternal or does he overwrite it?

If we focus on Stephen, it is easy to demonstrate his obsession

17. That this question has reached an exegetical watershed can be witnessed in the fact that Karen Lawrence's discussion and Maud Ellmann's lecture (both referred to above), as well as this essay, repeatedly turn to the same textual cruxes. A very different discussion of the same matters can be found in Christine van Boheemen's recent *The Novel as Family Romance: Language, Gender, and Authority from Fielding to Joyce*, Ithaca and London: Cornell UP, 1987. While each brings a different aspect to light, all concern themselves with language and gender and find the same textual loci illuminating.

with Woman's fleshliness and through his Jesuitical training with the flesh that betrays. The allusions proliferate: "woman's unclean loins" (*U* 1.421); "naked Eve ... Womb of sin" (*U* 3.41, 44); "tomb womb" (*U* 7.724); "Eve. Naked wheatbellied sin" (*U* 9.541).

Stephen's description of Anne Hathaway's betrayal of Will places him firmly in the Western philosophical, Judeo-Christian tradition. In this tradition, Woman is typically aligned with flesh, sin, and death. As Stephen explains: Anne Hathaway's sexual seduction of Will has been his first undoing: "By cock, she was to blame" (*U* 9.257), says Stephen, redistributing means and re-assigning guilt. "[T]he boldfaced Stratford wench ... tumbles in a cornfield a lover younger than herself" (*U* 9.259-60) and this "first undoing". No later undoing will undo" (*U* 9.459). After this first fall, all is mere repetition, for this first one left Will wounded and "ableeding", "[h]is belief in himself [having] been untimely killed" (*U* 9.455-56). To Anne remains "woman's invisible weapon", which acts on Will as "some goad of the flesh driving him into a new passion, a darker shadow of the first" (*U* 9.462-63).

Having been stripped of his manhood, he will be forever unsure of it; having sinned, he will be forever sinful; out of this uncertainty and sin, he will create. It was that "original sin that darkened his understanding, weakened his will and left in him a strong inclination to evil.... An original sin and, like original sin, committed by another in whose sin he too has sinned" (*U* 9.1006-09). (Notice the subtlety with which Stephen's Will-ful puns remove man from the corporeal to the rational at the very moment of his bodily shame). Stephen acknowledges his debt, "The words are those of my lords bishops of Maynooth" (*U* 9.1007-08); they are indeed, nearly a word-for-word transcription of those in the *Maynooth Catechism*.[18] The attribution merely gives the seal of authority to the already evident theological orthodoxy of Stephen's argument. The tradition of eliding the maternal, sexual sin and knowledge is even older than that of Christianity, as Sarah Kofman points out: "The Jewish tradition of the *Zohar* sets every sexual sin in relation to the unveiling of maternal nudity (*binah*). The same term also signifies

---

18. Don Gifford with Robert J. Seidman, *Notes for Joyce: An Annotation of James Joyce's Ulysses*, New York: Dutton, 1974, p. 180.

knowledge, understanding; the word *binah* is used to say 'Adam knew Eve'; committing a sin, discovering/unveiling the mother, eating the fruit of the tree of knowledge always go hand in hand" (p. 95). And what this knowledge ultimately brought was death. So it comes as no surprise that as Stephen's thoughts of Woman gather around mothers and whores the two merge and converge on death. When recounting Anne's care of Will, he recalls his own mother: "She [Anne Hathaway] bore him children and she laid pennies on his eyes to keep his eyelids closed when he lay on his deathbed. Mother's deathbed.... Who brought me into his world lies there, bronzelidded, under a few cheap flowers" (*U* 9.218-22). Birthbed becomes deathbed in one eternal female round. What man knows, when man knows Woman, is death.

But if Woman's maternal fleshly Truth signifies death, how does paternal incertitude signify an immortal and immortalizing Art? What model of writing does it provide? That it does, there is no mistaking, for this entire "aesthetic", this protracted exegesis of Shakespeare, hinges on the assertion that Shakespeare wrote out of the doubt left in him by that "first undoing" — he can never again be sure of either himself or Anne's fidelity. Doubt becomes belief that "Afar, in a reek of lust and squalor, hands are laid on whiteness" (*U* 9.654), belief that Anne cuckolds him by coupling with his two brothers Richard and Edmund. Will's inscription of their names in his plays as those of two of his greatest villains, Richard III and Edmund in *King Lear*, is the final transmutation of this doubt into art.

But Will's doubt is simply one instance of that greater doubt which attends all paternity. "Seed is a random thing", remarks Angela Carter in another context[19], so how can any supposed father be certain that his has not mingled with another's before the child is begotten? For that matter, "Who is the father of any son that any son should love him or he any son?" as Stephen asks (*U* 9.844-45). In Carter's words, " 'Father' is always metaphysics: a social artifact, a learned mode", or, as Stephen says, "a necessary evil", "a mystical estate", "a legal fiction" (*U* 9.828, 838, 844). Woman's body may

19. Angela Carter, "Doing it to Mama", *London Review of Books*, 19 May 1988, 6.

"know" the truth, but man's mind never can. And not knowing is the pre-condition of all art, which translates doubt into a greater truth through the imagination, the word, the Logos.[20] If woman's word is unreliable, man's is ultimately artistically profound.

Stephen's thoughts of his own creation make this point undeniably clear. In "Proteus", he has contemplated his own birth as a result not of sexual intercourse but of the coupling of a voice and a ghost: "Wombed in sin darkness I was too, made not begotten. By them, the man with my voice and my eyes and a ghostwoman with ashes on her breath. They clasped and sundered, did the coupler's will. From before the ages He willed me and now may not will me away or ever. A *lex eterna* stays about Him. Is that then the divine substance wherein Father and Son are consubstantial?" (*U* 3.45-8). The original sin which results in Stephen is soon lost in the etherea of ghosts, voices, wills and eternal laws. What Stephen would call the "maternal" truth of his material origins gives way to the eternal legal fiction of paternity. In fact, it is this law in which father and son are "consubstantial"; maternal physical substance has been refined out of existence.

She has, in fact, become a "ghostwoman". But how can his mother's ghostliness co-exist with her fleshliness? The ghost is the sign *par excellence* of absence, disturbance from the realm of the inessential, or, in Todorov's words, "the absolute and supernatural absence".[21] But neither Stephen nor his logic is to be so easily caught out.

Ulysses is a haunted text, and Stephen the one most haunted within it. His use of ghosts in his Shakespearean aesthetic exegesis is but one example of his attempt to incline them to his will. "What is a ghost?" he asks. "One who has faded into impalpability through death, through absence, through change of manners" (*U* 9.147-49). May Dedalus, mother ghost, clearly a ghost "through death", follows Stephen throughout the day, threatening him, taunting him

20. See Jacques Derrida, "Plato's Pharmacy", *Dissemination*, trans. Barbara Johnson, Chicago: U of Chicago P, 1981, pp. 61-171, especially "The Father of Logos", pp. 75-84.

21. Tzvetan Todorov, "The Structural Analysis of Literature: The Tales of Henry James", *Structuralism: An Introduction*, ed. David Robey, Oxford: Oxford UP, 1973, p. 87.

with the truth that he, too, must die. In "Telemachus" he recalls: "In a dream, silently, she had come to him, her wasted body within its loose graveclothes giving off an odour of wax and rosewood.... Her glazing eyes, staring out of death, to shake and bend my soul. On me alone.... Her eyes to strike me down.... Ghoul! Chewer of corpses! No, mother, let me be and let me live" (*U* 1.270-79). Her reappearance in "Circe" makes the point even more clearly: "I was once the beautiful May Goulding. I am dead" (*U* 15.4173-74). "All must go through it, Stephen.... You too. Time will come" (*U* 15.4182-84). Once again he names her — "ghoul", "corpsechewer. Raw head and bloody bones" (*U* 15.4200, 4214-15), "[S]trangled with rage", he screams "Shite!" desperately seeking through the excremental expletive to evacuate the deadly threat.

But when death threatens, it is ultimately to the trope of the insubstantial but immortalizing father that this patriarchal economy turns: "The intellectual imagination! With me all or not at all" (*U* 15.4227-28). For there are other ghosts more comforting than May's, ghosts "through absence, through change of manners" (*U* 9.148-49) which align themselves in this discourse with the father and the artist. Early on in the enunciation of his aesthetic, Stephen explains: "— As we, or mother Dana, weave and unweave our bodies ... from day to day, their molecules shuttled to and fro, so does the artist weave and unweave his image. And as the mole on my right breast is where it was when I was born, though all my body has been woven of new stuff time after time, so through the ghost of the unquiet father the image of the unliving son looks forth" (*U* 9.376-81). It is the artist's capacity to insubstantiate, to inhabit, "[i]n the intense instant of imagination" (*U* 9.381), past, present and future, to become, as Shakespeare does, both "the ghost and the prince ... all in all" (*U* 9.1018-19), which makes him artist. So, Stephen Dedalus, young artificer, can claim "If I call them into life across the waters of Lethe will not the poor ghosts troop to my call? Who supposes it? I, Bous Stephanoumenous, bullockbefriending bard, am lord and giver of their life" (*U* 14.1113-16). Mater's ghosts are of the body; pater's are of the mind, their only substance a textual body. Her death threat can be overcome by his promise of immortality through art.

True, Stephen does employ maternal metaphors of creation. Socrates learns "from his [midwife] mother how to bring thoughts into the world" (*U* 9.235-36). "As we, or mother Dana, weave and unweave our bodies ... so does the artist weave and unweave his image" (*U* 9.376), says Stephen thus appropriating even that one art which Freud left to women.[22] In *Portrait* Stephen has claimed "In the virgin womb of the imagination the word was made flesh" (*P* 217), anticipating his argument in "Oxen of the Sun": "Mark me now. In woman's womb word is made flesh but in the spirit of the maker all flesh that passes becomes the word that shall not pass away. This is the postcreation" (*U* 14.292-94). But the final movement is inevitably the same: Stephen "acknowledges" the materiality of Woman only to distinguish physical creation — giving birth out of the matter of the body to children — from artistic creation — giving birth out of the imagination to works of art.

In suppressing the maternal in favour of the paternal, Stephen keep good company. In *Moses and Monotheism* Freud writes: "Under the influence of external factors ... it came about that the matriarchal social order was succeeded by the partiarchal one.... [T]his turning from the mother to the father points ... to a victory of intellectuality over sensuality — that is, an advance in civilization, since maternity is proved by the evidence of the senses while paternity is a hypothesis, based on an inference and a premiss. Taking sides in this way with a thought-process in preference to a sense perception has proved to be a momentous step".[23] Stephen's momentous step allows him to create a new family for himself, based on a hypothesis that he is an artist, and a premiss that to be so he must realign his family tree. His true antecedents, he claims, are his mystical father, Daedalus, and the writers who have preceded him, those, like Brunetto Latini, who provide him with words when he needs them: "A basilisk.... Messer Brunetto, I thank thee for the word" (*U* 9.374-375).

Stephen seeks to purge or erase the materiality of the mother's body and his own material origins and replace them with a

---

22. Sigmund Freud, "Feminity", *New Introductory Lectures on Psychoanalysis*, trans. and ed. James Strachey, Pelican Freud Library 2, Harmondsworth: Penguin, 1973, pp. 166-67.

23. Sigmund Freud, "Moses and Monotheism", *The Origins of Religion*, trans. James Strachey, ed. Albert Dickson, Pelican Freud Library 13, Harmondsworth: Penguin, 1985, pp. 360-61.

genealogy of the father as (non-material) origin of writing. For him, fiction is engendered by the father in an attempt to transform woman's physical truth that betrays and lies into a higher truth. Of course, this whole movement is only necessitated because of the displacement of the father's own incertitude back on to Woman, and so can only ever be the creation of a lie which must then be overcome, the covering up of a lie rather than the revelation of a truth.

In like manner, Stephen's claim for the creator/artist as sexually double or androgynous, a claim which one might be tempted to suggest counters the masculinist discourse already examined (just as Woolf's concept of "androgyny" has been used by feminist critics to assert her feminism), quickly reveals itself to be similarly inscribed inside patriarchy: "The playwright who wrote the folio of this world ... is doubtless all in all in all of us ... glorified *man*, an androgynous angel, being a *wife* unto *himself*" (emphasis added; *U* 9.1046-52). The artist must incorporate (or to use Kristeva's phrase "ingest") Woman's truth into paternal incertitude, inscribe her "femininity" into his "masculinity" to produce the ostensibly gender neutral androgynous angel, who like Eliot's Tiresias, can in his now bisexual wisdom create the universal work of art. But we all know that Tiresias was really a man in drag. The true nature of Stephen's womanly man or maternal father is clear: *he* is glorified *man*. "Woman" as sign of sexual difference has been subsumed into the sexually neutral term "Man". Stephen's is a thoroughly patriarchal position.

What strikes one recurrently when disentangling the textual economy marked by "Stephen Dedalus" is its remarkable consistency throughout Joyce's texts. The same logical manoeuvres are repeatedly performed to the point that "Dedalus" comes almost to signify "aesthetic misogyny". In fact, I would argue, this textual strategy functions to provide the illusion that such an argument can have full and articulate voice.

If we elide Stephen and Joyce, we might prematurely conclude that Joyce's incorporation into his novel of Molly Bloom's fleshly words, like Stephen's insistence on the incorporation of "maternal" physical truth into the androgynous artist's aesthetic production, gives a place to the discourse of the Woman as Other within patriarchal discourse. Woman's fleshly word, her maternal/material language, Issy's "Gramma's grammar", seems to have pride of place in Joyce's texts. This is a certain feminist Joycean position which sees Joyce actually giving voice to Woman through Molly's bodily language; put slightly differently, this position sees Joyce as freeing or writing the language of Mater/Matter, as inscribing the (M)othertongue of, for example, Molly's discourse.

But the analogy between Stephen and Joyce would force one to admit such a reading only by suppressing the second movement: the subjugation of Woman's material "truth" to the paternal artist's triumphant imagination. If we take this move into account, this supposed giving of voice could only be seen as a textual strategy which, within the economy of the text, allows the "voice" of Woman to speak so the text can present itself as androgynous and as speaking an ostensibly new universal truth of sexual difference; Or put slightly differently, we could see this as a mere strategy which allows Joyce to take up his position within Modernism as He who embraces the language of sexual difference but inscribes it under the superior and proper sign of the ultimately paternal incertitude of language.[24] This is the Joycean post-feminist accusation: ultimately Woman can only be inscribed *within* patriarchal discourse, and Joyce is simply wilier than most in the subtlety with which he disguises the old (inevitable?) paternal trick.

But this conclusion is itself a result (as we have seen) of the too easy elision of Stephen and Joyce. How can we distinguish between the two? Insofar as we know Joyce, what we know is his text, his language. Running across the tropological field I have just described of Mother/Woman as flesh/truth, Father/Man as imagination/incertitude is a countering discourse, one which controls Stephen in his attempt to master it.

Stephen, as burgeoning artist finding himself placed in an episode the Art of which is Literature, concerns himself with signification, and is obsessed with finding his own sign, that specific configuration which would mark him as artist. "What's in a name?" he asks.

24. A different articulation of the "post-feminist" position — a far more highly sophisticated critique than this reductive characterization implies — can be found in Christine van Boheemen's *The Novel as Family Romance*.

"That is what we ask ourselves in childhood when we write the name that we are told is ours" (*U* 9.927-28). (You may remember that in *A Portrait* Stephen has gone searching for his father's initials — the same as his own — which he imagines will have been scratched in the school desk at Cork only to find the word *foetus*, signifier not of his connection with his father, but of the irevocability with his mother.[25] In *Ulysses*, Stephen asks "Where's your configuration?" only to answer his own question by locating his name in a nursery rhyme — "Stephen, Stephen, cut the bread even" — and an Italian phrase: "S.D.: *sua donna. Già: di lui. Gelindo risolve di non amare S.D.*" (*U* 9.940-41).[16] Clearly Stephen's initials are participating in the chapter's thematic concerns with Shakespeare's homosexuality and the androgynous artist, but of more interest to me here is the way in which Stephen's search for that which will afford him place and significance concludes only in the feminine signifier: "S.D.: *sua donna*": his woman.

But to demonstrate my point more persuasively, let us return to a passage to which I have already had recourse: "— As we, or mother Dana, weave and unweave our bodies, Stephen said from day to day, their molecules shuttled to and fro, so does the artist weave and unweave his image. And as the mole on my right breast is where it was when I was born, though all my body has been woven of new stuff time after time, so through the ghost of the unquiet father the image of the unliving son looks forth" (*U* 9.376-81).

Stephen, in choosing his mark, ignores the navel, that fleshly scar which signifies his maternal connection, and opts instead for "the mole on [his] right breast" which marks his flesh with the sign of the insubstantial paternal artist. The mole, when placed in this semantic configuration of "molecules shuttled to and fro" and a body "woven of new stuff time after time", aligns itself immediately with "entelechy, form of forms", Aristotle's "soul", as it has been articulated in a similar semantic formulation earlier in the episode.

---

25. For an important discussion of this foetal signature, see Maud Ellmann, "Polytropic Man: Paternity, Identity and Naming in *The Odyssey* and *A Portrait of the Artist as a Young Man*", *James Joyce: New Perspectives*, ed. Colin MacCabe, Brighton: Harvester, 1982, pp. 73-104.

26. "S.D.: his woman. Oh sure — his. Gelindo resolves not to love S.D." (*U* 9.940-941).

In his internal debate over whether he still owes AE the pound he borrowed five months previously, Stephen thinks to himself "You owe it," only to counter with "Wait. Five months. Molecules all change. I am other I now. Other I got pound" (*U* 9.203-06). But he resists the temptation to escape the debt at the price of erasing his continuing identity and concludes, "But I, entelechy, form of forms, am I by memory because under everchanging forms" (*U* 9.208-209). Stephen persuades himself of the persistence of selfhood through reliance on what he would identify as a paternal, insubstantial trace — memory. Molecules change and shuttle; bodies weave and unweave; moles, memories and entelechies persist.

Tracing their persistence in Stephen's mind takes us back to the trope's earliest appearance, in "Nestor", when Stephen thinks "The soul is in a manner all that is: the soul is form of forms" (*U* 2.75). His Aristotelian logic stands him and his aesthetic in good stead, for it finds an immortalizing paternal strand beneath the warp and woof of the maternally woven body. Whenever he finds himself or his aesthetic under threat, he returns to it as a protective fetish to guard himself against dissolution.

Take, for example, the next appearance of the "form of forms". in "Proteus". Here, Stephen begins a long meditation on creation with the appearance of two women whom he designates midwives. "One of [their] sisterhood lugged me squealing into life. Creation from nothing", (*U* 3.35) claims Stephen. Creation *ex nihilo*: Stephen imagines his own birth as truly original: "made not begotten" (*U* 3.45), he contends. There must have been an originating moment. But the very existence of the "navelcord", that which links him not only with the mother but with all humanity ("The cords of all link back, strandentwining cable of all flesh" (*U* 3.36, 37) asserts itself to the denial of this originality. The attempt to imagine a non-navelled belly takes him not to Adam, but to Eve: "She had no navel.... Belly without blemish, bulging big, a buckler of taut vellum ..." (*U* 3.41-42). "Vellum", writing space, that on which Stephen would write the fiction of his own origins. For the endless regression threatens ownership of the signature.

"My soul walks with me, form of forms" (*U* 3.279-80), Stephen asserts in the face of his threat. And this "form of forms" persists, does not change when all else does, has end, as Stephen reformulates it here: "His shadow lay over the rocks as he bent, ending. Why not endless to the farthest star? ... I throw this ended shadow from me, manshape ineluctable, call it back. Endless would it be mine, form of my form?" (*U* 3.408-09, 412-14). Clearly, the implied answer is "No", else it could not be "manshape ineluctable". Ownership demands finitude. Soul, shadow, form of forms complies.

But try as he might to suppress it, the endlessness of Woman reasserts itself again and again. The "unspeech" which non-origin implies encroaches upon the lingua partia. As Stephen contemplates his own poem he slides from "Mouth to her mouth's kiss" (*U* 3.400) to "mouth to her woomb. Oomb, allwombing tomb" (*U* 3.401-02) to "breath, unspeeched: ooeeehah: roar of cataractic planets, globed, blazing, roaring wayawayawayawayaway" (*U* 3.402-04). While Stephen can reach for paper on which to inscribe these words, he can not contain the threat of endlessness which their very repetition portends. What authority demands is that the words remain "Signs on a white field", sent "[s]omewhere to someone" (*U* 3.415). It demands that Stephen's question, "Who ever anywhere will read these written words?" (*U* 3.414-15) remain the modest, rhetorical denial that his egoistic "Signatures of all things I am here to read" implies (*U* 3.2). But the very hypothesizing of himself as reader demands an *a priori* writing to be read. And the spiralling vortex of reader/writer/reader has its relation in the endlessness of Woman as Stephen constructs her, not the finitude of man.

Earlier in this scene, "[a] bloated carcass of a dog" floated onto the beach before Stephen, whom Mulligan has already named "dogsbody" (*U* 3.286, 1.112). "Ah, poor dogsbody! Here lies poor dogsbody's body", thinks Stephen, implicating himself in the death he sees (*U* 3.351-52). But dead dog is supplanted by live dog (Tatters) which, oblivious to the fact that it is his future self it approaches, sniffs, stalks, noses its brother, then lollops off, smells a rock, cocks a hindleg and pisses against it. Like his nominal relation, Stephen too pisses, this time into Cock lake (*U* 3.453-60). Cocked leg and Cock lake, dog's body and dogsbody inevitably "[move] to one great goal": urination (*U* 3.351). Stephen's act differs from Tatters' only in that he articulates his into "fourworded wavespeech: seesoo, hrss, rsseeiss, ooos" (*U* 3.456-57). When, in "Scylla and Charybdis", Stephen describes to himself his aesthetic ("Just mix up a mixture of theololologicophilolological"), he concludes with a linguistic urination: "*Mingo, minxi, mictum, mingere"* (*U* 9.762). He philologically conjugates in he Latinate language of theology the verb "to urinate". But what logic informs this urinary aesthetics? What has it to do with dogbodies? And what has any of this to do with guarding oneself against maternal threat?

The seahorse is an odd place to find Stephen, for he is, as we learn later, hydrophobic (a diseased condition to which dogs' bodies are particularly prone — see Garryowen, for example (*U* 12.710)). When he refuses Bloom's offer of water with which to wash, we are told why: "[H]e was hydrophobe, hating partial contact by immersion or total by submersion in cold water, (his last bath having taken place in the month of October of the preceding year), disliking aqueous substances of glass and crystal, distrusting aquacities of thought and language" (*U* 17.236-40). Surely Sandymount strand brings him within pissing distance of that which most threatens, which he most fears ("great sweet mother" (*U* 1.80)), which he and Hamlet's father's ghost hear as "Elsinore's tempting flood" (*U* 3.281). Stephen feels the pull of the sea, and his mind is filled with thoughts of drowning: "Full fathom five thy father lies.... Found drowned.... A corpse rising saltwhite from the undertow.... Sunk though he be beneath the watery floor" (*U* 3.470-74). The fear of being invaded by effluent/refluent waters focusses itself: "Bag of corpsegas sopping in foul brine. A quiver of minnows, fat of a spongy titbit, flash through the slits of *his buttoned trouserfly*" (emphasis added; *U* 3.476-77). Buttoned, he is still undone. The sea, like the cannibal chief, "consumes the part ... of honour" (*U* 8.746). Threat of castration and threat of invasion — "Dead breaths I living breathe ... he breathes upward the stench of his green grave" (*U* 3.479-81) — combine to reveal the ultimate threat: dissolution: "God becomes man becomes fish becomes barnacle goose becomes featherbed mountain" (*U* 3.4777-79).

But dissolution is quickly redesignated, "seachange", and so resignified as working not to the ends of the maternal but to those of the paternal: "Seadeath, mildest of all deaths known to man. Old Father Ocean" (*U* 3.482-83). By erecting a fetishistic barrier between himself and the threat, Stephen can delude himself that he is managing and controlling it to his own paternal ends.

The same mechanism of creating a (maternal) threat, bringing oneself into proximity with that threat, then "mastering" it through the name of the father operates throughout. Why, fearing water, would Stephen delineate an aesthetic theory which suggests artistic creation is synonymous with "making water"? (It strikes me as odd that in this economy Denis Breen takes "U.P.: up" as an insult.) Because "making water" is a euphemism; urination is actually ridding the body of water; expelling it, not creating it. Thus, his theory is entirely commensurate with his psychic state and can easily be seen to be linked with his intellectual predisposition — "distrusting aquacities of thought and language" (*U* 17.240). To rid the body of water, to rid the mind of aquacities: the movement is the same. And he has the double bonus of having tamed the menacing "maternal".

But why would Stephen, water-hater, expeller of water, choose not only to urinate but to do so into the watery waves? The only thing which stands between him and the waves is a breakwater of boulders, stones which simultaneously separate Stephen from the threatening maternal sea and provide a pissoir for the lolloping dog. If proximate or simultaneous urination signifies bonding between male and male (surely that is the Ithacan symbolism of Stephen's and Bloom's "first sequent, then simultaneous, urinations" (*U* 17.1192)), dog's body and dogsbody bond in their acts as well as their appellations. And what they piss into or against is that which protects them from engulfment: in Stephen's case water safely removed from threat by its re-designation "*Cock* lake", in Tatters', the "*mole* of boulders" (*U* 3.453, 279).

For this is very much a cock-and-mole story. Or call it cock-and-bull (remember Bous Stephanoumenous?); it amounts to the same thing. The rationale: the mole/the alternative cock/the patronymic signifier protect the *cogito* from dissolution and facilitate creation. They provide a paternal prophylactic periphery against the threat of invasion and deliquescence and an illusory arena within which paternal creation as the expulsion of the maternal will be sanctioned. Stephen's logic is both complex and ingenious: Find the threat, label it maternal, place it on the other side of a paternally labelled protective barrier, proceed with your project, a project with which it is only possible to proceed because one has fictively banished that which would prevent its progress and, since this project itself is designated as controlling the threat, gain the extra bonus of a fantasy that one has conquered it. The sleight-of-mind becomes more inventive as the elusive Other refuses to remain fixed. For try as this discourse might to master them, these signifiers will not stay put.

Let us return to the paternal mole's penultimate appearance, happily sitting on Stephen's right breast. Stephen has just redesignated the physical sign (that which according to his theory should be "maternal") as the mark of the Father: "as the mole on my right breast is where it was when I was born, though all my body has been woven of new stuff time after time, so through the ghost of the unquiet father the image of the unliving son looks forth" (*U* 9.378-81). The signifiers of physicality and those of incertitude have already begun to blur; physical sign becomes sign of the immortal.

Very soon within the economy of this episode the mole was moved again — onto woman's breast. "Ravisher and ravished, what [Shakespeare] would but would not, go with from Lucrece's bluecircled ivory globes to Imogen's breast, bare, with its mole cinquespotted" (*U* 9.472-74). The allusions of course are to Shakespeare's "The Rape of Lucrece" and *Cymbeline*, and are used here by Stephen as tropes of Woman's castrating powers: through her seduction, rendering impotent and final betrayal of Will, Anne has fulfilled the threat of castration, ravishing Will and leaving in him a need to ravish, her lasting influence being felt in the transference of the trope from Shakespeare's life to his writing. So he creates Lucrece, a woman of absolute virtue who is violently raped, and her obverse, Imogen, very type of the unfaithful Woman. Of course, Imogen is not unfaithful, as we shall see. It is the masculine incertitude, fully in the grip of patriarchal distortion, that turns a virtuous woman into a whore and displaces the responsibility for the violation of Lucrece's virtue from the male perpetrator onto the female who left him wounded. But let's follow Imogen's mole, lately on Stephen's breast.

In *Cymbeline*, Posthumus makes a bet with Iachomo that Imogen, Posthumus's wife, will remain faithful to him against Iachomo's attempts to seduce her. Through trickery Iachomo secures entrance to Imogen's chamber while she is asleep, notes the features of the room, removes from Imogen's wrist the bracelet Posthumus had given her as a token of his love, and finally spies the physical sign to which Stephen will later allude: "On her left breast/ A mole cinquespotted, like the crimson drops/ I' th' bottom of a cowslip: Here's a voucher,/ Stronger than ever law could make; this secret/ Will force him think I have pick'd the lock and ta'en/ The treasure of her honour".[27] Note, for the nonce, that the mole's is "a voucher, stronger than ever law could make" — a fleshly sign more potent than a legal fiction. This should sound familiar. Note too that this physical sign will *force* the *thought* that woman has been unfaithful.

On meeting Posthumus later, Iachomo attempts to persuade him that Imogen has betrayed him. The villain begins by detailing the physical facets of Imogen's room as proof that he's violated more than her bed chamber. When this fails, Iachomo presents Posthumus with the bracelet he had removed from Imogen's wrist. This stronger evidence nearly convinces, but Posthumus resists and ultimately asks for "some corporal sign about her,/More evident than this". Having carefully laid his trap, Iachomo springs it:

> If you seek
> For further satisfying, under her breast,
> Worthy the pressing, lies a mole, right proud
> Of that most delicate lodging: by my life,
> I kiss'd it, and it gave me present hunger
> To feed again, though full. You do remember
> This stain upon her?

Posthumus: Ay, and it doth confirm
> Another stain, as big as hell can hold,
> Were there no more but it (II. iv. 133-41).

The mole suffices as the "more evident" "corporal sign" Posthumus demanded; he is undone. So undone, in fact, that he wishes to undo his maternal origins:

> Is there no way for men to be, but women
> Must be half-workers? We are all bastards,
> And that most venerable man wich I
> Did call my father, was I know not where
> When I was stamp'd. Some coiner with his tools

27. William Shakespeare, *Cymbeline, The Riverside Shakespeare*, ed. G. Blakemore Evans et al., Boston: Houghton Mifflin, 1974, pp. 1517-1563, II, ii, 37-42. All future references will be cited by act, scene, lines, and incorporated in the body of the text.

Made me a counterfeit; yet my mother seem'd
) The Dian of that time. So doth my wife
The nonpareil of this....
                    Could I find out
The woman's part in me — for there's no motion
That tends to vice in man but I affirm
It is the woman's part: be it lying, note it,
The woman's; flattering, hers; deceiving, hers;
Lust and rank thoughts, hers, hers; revenges, hers;
Ambitions, covetings, change of prides, disdain,
Nice longing, slanders, mutability,
All faults that man may name, nay, that hell knows,
Why, hers, in part, or all; but rather, all;
For even to vice
They are not constant, but are changing still;
One vice but of a minute old, for one
Not half so old as that. I'll write against them,
Detest them, curse them (II. v. 5-8, 19-33).

Man names and writes; what he names which allows him to write is
Woman's fleshly sin. Woman's presumed infidelity leads immediately to man's fears as to his origin: once the breach is opened, the
fiction that man can know his fathers dissolves. Posthumus's
prematurely accepted belief in his wife's infidelity leads him
immediately to suspect his mother. If one lacks virtue, mightn't they
all? If all, mightn't I be a bastard? So, Posthumus assumes that,
rather than being truly made, he has been stamped and sent into
circulation by a counterfeiter, whose tools his mother let into the
mint in his father's absence. And his final impulse is to banish the
Woman in him. Paternal incertitude and its misogynistic effects are
remarkably pervasive.

But we all know Posthumus errs. Where does he go wrong? He
has assumed that the signifier, Imogen's mole, can only have one
signified, her infidelity. It is precisely because he accepts that this
sign is "more corporal" that he is so quickly gulled. But moles, like
blood on the sheets, can have more than one meaning. Posthumus's
failure to recognize that the mole, wielded as figure by Iachomo,
could signify Iachomo's rather than Imogen's deception leads to his
undoing. Posthumus's mistake lies in his faulty reading. He has too

willingly believed Iachomo's tale precisely because Iachomo has employed the timehonoured tradition of Woman's body signifying man's betrayal.

But what interests me most here is Imogen's mole, for the mole is the stain that supposedly confirms Woman's sin. Shakespeare knows his English well, for "mole" is an Old English word: "I looked it up and find it English and good old blunt English too", remarks Stephen (*P* 251). "Mole", or in Anglo-Saxon "mal", meant "stain" and from that it became, in late Middle English, "a spot or blemish on the skin."[28] Sin stains the flesh and opens a chasm "as big as hell" — Woman's sin, Woman's flesh, Woman's hell — all ultimately lead to man's demise.

This is the meaning Stephen wishes to convey as he cites Imogen's mole as evidence of Shakespeare's having been ravished by Ann. The mole is the trope of betrayal for Stephen, and betray it does. *Cymbeline* teaches that he who would too readily assume the fixity of the sign, particularly when it comes to Woman, will merely be the instrument of his own destruction; and Stephen's aesthetic comes tumbling down. For within *Ulysses* the mole has been, first, the fleshly mark of Stephen's persistent existential self; second, the figure of the paternal artist's power to control figuration by weaving and unweaving selves through the mastery of signs; and third, the ostensibly irrefutable physical sign of woman's fleshly betrayal, the sign of that which undoes man. Thus ultimately it merely signifies the betrayal of him who would attempt to deceive by presuming to prove the mastering power of the paternal by fixing the meaning of Woman as sinister corporeality.

The only distinction between Stephen's mole and Imogen's is that his is dexter, hers sinister: the same mark, differently gendered, signified other to void the threat. But it is the very dexterity of his which turns it sinister as it ultimately becomes the site of his frustration. The sign that fastens itself to Stephen's right breast proves neither his own existence nor that of the pater's absolute power to control language nor that of some truth of Woman's physical betrayal of man; instead it merely proves Stephen's undoing.

28. William Little et al. eds. *The Shorter Oxford Dictionary on Historical Principles*, 1933; Oxford: Clarendon Press, 1973, p. 1344.

Stephen's argument is undone but so is the entire aesthetic he has erected on the opposition Mother/Physicality/Truth, Father/ Incertitude/Art. This argument depends on his capacity to fix the sign steadfastly in such an alliance: Woman:Truth; Man:Imagination. But the only "Truth" signified by the sign of Woman is a truth that betrays. And it betrays at the very moment that one attempts to fix it. Whether this fixing takes the form of eliding the sign of corporeality with corporeality, the sign of Woman as physical truth with physical truth, or that of the more sophisticated linguistic fixing of Woman as Other against which a masculine aesthetics is then erected, the result is the same. Woman will always escape. For as Sarah Kofman has argued (paraphrasing Simone de Beauvoir): "*Woman* as such, as eternal essence, does not exist, she is the (possible) product of a specific constitution and history that vary with the individual. One is not a woman, one is not born a woman, one becomes a woman" (p. 122).

What I want to suggest here, is that in the language or rhetorical troping of *Ulysses* we see the only "Truth" of the "figure of Woman" revealed. This "Truth" is that the acts of reducing Woman to physicality, of mistaking language for materiality, of believing the sign of the thing is the same as the thing, are acts of reduction which language, Joyce's language specifically, will belie. And it is precisely in the figure of Woman that this drama is played out. For the figure of Woman is that through which meaning in the text does not come off quite as Stephen had planned. This trope is that through which the text fails to mean what it pretends to mean, that which, as Shoshana Felman has argued in another context, "can engender but a conflict of interpretations, a critical debate and discord."[29] To reduce Woman within language to an object in all its physicality which must be located and then measured against real Woman is a project doomed to failure.

For what Joyce's language knows is that this fixed Truth can only be achieved through the suspension of a veil between the masculine

29. Shoshana Felman, "Turning the Screw of Interpretation", *Yale French Studies* 55/56 (1977), rpt. in *Literature and Psychoanalysis: The Question of Reading: Otherwise*, ed. Shoshana Felman, Baltimore: Johns Hopkins UP, 1982, p. 112.

and its other, which allows it to assert a Truth of Woman (as matter, or sin, or even endlessness) against which the masculine can define itself, and which thus allows it to carry off the illusion of self-sufficiency, rationality, self-identity. But the figure of Woman is ultimately not that physical Truth which lies the other side of the veil, but that which reveals the trick of the veil. Joyce's language and the feminine figure know what Stephen doesn't, that: "... women are not concerned with Truth, they are profoundly skeptical; they know perfectly well that there is no such thing as 'truth', that behind their veils there is yet another veil, and that try as one may to remove them, one after another, truth in its 'nudity', like a goddess, will never appear"(Kofman, p. 105).

So where does all his leave the debate between Gilbert and Kristeva, or between the feminist and post-feminist Joyceans? What I would like to argue finally is that these positions represent a division within feminist readings of Joyce that is generated in and by Joyce's text. They are symptomatic readings produced by the text rather than cures for or resolutions of the "problem" of Joyce's figure of Woman. The truth of Woman in Joyce's text can precisely only *not* be known. As long as the critic seeks either to find the true Woman or to reveal her inevitable reappropriation by the masculine, she will be merely sustaining the enigma that the text has not only produced but exposed. I borrow an explanation from Felman's "Turning the Screw of Interpretation": "Criticism, to use Austin's terminology, here consists not of a statement, but of a performance ... of the text; its function is not *constative*, but *performative*. Reading here becomes not the cognitive observation of the text's pluralistic meaning, but its 'acting out'. Indeed it is not so much the critic who comprehends the text as the text that comprehends the critic. Comprehending its own criticism, the text, through its reading, orchestrates the critical disagreement as the performance and the 'speech act' of its own disharmony" (Felman, pp. 114-15).

In one sense, both Gilbert and Kristeva have been right for both have identified operations which do occur in *Ulysses*: in the case of the former, the elision of the sign of the physical with the physical at the locus Woman; in that of the latter, Woman functioning within the text to allow a masculine identity formation. But this is not an either/or dilemma. Rather, it is a dilemma which can never be resolved because it is both/and. Both Gilbertian and Kristevan positions are true and this very simultaneity makes either, on its own, false. The extent to which any reading of *Ulysses* ignores the figure of Woman as that which prevents either Gilbert or Kristeva from speaking the whole truth, is the extent to which that reading will fail to be other than a performance of an irresolvable debate already immanent in *Ulysses* itself.

Oxford